New Investigations
of Marx's Method

New Investigations of Marx's Method

Edited by
Fred Moseley
and
Martha Campbell

HUMANITIES PRESS
NEW JERSEY

First published in 1997 by
Humanities Press International, Inc.
165 First Avenue, Atlantic Highlands, New Jersey 07716

This collection © 1997 by Humanities Press International, Inc.

Library of Congress Cataloging-in-Publication Data
New investigations of Marx's method / edited by Fred Moseley and
  Martha Campbell.
    p. cm.
  Includes bibliographical references and index.
  ISBN 0-391-04021-9 (cloth)
  1. Marx, Karl, 1818–1883. Kapital. 2. Marxian economics.
  3. Dialectical materialism. I. Moseley, Fred, 1946– .
  II. Campbell, Martha, 1946– .
  HB501.N39823 1997
  335.4'1—DC21   96-48493
                                                                        CIP

Printed in the United States of America

Contents

Introduction

Fred Moseley

This book is a successor to an earlier book by the same group of authors which was entitled *Marx's Method in Capital: A Reexamination* (1993). Like the first book, this book is also concerned with the methodological principles that underlie Marx's theory in *Capital*, a subject which is essential to an understanding of *Capital*, but which so far has received very little attention, and certainly insufficient attention. These authors do not think that "Marx was always right"; indeed they all have criticisms of Marx's theory, some of them quite significant. However, they do all insist that a proper evaluation of Marx's theory, and especially its logical coherence, requires first and foremost a clear and thorough understanding of Marx's theory in terms of its own logical structure.

There are three main prevailing interpretations of Marx's logical method in *Capital*: (1) the logical-historical interpretation suggested first by Friedrich Engels and later developed by R. L. Meek; (2) the "successive approximations" interpretation introduced by Henryk Grossman and adopted by Paul Sweezy; and (3) the neo-Ricardian or Sraffian interpretation based on linear production theory and represented by M. Morishima and I. Steedman, which has been widely adopted in recent years. The authors of this book reject all three of these prevailing interpretations of Marx's logical method, for various reasons. This rejection of these interpretations implies that the voluminous secondary literature on Marx's theory must at least be reexamined and is probably largely erroneous.[1] This recognition in turn implies the urgent need to return to Marx's own writings and to thoroughly reexamine the methodological principles of Marx's economic theory.[2] If the prevailing interpretations are erroneous, what is the logical structure of *Capital*?

This book deals with many of the same methodological issues addressed in the first book, including: the meaning of dialectical logic, the relation between Marx and Hegel, criticism of the "logical-historical" interpretation of Marx's method, Marx's emphasis on social forms, the historical specificity of Marx's concepts, the commodity as the starting point in Marx's theory, Marx's theory of money, Marx's distinction

1

between capital in general and competition, and Marx's critique of bourgeois economics. This book also addresses several important additional methodological issues, including: Marx's concept of totality, Marx's concept of tendency (especially the tendency of the rate of profit to fall), and an appraisal of Marx's theory in terms of Lakatos's methodology of scientific research programs. All in all, this book represents continued progress on these important topics and toward a better understanding of Marx's logical method in *Capital*.

This group of authors has met annually for the last four years at Mount Holyoke College. The seven authors consist of three economists and four philosophers, reflecting the interdisciplinary nature of the subject of the logical method of Marx's economic theory. It should be emphasized that this group does not represent a new monolithic point of view on Marx's theory. As should be apparent from the previous book and from this book, there are many disagreements among these authors, some of them quite fundamental and important (see the introduction to the first book for a discussion of the important agreements and disagreements among these authors). However, these authors do share the rejection of the prevailing interpretations of Marx's logical method mentioned above and they also share the desire to rediscover Marx's method.

The first paper, by Chris Arthur, critically examines Engels's influential interpretation of Marx's method as a "logical-historical" method, according to which the order of Marx's categories in *Capital* correspond to an idealized periodization of history, such that the subject of Part 1 of Volume 1 is not capitalism, but rather a precapitalist "simple commodity production." Arthur argues that Engels was mistaken in attributing such a "logical-historical" method to Marx. Arthur first critically examines the three texts in which Engels presented his interpretation of Marx's method: his 1859 review of Marx's *A Contribution to the Critique of Political Economy*, his preface to Volume 3 of *Capital*, and his supplement to Volume 3. Arthur then presents his own interpretation of Marx's method, and especially of Part 1 of Volume 1, which is based on systematic dialectics and the Hegelian concept of "totality." Arthur argues that the subject of Marx's theory throughout *Capital* is a "structured totality," the system of capitalist production. The starting point of such a dialectical analysis of a structured totality is the most abstract, universal element of this totality, which provides the basis for the derivation of the other key elements of this totality. Thus, the commodity in Chapter 1 of *Capital* is an abstract element of the totality of capitalist production, the starting point for the analysis of this totality, not the product of an earlier historical mode of production.

Patrick Murray argues that Marx's philosophical method can be characterized as "redoubled empiricism." "Redoubled empiricism" is concerned not only with the empirical validity of theories, but also with the connection between theoretical concepts and the social forms of a historically specific type of society. Ordinary empiricism does not examine the empirical foundations of its concepts because it is trapped in the dualist split between subject and object, a split which is characteristic of modern philosophy in either its rationalist or empiricist branches. Murray argues that Marx's method of "redoubled empiricism" enabled him to overcome this pervasive dualist split. Marx's emphasis on social forms and formal causality places him within the tradition of Aristotle and Hegel, and his "redoubled empiricism" places him in the company of pragmatists such as James and "post-dogmatic" empiricists such as Quine and Davidson. Murray then examines two prior comparative appraisals of Marx's theory and neoclassical economic theory by Moseley, and argues that, while correct in so far as they go, these appraisals miss the crucial feature that Marx's theory explains the nature and effects of social forms and neoclassical economics does not. Murray argues further that both classical and neoclassical economic theory are incapable of analyzing social forms and their effects precisely because they remain trapped within the dualist split of objectivism (classical economics) or subjectivism (neoclassical economics). Murray concludes that all these considerations suggest the scientific superiority of Marx's theory.

Paul Mattick emphasizes that *Capital* not only presents Marx's theory of capitalism, but also presents a thorough-going critique of "classical" and "vulgar" economics (it is to be recalled that the subtitle of *Capital* is *A Critique of Political Economy*). Indeed, these two aspects of *Capital* are directly linked in that, according to Marx, the reality of capitalism, which his theory explains, itself determines the limited and mistaken theoretical expressions of this reality by those who take this reality as the natural form of social life. In the words of Marx's famous "Preface" to *A Contribution to the Critique of Political Economy*: "social being determines consciousness." Mattick argues that Marx's critique of political economy in *Capital* is an application of this "guiding principle" to the reality of capitalism. With regard to the structure of *Capital*, Mattick argues that Marx begins with the commodity, not because the commodity is logically prior to money or capital (thus disagreeing with most of the other authors in this book), but because the commodity represents the classical economists' understanding of capitalism as a system of market exchange, which implies the freedom of individuals and the exchange of equivalents. Marx's theory then proceeds to explain the reality of the exploitation of workers beneath this appearance of equal exchange. However, *Capital* does not simply reveal the reality of exploitation. It also explains how this reality is necessarily misperceived as characterized by freedom and equality. The argument continues in Volume 2 to explain how the circulation of capital as a system of extracting surplus labor necessarily appears on the market as the demand for commodities by capitalists and workers. The climax of Marx's critique is in Volume 3, in that it is explained how the reality of surplus-value necessarily appears to capitalists and their theoretical representatives as the particular forms of income to capital (profit, interest, and rent), and as originating from capital itself (and land). Mattick concludes that, according to Marx, these normal forms of understanding break down when social reality itself breaks down (i.e., in times of economic crisis), thus opening the possibility of a new understanding of society and of the transformation of society.

Martha Campbell defends Marx's theory of money against influential recent criticisms presented by Levine and Ong. Both of these critiques have to do with Marx's theory of commodity money. Levine and Ong argue, first of all, that Marx's derivation of commodity money is invalid because it is based on an artificial barter economy. Campbell carefully reviews Marx's arguments in Chapter 1 of Volume 1 of *Capital* and shows that this criticism is mistaken and is based on ignoring Marx's theory of value, from which his theory of money is derived. Secondly, Ong also argues that money cannot be a commodity in capitalist economies because the supply of the precious metals is exogenously determined and too limited to accommodate the needs of capital accumulation. Campbell again reexamines Marx's texts and shows that this criticism is based on a failure to distinguish between two different functions of money—as measure of value and as means of circulation. According to Marx's theory, money must be a commodity only in its function as a measure of value. As a means of circulation, commodity-money can be replaced by a mere symbol. Indeed Marx himself argued that the needs of capital accumulation would have to be met by credit money, thus anticipating Ong's argument. Campbell also argues that the main point of Marx's theory of money is that social labor must be represented as money in an economy of private and independent producers. Marx made the assumption that money is a commodity in order to emphasize that, in such a private economy, it is beyond social control. Money need not be a commodity, but whatever form it takes must remain beyond social control.

Fred Moseley examines the development of Marx's theory of the distribution of surplus-value, which is eventually presented in Volume

3 of *Capital.* Moseley reviews the various drafts of *Capital* and especially the recently published (in English) "1861–63 Manuscript," in which
Marx began to work out his theory of the distribution of surplus-value
for the first time in detail. Moseley argues that Marx's theory of the
distribution of surplus-value is based on the fundamental methodological premise that the total amount of surplus-value is determined
prior to and independently of the division of this total amount into
individual parts. The individual parts of surplus-value are then determined at a subsequent stage of the analysis, with the predetermined
total amount of surplus-value taken as a given magnitude. The paper
provides substantial textual evidence that Marx consistently adhered
to this methodological premise throughout the various drafts of *Capital,* both in his theory of equal rates of profit and prices of production
and in his theories of merchant profit, interest, and rent, the other
individual parts into which surplus-value is divided. This conclusion
has significant implications for the debate over Marx's solution to the
"transformation problem." Moseley argues that if Marx's theory of prices
of production is correctly interpreted to include this premise of the
prior determination of the total amount of surplus-value and hence of
the rate of profit, then there is no logical error in Marx's theory, contrary to the widely-held contrary view, based on the neo-Ricardian interpretation of Marx's theory.

Geert Reuten examines the concept of "tendency" in economic theory
in general and especially in Marx's theory of the tendency of the rate
of profit to fall. The main question addressed is whether Marx's concept of tendency refers to a "power" or "force" which may not be directly observable or to an "expression" or "result" which is directly
observable. Reuten first reviews related notions of tendency in the works
of Roy Bhaskar and J. S. Mill. He then carefully examines all the editions of Volume 3 of *Capital,* including a recently published German
edition of Marx's 1864–65 manuscript without Engel's editing. Reuten
concludes that Marx's texts are ultimately ambiguous. One can interpret the texts as supporting either the "power" notion of tendency or
the "expression" notion of tendency. Reuten concludes by briefly sketch-
ing the implications of the "power" notion of tendency for empirical
research, and argues that the cross-fertilization of methodological, theoretical, and empirical research is the most promising way to reclaim a
"real world political economy" whose aim is to provide theoretically
informed explanations of important empirical phenomena.

Finally, Tony Smith argues that a consideration of Marx's theory
from the perspective of Lakatos's methodology of scientific research
programs clarifies the crucial role of systematic dialectics in Marx's

theory and, at the same time, reveals some important weaknesses of Lakatos's methodology. Smith first argues that Marx's systematic dialectics of social form (discussed in Smith's paper in the first collection and at length in an earlier book by Smith) can be interpreted as the "hard core" of Marx's theory, i.e., as the basic postulates that are taken for granted and as mostly inviolable by those working within the Marxian research program. However, Smith argues further that Lakatos's conception of the hard core is mistaken because it assumes that the hard core by itself has no explanatory power, whereas Marx's hard core of systematic dialectics has significant explanatory power, and much greater explanatory power than the hard core of neoclassical theory, the rational maximizing choices of atomized individuals. Smith argues further that from the hard core of systematic dialectics one can derive the "positive heuristics" of Marx's theory, i.e., the set of questions that should be pursued. These consist of questions that emphasize the nature of class relations in capitalism and the historical development of capitalism. The hard core of systematic dialectics can also be used to derive the more concrete theories in the "protective belt" of Marx's theory, e.g., the source of profit, the persistence of class conflict in capitalism, inherent technological change, the increasing concentration of capital, recurring crises, etc. Finally, Smith argues that, on the Lakatosian appraisal criterion of the prediction and corroboration of "novel facts" derived from the hard core in the protective belt, Marxian theory more than holds its own against the competing neoclassical theory. However, Smith argues that the usefulness of novel facts as a criterion for theory appraisal is limited because of the complexity and interrelatedness of the open system of capitalism, which makes it very difficult for theories of capitalism to make definite predictions. Smith suggests that a more appropriate criterion of theory appraisal is "retroduction" (as developed by Andrew Sayer), or the explanation of phenomena by postulating the real mechanisms which are capable of producing the phenomena (e.g., the law of value, exploitation, the distribution of surplus-value, etc.). On the basis of this broader criterion, Smith argues that Marxian theory is far superior to neoclassical theory.

Further research is clearly needed on all the important topics addressed in these papers: the reason(s) why Marx began his theory of capitalism with the commodity; the double character of *Capital* as both a critique of bourgeois economics and the presentation of an alternative theory of capitalism; the relation between concepts and empirical reality in Marx's theory; whether Marx's theory of money requires that money be a commodity; Marx's distinction between capital in general and competition and the challenge implied by this distinction to the currently dominant neo-Ricardian interpretation of Marx's theory; the precise logical and empirical status of Marx's theory of the tendency of the rate of profit to fall; the comparative methodological appraisal of Marxian and neoclassical theories, programs in this comparative appraisal. The authors of these papers hope that the papers will serve to stimulate further research and discussion of these and other important issues related to Marx's method in *Capital*.

I would like to express a special thanks to my co-editor, Martha Campbell, who was a very capable and thoughtful collaborator throughout the process of putting this book together. I would also like to express appreciation to Mount Holyoke College for its ongoing and generous financial support of our working conferences. I also thank various members of the Mount Holyoke staff, especially Dawn Larder, who have very ably assisted in the logistical arrangements for these conferences.

Notes

1. This view is also expressed by Scott Meikle (1985): "Much of what is written today from within the Marxian tradition is as deeply flawed in method and conception as most of what is written about Marxism from outside it. This is true in political economy, in sociology, and in political, historical, and philosophical analysis. There is little today that can be viewed as constituting the regeneration of Marxism that was expected and hoped for in the 1960s, in spite of the enormous increase in published material which is in one way or another Marxist. On the contrary, there is no shortage of evidence of profound and pervasive methodological disorientation, and it shows itself most starkly in the spectrum of attitudes taken to dialectics" (p. 1).
2. Meikle (1985) again writes: "What is needed, and missing, is the underpinning philosophy upon which Marx's now unfamiliar concept of science and explanation are founded" (p. 5). Other works that have pioneered this reexamination of Marx's logical method (besides other works by the authors of these papers) include: Rosdolsky (1973), Zelený (1977), Eldred and Roth (1978), Echeverria (1980), Sekine (1982), Albritton (1986), and Shamsavari (1991).

References

Albritton, Robert (1986). *A Japanese Reconstruction of Marxian Theory*. London: Macmillan.

Echeverria, Rafael (1978). "The Later Marx and Hegel: A Study on the Development of the Marxian Concept of Science," *Research in Political Economy* 3, 155–208.

Eldred, Michael and M. Roth (1978). *A Guide to Marx's 'Capital'*. London: CSE Books.

Meikle, Scott (1985). *Essentialism in the Thought of Karl Marx*. La Salle, IL: Open Court Publishing Co.

Moseley, Fred ed. (1993). *Marx's Method in 'Capital': A Reexamination*. Atlantic Highlands, NJ: Humanities Press.

Rosdolsky, Roman (1977). *The Making of Marx's 'Capital'*. London: Pluto Press.

Sekine, Tom (1982). *The Dialectic of Capital*, vols. 1 and 2. Tokyo: Yushindi Press.

Shamsavari, Ali (1991). *Dialectics and Social Theory: The Logic of Capital*. Braunton, Devon: Merlin Books.

Zelený, Jindřich (1980). *The Logic of Marx*. New York: Rowman and Littlefield.

1

Against the Logical-Historical Method: Dialectical Derivation versus Linear Logic

Christopher J. Arthur

1. Introduction

In the 1873 *Afterword* to the second edition of *Capital* Marx complained that his method had been little understood; but this *Afterword* itself raised more questions than it solved, especially with regard to some notoriously ambivalent and opaque remarks on Hegel's dialectic. To-day the question of Marxist method is still open to interpretation.

In the first part of this paper the views of Engels are examined. Partly on the basis of a particular reading of Hegel, he put forward what came to be known as the "logical-historical method." According to him the structure of *Capital* is simply a corrected reflection of the historical development of the capitalist system, in which each moment is exhibited at the stage when it attains its "classical form." This interpretation was dominant until recently and influenced the understanding of *Capital* even by those cautious enough not to rely on the historical claims made by Engels; for they replaced the historical story with what Meek colorfully described as "mythodology," or with what Sweezy designated the "method of successive approximations." It will be shown below that Marx did not adhere to such methods, however.

The paper will conclude with a discussion of the substantive issue of Marxian method, of what has been made of it, and what it should be. The structure of the readings by Engels, Sweezy, and Meek, is logically the same. It is based on a *linear* logic. I counterpose to this a *dialectical* logic.

2. Origin of the Logical-Historical Method

The orthodox way to understand Marx's work descends from Engels's review of Marx's 1859 *Contribution to the Critique of Political Economy.*[1]

9

The extraordinary thing about the review is that, without much evidence from the book, Engels situated Marx's work in the context of Hegelian speculative science; he went on to foist on the book a "logical-historical method."[2] Why did Engels bring Hegel into his review when Marx's text barely mentions him? To begin with, Engels had the evidence of a letter from Marx, in which it is noted that Hegel's *Logic* was of assistance in "the method of analysis."[3] Furthermore, as Engels noted in his review, in the *Contribution* Marx employed the notion of "contradiction" as a term of art in a manner reminiscent of Hegel in his *Science of Logic*. It seems, then, that Engels was entitled to refer to Hegel.

However, what exactly was the lesson that Marx learned from Hegel? A distinction can be drawn between systematic dialectic (a method of exhibiting the inner articulation of a given whole) and historical dialectic (a method of exhibiting the inner connection between stages of development of a temporal process), of which examples of both are found in Hegel. The problem with Engels's account is that he conflated the two. It is clear that Marx was influenced in his work by Hegel's method of developing concepts from one another in accord with a logical principle. But in his review, Engels tried to restore Hegel's reputation by pointing to his "tremendous historical sense."[4] Engels was thereby led to invent a method of exposition which, while "logical," is yet "nothing but the historical method, only stripped of . . . disturbing fortuities."[5]

I say "invent" because this is not something that can properly be derived from Hegelianism as Engels seems to imagine;[6] for Hegel, in his systematic dialectics, such as *The Philosophy of Right*, is to be found developing logical orders differing from historical orders, as Marx knew.[7] If Engels had taken seriously the *Logic* as a guide to method, then he would have been led to stress the *systematicity* of Marx's approach; instead, harking back to his youthful enthusiasm for Hegel's philosophy of history, Engels saw the unity of the text as established historically.

However, Engels *did* have on file an extremely confusing outline by Marx of his projected book, in which he spoke of transitions which were "also historical."[8] Possibly the idea of a "logical-historical method" may have occurred to Engels when trying to make sense of Marx's text because of this.

Furthermore, in the 1859 text we find three interludes on economic literature, the first explicitly historical. This seems to have been why Engels stated that "even according to the method won, the critique of economics could still be arranged in two ways—historically and logically."[9] For the double exposition of the *Contribution*, in which the substantive critique is followed by a survey of the relevant literature, seems to have been interpreted by Engels as a straight comparison of logic and history since the literature was "reflected history" so to speak. However Marx criticized this literature for its vacillating between categories of different levels of analysis, in his final word on it.[10] But he could only do this having *independently* grasped the hierarchy of categories with his own logical apparatus.

Engels's view dominated Marx scholarship this century, but is now widely contested, for it flatly contradicts Marx's explicit statement in his unpublished *Introduction to the Critique of Political Economy* of 1857 (presumably unknown to Engels) that the categories should not be presented in order of historical evolution, but in accordance with the articulation of the existing system.[11] For "in examining the development of economic categories it is always necessary to remember that the subject, in this context modern bourgeois society, is given, both in reality and in the mind, and that therefore the categories express forms of being . . . of this particular society."[12] But what is also apparent is that at this time Marx was by no means clear about the relation between logic and history; the piece has very much the feel of an exploratory discussion, and it was very possibly suppressed *just because* Marx felt the whole issue needed further thought. Nevertheless, the draft *Introduction* stated clearly that "it would be . . . wrong to let the economic categories succeed each other in the order in which they were historically decisive."[13]

The assumption of many commentators, who rely on this as summarizing Marx's real view of the matter, is that Engels's promotion of a logical-historical method must be an unwarranted imposition on Marx's text. Such a charge against Engels is put in question if we attend to the circumstances of the publication of the review in *Das Volk*. Marx was acting editor of the paper at that time, and when submitting the first part of his review to Marx, Engels specifically advised him that he could "tear it up," or "knock it into shape,"[14] if he did not like it. Thus it seems that the review had Marx's *imprimatur*: why else did Marx allow the review to pass, and exult when it was widely reprinted?[15]

I think Marx let the review pass, not just because of the urgency of deadlines, but because he was still undecided about the relevance of his logical arrangement of the categories for historical research. According to Hans-Georg Backhaus:

The Engelsian statements on method in the 1859 review have scarcely anything in common with Marx's actual procedure. If Marx did not "tear up" or "rectify" even this passage of the review then one can only see in this a further index for the fact that he was not able to win any proper clarity about the distinctiveness of his procedure.[16]

But this way of putting the matter conflates two issues. There is no doubt that Marx was clear about his procedure in the *Contribution*; what he was not clear about was what light it threw on history. However, what we can say is that if the relation to history of the logical development is variable, then we cannot, as Engels seems to think, take history as a *guide*.[17] We can perhaps say of an early stage that it is what will have become capitalism. But this cannot be read as a historical explanation for the development if the movement of history lacks the *necessity* for it; whereas in a dialectical derivation there is supposed to be immanent necessity. Engels was right to refer to Marx's dialectical development of categories, and to name Hegel as an important source for dialectical method. But he should have looked to Hegel's logic rather than to his philosophy of history.[18]

What probably impressed Engels (and his followers, like Meek) is that if one considers the basic forms of circulation, then the sequence commodity-money-capital could be both logical and historical; each cannot be understood without its predecessors, with luck the concept of each could be derived from its predecessor through a dialectical development, and historical contingencies did indeed make this progression possible. But (as I shall argue) starting *historically* with the commodity would *not* mean starting historically with value in Marx's sense, because under the contingencies operative in underdeveloped forms of commodity exchange we would have price, to be sure, but not yet labor values (unless one means something relatively indeterminate by value)[19] for, as Marx allows in the *Contribution* itself, "the full development of the law of value presupposes a society in which large-scale industrial production and free competition obtain, in other words, modern bourgeois society."[20]

3. Simple Commodity Production

In his 1859 review Engels argued that the logical development was "nothing but the reflection of the historical process in an abstract and theoretically consistent form," in which each moment is "examined at the point of development of its full maturity, of its classical form."[21] But when is a moment in "its classical form?"—Value itself, for example? Engels came back to this question in his commentaries on *Capital*, Volume 3, where he claimed that Marx started by describing a historical stage of "simple commodity production," that there value attained its classical form, but that subsequently the picture changed when, with capitalist production, commodity value appears in a secondary derivative form.

In his preface to Volume 3 Engels explained that "where things and their mutual relations are conceived not as fixed but rather as changing, their mental images, too, i.e., concepts, are . . . not to be encapsulated in rigid definitions, but rather developed in their process of historical or logical formation." He concluded that, in view of this, "it will be clear, then, why at the beginning of Volume 1, where Marx takes simple commodity production as his historical presupposition, only later, proceeding on this basis, to come on to capital—why he proceeds precisely there from the simple commodity and not from a conceptually and historically secondary form, the commodity as already modified by capitalism."[22] In this passage, then, Engels again supposed that the logic of Marx's exposition parallels a historical process, namely, that from the historical "presupposition" of "simple commodity production" to capitalist production. Furthermore, in a supplement to the second edition of *Capital*, Volume 3, he insisted once again that "Marx's law of value applies universally, as much as any economic laws do apply, for the entire period of simple commodity production, i.e., up to the time at which this undergoes a modification by the onset of the capitalist form of production."[23]

The context in which Engels became involved in this discussion was that in which it seemed to many that Marx's Volume 1 "values" were merely a stage in the process of generating the Volume 3 "prices of production." Faced with the objection that, if such values were not *empirically* present because they were superseded in the presentation by these prices of production, then they had no substance, being, indeed, mere "fictions," even if convenient or necessary fictions, Engels reacted by interpreting the stages of Marx's presentation *historically* in order to ensure that the values were indeed empirically visible, but of course, in the past, before capitalism "modified" the relationships involved.

Before discussing the merits of Engels's view, it has to be noted that there is precious little textual support for it. Marx certainly did not develop the idea of "simple commodity production" at the point where it was supposed to be under discussion, namely the first few chapters of Volume 1. In truth, Marx never used the term in any of his work.[24] Likewise, it is certain he never referred to the capitalistically produced commodity as a secondary derivative form.[25] On the contrary, over and over again he stated that only with capitalism is the value-form fully developed. For example: "the concept of value is antecedent to that of capital but, on the other hand, its pure development presupposes a mode of production based on capital;"[26] thus "the concept of value wholly belongs to the latest political economy, because that concept is the most abstract expression of capital itself and of the production based upon it."[27]

It is true that Engels was able to cite a passage from the manuscript of the third volume in which something like the content of the idea of a stage of simple commodity production was discussed by Marx. Seizing enthusiastically on this, Engels claimed that "if Marx had been able to go through the third volume again, he would undoubtedly have elaborated this passage significantly;"[28] however, it is just as possible that he would have decided that it was a false trail and eliminated it![29]

Engels rightly drew attention to the fact that, in a dialectical movement, concepts must be grasped in their "formation." But *when* do we have a fully formed concept? I shall not enter on a discussion as to the historicity of "simple commodity production;" for there is a prior more interesting question from a theoretical point of view: does the model work *conceptually?*—Does the law of value really attain its maturity at such a posited stage of development of commodity exchange, or rather, does it attain its complete development only with capital?— Is it correct to view the "simple" commodity as in some sense primary, and the product of capital as in some sense "secondary"?—a derivative form presenting us with a less than "pure" case?

The truth is that, because in such a "society" as Engels imagines there is no mechanism enforcing equivalent exchange, there is no necessity for value to emerge as anything more than an empty form with the potential to develop a meaningful content with capitalism.

There are two cases to consider: either there is mobility of labor or there is not. In the latter case exchange in proportion to labor times expended could only occur on the basis of a *normative* principle. It might have been a widely followed *rule*, but not an objectively imposed *law* to be grasped in its necessity by science. Even if one could find historical examples of this rule, it is clearly irrelevant to commodity production in a market economy based on driving hard bargains. In the former case, exchange at "value" is supposed to take place because otherwise people would switch into the better rewarded occupation. As with the other case, it should be noted that this presupposes that everyone knows what labor is expended by others; this is a very doubtful proposition historically. However, even if it is accepted as an idealizing assumption it is still true that we have nothing like an objective law operative. For the assumption is here that the *only* consideration affecting the choices of individuals is avoidance of "toil and trouble," as Adam Smith originally argued. This *subjective* premise has little to do with Marx's hypothesis that there exists in capitalism an *objective* law of value which makes exchange at value *necessary*. If one relies merely on subjective perceptions of producers, then other subjective preferences to do with the trouble of learning new methods, or the preference for one occupation rather than another, may be operative also. Just because there is an exchange of goods produced, this does not mean any law of value governs the ratio of exchange. According to Marx the law of value is based on exchange in accordance with socially necessary labor times, but in the case of simple commodity production there is no mechanism that would *force* a given producer to meet such a target or be driven out of business. When all inputs, including labor power itself, are monetized, that is to say, have a value form, then an objective comparison of rates of return on capital is possible and competition between capitals allows for the necessary enforcement of the law of value.

If it is granted that value is not a substance given prior to exchange (as is use value), but one which develops only in and through the forms of exchange, then it is fully developed only when these forms have reached the point at which it can be demonstrated that value has become a reality in both form and content and that its logic has imposed itself on the movement of the economy to the extent that there emerges a quantitatively determinant law of commodity production. For the reasons explained above this law cannot hold in the postulated model of simple commodity exchange.

It is important to understand that the problem of the "fictional" status of value remains even for presentations of the argument more sophisticated than that of Engels. The same problem arises for those who ignore the historicity of the superseded stage and take it as a convenient myth.

R. L. Meek, for one, argued that "to understand capitalism . . . one must understand first and foremost that it is a particular type of *commodity-producing* society."[30] Thus "the capitalist stage" is a special case of "the broad basic relation between men as producers of commodities which persists throughout the whole period of commodity production." The way to proceed (he thinks Marx held) "was to begin by postulating a society in which . . . the laborers still owned the whole produce of their labor." Next, "having investigated the simple laws which would govern production, exchange, and distribution in a society of this type, one ought then to imagine capitalism suddenly impinging upon this society."[31] In doing just this, Meek believed, "Marx's procedure becomes formally similar to that of Adam Smith and Ricardo, who also believed that the real essence of capitalism could be revealed by analyzing the changes which would take place if capitalism suddenly impinged upon some kind of abstract pre-capitalist society." This was the main reason why Marx "starts with values," and why, having transformed them into prices of production, "he still insists that the 'values' play a determining role."[32]

This reference back to a supposed precapitalist society of simple commodity production Meek said was "not a *myth* . . . but rather *mythodology*."[33] In spite of criticisms levelled against him, as late as 1973 Meek reiterated his position:

> I still think I was right in laying special emphasis on Marx's "logical-historical method;" indeed, if anything I think I underestimated the extent to which Marx's economic work was guided by it. . . . Marx's *logical* transition in *Capital* (from the commodity relation as such to the "capitalistically modified" form of this relation) is presented by him as the "mirror-image" of a *historical* transition (from "simple" to "capitalist" commodity production).[34]

One thing Meek correctly pointed out is that "the analysis of economic categories ought so far as possible to be conducted in terms of, rather than in abstraction from, 'relations of production' in Marx's sense."[35] Yet Meek clearly abstracted a stage too far in leaving out the key relation—the capital relation—and expecting that the essence of capitalism can be derived therefrom.

The problem about the actuality of value remains even for those (to be considered shortly) who abjure any talk of a real or supposed *historically* prior stage of simple commodity production, but still treat value as a "logical" stage in the derivation of prices, if they cling to the view that it is in the "first" stage, namely a noncapitalist model, that true value relationships obtain and that adding capitalist competition to the model changes nothing essential about value, but merely "moves it around" in accordance with the complications induced by the effects on prices of the tendency to equalize the rate of profit for capitals of different composition.

It will be recalled that Engels distinguished between a logical and historical method before he identified them. Others who deny this identity, and the relevance of historical shapes of exchange, must of course rely on a purely logical method of appropriating and explaining the inner nature of capital. But far too little attention has been paid to the question of just what this "logic" should be. Because of the lack of familiarity of thinkers with dialectic since Marx, it is not surprising that other logics were employed. Methodologically sensitive Marxists such as Grossman and Sweezy put forward the method of "successive approximations." As they explained it, this depended on the notion that in order to exhibit value in its pure form a number of simplifying assumptions could be made. After this simplification of the forms, a model of value relationships could be outlined in which the law of value would be perspicuous. Then a series of stages could be exhibited, in which the initial simplifications were gradually dropped, and new models of greater complexity could be introduced which would demonstrate both that the phenomena might look different, but that nothing essential is changed, when the more complex model is built on the basis of the simple one. This is a perfectly respectable scientific procedure: but it works only *if* it is true that the reality concerned is so ordered that it can be grasped by such a linear logic.

Henryk Grossman, in his 1929 book, *The Law of Accumulation*, first put forward what became the typical analytical-linear view of Marx's method. He argued that one can only approach a complicated reality by stages; one begins by making "various simplifying assumptions"; the result is the first stage of Marx's "approximation to reality." It follows that conclusions established on such a structure of assumptions "have a purely provisional character," he admitted, and "must go together with a subsequent process of correction that takes account of the elements of actual reality that were disregarded initially." Thus, "stage by stage, the investigation as a whole draws nearer to the complicated appearances of the concrete world and becomes consistent with it."[36]

Paul Sweezy took up this same method to characterize Marx's theory of value. According to him, Marx practised the method of "successive approximations": this "consists in moving from the more abstract to the more concrete in a step-by-step fashion" removing simplifying assumptions at successive stages of the investigation so that theory may take account of, and explain, an ever wider range of actual phenomena.[37] As Sweezy said, this leaves the problem of "what to abstract from and what not to abstract from," a distinction he interpreted in terms of what is "essential" and what is "inessential."[38]

At first, it seems that the capital relation was to be isolated as essential;[39] but then he concluded that since this is "in form" an exchange relation it is "clearly a special case of a large class of such relations which have a common form and structure;" therefore a beginning should be made with "analysis of the general phenomenon of exchange."[40] Sweezy, however, could think of no way this could be done except on the assumption that "Marx begins by analyzing 'simple commodity production.'"[41] Inevitably this analysis was understood by Sweezy to show that "the law of value is essentially a theory of general equilibrium developed in the first instance with reference to simple commodity production and later on adapted to capitalism,"[42] and that "to apply our theory of value to the analysis of capitalism it is first necessary to inquire carefully into the special features which set this form of production off from the general concept of commodity production."[43]

Notice that the theory is merely "adapted" or "applied" to capitalism because we already have the "essentials" in the "general" account, which assuredly apply to the "special case." What is wrong with this is the way the problem is set up as a movement from the "general concept of commodity production" to the "special case," which in spite of its "special features," shares "a common form and structure" with the generality of cases. This is decidedly *not* what Marx's development of the value form shows; on the contrary: the C-C' (C=commodity) structure is thoroughly *transformed* when C-M-C' (M=money) is developed, *transformed* again with M-C-M', *transformed* again with M-P-C-M' (P=capital in the phase of production), and *transformed* again with the formation of an average rate of profit resulting in so-called "prices of production."

Yet this "finished form" of value cannot be artificially held apart from its predecessors. From a systematic dialectical point of view, when the movement to prices of production is undertaken, the law of value is realized only in its negation; for the condition which grants it determinacy, namely, capitalist competition, brings with it differences that transform actual values. But the law still holds in an important sense, even in the mode of being denied, because prices of production can properly be understood only as the *outcome* of this dialectical unity in difference: of the potential and realized values. Indeed, even in the case of the simple circulation of commodities, prices will rarely be immediately reducible to values. This is because we do not have before us a hypostatized equilibrium, but a constantly moving system in which the prices should *not* be seen as "deviating" from value because of unimportant "frictions"; for the price variations are essential to the system's dynamic. If someone is consistently underselling the market, this cannot be due to a temporary surplus, but a new method of production. Or, again, if everyone has surpluses that may indicate a permanent shift in the pattern of demand. It is the gap between "idea" and "reality" that indicates a new shape of the idea is at hand.

The "general phenomenon of exchange" (in Sweezy's locution), *just because* it is general (and especially when "general" is confused with "simple" to produce the notion of "simple commodity production"), is too indeterminate in its effectivity to ground a determinate realm of values; only when commodities are products of capital is the "empty" form of value infused with a determinate content under the force of valorization. As with Meek, Sweezy has undertaken "an abstraction too far," and instead of deriving the actuality of value he has illegitimately built it in from the start.

The key to all these views (Engels's, Sweezy's, Meek's) is that whatever is supposed as essential in the earlier model is carried through *un*transformed in its nature, even if "hidden" behind confusing "surface" phenomena, in later versions. All such approaches are based on a *linear* logic, not a *dialectical* logic.[44] The question is whether value relationships are conformable to such a linear logic in their development from simple forms of value to more complex ones, or whether, as I argue, value becomes a truth only with the full development of capitalism.

In the latter case the exposition of value forms begins with a concept of value that is thoroughly *inadequate* and would have to be *substantiated* in its further development. On this account much more than a complicated secondary form of value is arrived at in the capitalist relationship. It is rather that the true form of value *results* from the exposition, and the original seen from this perspective is precisely the overly simple, utterly abstract, appearance of the concept, whose validity as a starting point is only secured in the result.

The problem is not at all that of a pure or simple case to be isolated from concrete complexity. It is a matter of how to articulate a *complex concept* that cannot be grasped by some sort of immediate intuition. To use Engels's own words, concepts like value and capital "are not to be encapsulated in rigid definitions"; but unfortunately, in his application of this insight, Engels himself did not reformulate his *concept* of value; he merely suggested that its apparent magnitude is modified. The same is true for Sweezy and Meek. All share a linear logic, in which each stage supposedly embodies value relationships in a perfectly adequate fashion and thus provides a ground for the next one to "add on," so to speak, new external causes of variation.

Furthermore, it is worth noting that Engels set the terms of the debate wrongly. There was no need at all to theorize "simple commodity production." For what was at issue in the movement from Volume 1 to Volume 3 was the transition from capital in general to many capitals, from capital in its identity with itself to differentiable capitals; for this a movement of particularization was required. The problem that upset Engels was not this movement as such, for which he was evidently happy with Marx's "transformation," but that capital in general (especially if it was interpreted as a system of capitals of identical composition) was "fictional"; hence his concern that value had to have empirical reality. But since value in Volume 1 was not such an empirical concept he had to go back further to a precapitalist stage of history. Unfortunately, people like Sweezy followed this route even though for them there was no problem about setting up models with no historical or empirical referent. Thus for Sweezy the virtue of "simple commodity production" was not its supposed empirical reality (as it was for Engels) but its supposed theoretical perspicuity as the starting point for a linear derivation.

In assessing the faithfulness of Engels's commentary to Marx's intentions, two distinct issues must be separated.

a) Do the early chapters of *Capital* refer to simple commodity production? That is to say, even if no such historical stage ever existed, did Marx suppose it as an imaginary paradigm of pure value production, for the sake of clarifying his exposition? Here, I think that the evidence is clear that Marx is *from the start* presupposing that his object is capitalist production and that he begins with the commodity because that is its basic unit of output whose conditions of existence he traces. The very first line of *Capital* shows this: "The wealth of societies in which the capitalist mode of production prevails appears as an immense collection of commodities. . . . Our investigation therefore begins with the analysis of the commodity."[45]

b) Notwithstanding this last point, namely that Marx was interested in the commodity as a product of capital, might it not be true that the laws he adduced can nonetheless be referred back to a real (Engels), or imaginary (Meek), or modelled (Sweezy) stage of simple commodity production? I have previously argued that the law of value could not govern such a mode of production.

Thus, taking the two points together, Engels's view that the logical development of Marx's argument is a "corrected history" of a development to capitalism out of "simple commodity production" fails both at the textual and substantive level. This is now recognized. Let us mention a couple of examples.

Martha Campbell has shown that, if Marx's starting point is taken to be the universality of the commodity form of the product of labor, his procedure is to demonstrate that a necessary condition of such universality is the existence of an economic system whose sole regulating principle and goal is value, that is to say, a system of capitalist production. Thus the commodity with which his analysis begins cannot be a product of a precapitalist form of economy; rather it must be considered as the simplest immediate universal element presented by capital in its process of production.[46]

Jairus Banaji, utilizing the resources of Hegel's logic, argues that the first sentence of *Capital* (quoted just now) has the following obvious consequence:

The conceptual regime of Part One, Volume One, is not some "abstract precapitalist society" of "simple commodity producers;" it is the sphere of Simple Circulation, or the circulation of commodities as such, and we start with this as the process that is "immediately present on the surface of bourgeois society," we start with it as a reflected sphere of the total process of capital which, however, has still to be determined *as reflected*, i.e., still to be posited. When we examine the simple commodity, or the commodity as such, we only examine *capital* in its most superficial or immediate aspect.[47]

As he rightly observes, "simple commodity production" is not Marx's myth but a fiction of the mythodologists, Meek and company.[48]

These authors are selected for citation because, if Engels is wrong, an *alternative* reading of the argument is required, and their criticism is rooted in such an alternative view. A view similar to theirs is expounded in the next, and final section.

4. The Problem of Totality and Dialectical Exposition

Following Engels's lead, the main dialectical theorists presented dialectic as a principle of movement, primarily of history. Yet dialectical argument is better suited to reconstruct the articulation of a structured whole. If we look at Hegel and Marx it is clear that analysis of wholes through systematic dialectical argument is what is most important in their work. This is the issue when it is considered in what exactly consists the logical development of the argument of *Capital*.

It must be adequate to its object: but here the object is a certain sort of *whole*. It is not a mere aggregation; this we have in a pile of bricks where one brick rests casually on another. It is, rather, a *totality* where every part clearly requires complementing with others to be what it is; we cannot say "what it is" without reference to the whole context of its relations and determinants; hence internal relations typify the whole, such that the very essence of each element depends on its relation to others and the whole. A thing is internally related to another if this other is a necessary condition of its nature. The relations themselves are not independent individuals but situated as moments of a totality, and reproduced through its effectivity. If the elements are bound together in such a whole, we can then speak of holistic causality bringing about a substantial transformation of all the relations involved.[49]

The problem we face is that a totality cannot be presented *immediately*; its articulation has to be exhibited; in doing that we have to make a start with some aspect of it. But in the exposition the argument can move through the reconstruction of the whole from a particular starting point because we can move logically from one element to another along a chain of internal relations; in strict logic if the very meaning of an element is at issue (which I shall argue is the case in the value forms commodity-money-capital each of which requires the others to complete its meaning or develop its concept), or with a fair degree of confidence if material conditions of existence are involved (as with the relation of valorization to production).

Thus in a dialectical argument the meanings of concepts undergo shifts because the significance of any element in the total picture cannot be defined for good at the outset. In an analytical argument this last is the assumption, namely that the analysis of the whole into its elements results in a set of "atomic facts," and then the whole is grasped as the resultant of the aggregate influence of these elements on each other. But if, contrary to this, each element is significant only insofar as it is itself determined by its place in the totality as well as contributing to the movement of the whole, then, in the exposition, forced as it is to start somewhere, with some more or less isolated (and hence to that extent falsified) relation, the initial moment can only be characterized in a provisional under-determined way. As the presentation of the system advances to more complex, and concrete, relationships the originating definition of a concept shifts accordingly, normally towards greater definiteness, although sometimes new and broader applications of the concept come into view.[50] Instead of foreclosing on reality, the dialectical method remains open to fundamental reorganizations of the material thus far appropriated, as it gets closer to the truth of things.

For a linear logic value is real from the start of the exposition, and its truth is transparent at that point, only to become clouded when later modifications impact on the initial postulate. The reason I argue that this logic is inappropriate is that capitalism is constituted as a totality. This totality forms its elements in such a way that taken apart from it they are denatured.

The exposition of the system, starting with some simple yet determinate relation (such as the commodity form), is thereby forced to abstract it violently from the other relations that in reality penetrate it and help to constitute its effectivity; thus it is necessary at the end to reconceptualize the significance of the beginning. Given this, the concepts of Marx's first chapter can only have a provisional and indeterminate character, and the argument as it advances changes the meanings of these concepts, through grounding them adequately in the comprehended whole. To expound complex truths, where everything, as we say, "hangs together," a suitable method of presentation, or dialectic of exposition, is required. It necessarily must *start* somewhere; but if this starting-point is ripped out of the whole, as abstracted thus, it is necessarily inadequate as a characterization both of itself and the whole. However, the exposition can then proceed precisely by questioning its status. Insofar as this abstracted element has no meaning outside the structure to which it belongs, only at the end of the reconstruction of the totality is its truth unfolded: truth is system from an expositional point of view.

It is noticeable in the linear logic that there is no genuinely immanent development from the posited stage of simple commodity production to capitalist commodity production. Rather, simple commodity production and capitalist commodity production are counterposed and compared on the assumption that the capital relation impacts on the simpler model because the theorist introduces it; the shift from one "level of analysis" to another is due to their *decision* to add a further determination, e.g., "let money be invented," "let labor-power be a commodity," "let different organic compositions prevail." But in a dialectical argument successive stages are introduced because they are demanded by the *logic of the exposition*.

If we are dealing with a totality, the problem is how to articulate this systematically in such a way that a move from a suitable starting point may be made by a dialectical derivation to the result that the totality is now grasped as the unity of its internal relations. There are, then, two things to settle: the choice of a starting point, and the method of advance from it.

Postponing the second question, let us address the first. Marx asserted in his 1857 *Introduction* (and reasserted in the very title of his big book) that the whole contains within it industrial capital as its "overriding moment." This leaves the problem of how to start the first volume given that capital is a complex concept, even in its most abstract form as self-valorization. As Marx said, it is necessary to employ "the power of abstraction" to arrive at the "cell-form" equivalent of the body of the capitalist totality. The sequence of thought in carrying through this abstraction must be such that it arrives at a starting point which is sufficiently *simple* to be grasped immediately by thought and yet sufficiently historically *determinate* to lead to the other categories that structure this specific society, i.e., bourgeois society based on the capitalist mode of production. While Marx said in the 1857 *Introduction* that the scientific method of exposition starts with something abstract he also pointed out that generic abstractions of an ahistorical type would tell us nothing of any importance (there is no "production in general" for example).

What is required, then, is that the movement of abstraction retain in the proposed immediacy of the beginning some sign of its origin in a historically determinate set of relations of production. It must seize upon some *particular* aspect of the whole under consideration which, while simple, is also so implicated in the whole from which it is separated out that it still bears this trace of its origin.

Bearing these considerations in mind, let us now reconstruct the sequence of Marx's thought. He is faced with capital; he cannot start with that because even if its concept is stripped to its bare essentials it still has the complexity of self-valorization, whose immediate appearance is an increment in the reflux of money. So he abstracts from this complex relation the figure of money. But what is money? The fact that this is no simple matter, and that any show of immediacy that might be given by the tangible quality of coins in the pocket is illusory, may be demonstrated by reviewing the weird and wonderful ideas of it that have been advanced, both by the vulgar and by the theorists; furthermore it seems to have a bewildering variety of functions. It is not a suitably simple beginning. (Although it is interesting to note that it seems to have formed the beginning of Marx's first serious draft of his economics in 1857.) It is also clear that money is essentially an incomplete idea, having no sense except in its various relations with commodities, such as medium of their circulation. In a way it is clear that the commodity is, as he himself stated, the "cell-form" Marx needed. The research program therefore took the form of deriving from the commodity first money and then capital.

But what more precisely are we starting from?—and how do we advance? To begin with, it may very well seem to be the case that the commodity cannot be a suitable starting point because it is disqualified for failing to meet both the criteria earlier established, namely simplicity and historical determinacy.

a) The first because, upon analysis, it turns out the commodity itself embodies a puzzling dichotomy: it is a good in that it serves as a use-value, and on the other hand a different, even contrary, determination is found in it, that of exchangeableness.

b) The second because this commodity form attaches to things that are not even products of labor, and, even if these are excluded by fiat,[51] it is still obvious enough that commodity exchange appears in a whole set of epochs of history, possibly including Engels's "simple commodity production." It seems then Sweezy may be right in saying Marx's starting point was the general class of exchange relations, not the specifically capitalist, and that the theory of value antedates that of capital in the argument.

However, to deal with the second point first, when we examine Marx's work more closely we see that in Chapter 1 implicitly, and in other writings explicitly, Marx so determines the commodity taken as the starting point as to exclude any such precapitalist formations. The key point to grasp is that the simple category of *universality* is built into the starting point. Over and over again he explicitly excludes as relevant to the theory social formations in which only *surpluses* appear on the market. The key point about choosing a sufficiently simple start is that "simple" here means *logically* simple, i.e., pure and universal; but if this sort of abstraction is *produced* by the historical development of a concrete whole to maturity it is really, although in the logic a beginning, in the history a result, as Marx said (in his 1857 *Introduction*) was the case with the general category of labor. This requirement of simple universality is implicit in the first line of *Capital* where it is specified that wealth takes the form of commodities in bourgeois society.

Thus the starting point is not some vague notion of "commodity," but the commodity taken in the characteristic form in which it appears in capitalism. Then the way is open to *derive* capitalism; for, in Marx's own words: "a highly developed commodity exchange and the *form of the commodity as the universal necessary social form of the product* can only emerge as the consequence of the capitalist mode of production."[52] The underlined phrase is the historically determinate beginning of *Capital*, therefore. But only in one sense.

Certainly the question to be asked is: How could it possibly be the case that the commodity form be *universal* and *necessarily* so? And the ground for this can be demonstrated to be capitalist production. But, to *answer* this question thus, it turns out that one needs to focus on that aspect of the commodity that betrays its social origin, namely exchange value. It will be recalled that a moment ago we pointed out that the commodity was itself a unity of use-value and exchange value. Should it not therefore be stated that Marx's true starting point was value, something suitably simple and universal which we can show to be grounded in capitalism? (Indeed it is interesting to note that in the various plans of the period Marx changed his characterization of his starting point in the process of publishing his 1859 *Critique*. Throughout 1858 his plan began: Value-Money-Capital[53] but his publications in 1859 and 1867 use the titles Commodity-Money-Capital.)

However, while simplicity and universality are certainly advantages for a starting point, another still more important is lacking, namely *immediacy*. How do we *know* that we are dealing with value? Value is in truth something posited (though not yet grounded) only through the mediation of the totality of relationships of the commodities exchanged one with another. Faced with this ceaseless movement of exchange, the idea arises that some *identity* in essence is present behind the heterogeneous appearances of commodities. Such an analytical reduction of the observed phenomena may be mistaken, but it suggests the following research program: On what conditions of existence can value be shown to ground itself, so as to validate itself as this universal property of commodities? As we shall see shortly, a dialectical derivation of the necessity of money and capital may be undertaken to answer this. The upshot establishes that if the commodity is the product of capital it instantiates value.

So what *is* the starting point? The commodity has immediacy in our experience (popular consciousness is aware that in this society practically everything is bought and sold) yet it is susceptible of further analysis. Value is a simple universal but, while an immediacy for thought is so only as a mediated immediacy, a thought arising from the contemplation of a systematic regular, reproduced set of exchanges. But on the other hand, it is clearly something which, in virtue of its problematic status as an abstraction from the heterogeneity of the shapes in which commodities appear, cries out for a grounding movement.

In these circumstances we may gratefully accept Banaji's ingenious suggestion that *Capital* has a double starting point: the commodity forms the *analytical* starting point, from which we separate out value; while this value forms the *synthetic* point of departure for deriving more complex relationships in the course of seeking how to ground it as the pure universal essence of the commodity.[54] Once the commodity has been established as a *form of value* necessarily linked to money and capital, we have a very different commodity under discussion than that originally grasped in the immediacy of experience as a mere aspect of an uncomprehended totality.

It is perhaps worth noting that in *Capital* Marx himself supplied a somewhat ambiguous characterization of his starting point: he stated that just as biology got properly underway when the microscope resolved the body into cells so "the power of abstraction" reveals that "for bourgeois society the commodity-form of the product of labor [*die Waarenform des Arbeitsproduckts*] or the value-form of the commodity [*die Werthform der Waare*] is the economic cell-form."[55] Is the "or" asserting an identity or disjunction? What is clear is that in the first case Marx is interested in the fact that in bourgeois society products take the form of commodities whereas in the second case he is interested in the fact that commodities have values. This seems to fit Banaji's suggestion that there is a double point of departure.

Furthermore, in the original draft of Marx's 1859 *Critique* there are some interesting passages on the nature of his dialectical derivation of capital. If we begin with commodities and their circulation we see that: "In the C-M-C movement, the physical matter appears as the actual content of the movement; the social movement, only as a fleeting mediation for the satisfaction of individual wants."[56] Therefore it is exchange value that is "the social form as such;" its further analysis, therefore, leads us into "the social process which throws the commodity onto its surface;" thus we now "proceed from exchange value as such, as we earlier proceeded from the commodity."[57] Notice that in this passage Marx in effect provides evidence supporting Banaji's suggestion that there are two starting points in Marx's argument.

It is clear to all Marxists that in its formal definition capital is a monetary form, money which breeds money; it is also clear that money essentially mediates commodity exchange; thus it is concluded that a beginning must be made with the commodity. What is not often realized is that, if these forms are to be forms *of value*, the reverse sequence of internal relations must also hold. For, as was demonstrated above, the concept of value cannot be convincingly posited as objectively grounded at the level of commodity exchange alone.

The method of advance in systematic dialectic is based on observing whether or not the characteristic identified, in this case value as a universal property of commodities, can be objectively grounded in the stage of development (e.g., of exchange) under review. It may well turn out to be the case that the determination (e.g., of value) imputed to such relations gives rise to a contradiction. This in turn gives rise to the immanent necessity to transcend the contradiction and thereby produce a more complex set of relations to which an adequate actualization of value may be imputed; the process may be repeated several times.[58]

In order to illustrate the point let us say something briefly about the value form as it develops from commodities to money to capital.

With respect to Marx's handling of these crucial transitions between value forms, his best is that, in Section 3 of Chapter 1, from value to money; here he shows that value cannot be actualized in an accidental exchange but requires the unification of the world of commodities through the establishment of a universal equivalent. Marx starts with the simple relationships of commodities and demonstrates the "defects" or "deficiencies" involved in the attempt to present as a universal property of the commodity something that is only immanent in their relations.[59] This contradiction is solved by the doubling of the value form into commodities and money whereby the value implicit in commodities appears explicitly in money, which as immediate exchangeability actualizes value; as a mere immanence, the abstraction of value from commodity relations must be grounded in something explicitly positing it, money, which, Marx noted in his *Grundrisse*, is "value for itself."[60]

Money in turn, however, runs into the contradiction that, to express its universality over against the particular manifestations of value in the commodities it unites, it must both stand apart from this world of particulars as "autonomous value," but assert itself as value through actualising its immediate exchangeability in practice, i.e., alienating itself in exchange, thereby dissolving into particularity.[61] So if money is to actualize the concept of value in autonomous form it must be independent of its function as mere medium of circulation; it must be somehow counterposed to circulation of commodities as value "for itself," as distinct from merely relating these values "in themselves" to each other. But if it is withdrawn from circulation and hoarded to preserve itself as autonomous value then it ceases to be money, it reverts to its gold shape as a mere natural object; gold is only money if it is gold *used* in circulation; but if it *is* alienated then once again it metamorphoses into a mere good lacking in the character of value for itself. Thus money cannot realize the concept of value because of the contradiction that in striving to be value for itself it must be alienated but cannot be. The solution to this contradiction is to alienate for the sake of realizing more money, by making *itself* the object of its entry into circulation. This, however, is a new value form, that of capital. That is to say, through a dialectical development the money form gives rise to the new form of value, value as the aim of exchange in the capital form.

Finally the key move from circulation to production is motivated for Marx by the search to ground satisfactorily the regular production of surplus-value. For a new contradiction arises when the source of surplus-value must arise in this circulation form, yet cannot on the working assumption of equivalent exchange. Thus in *Capital* he points to the contradiction that "capital cannot arise from circulation, and it is equally impossible for it to arise apart from circulation."[62] The solution is stated to lie in the purchase and consumption of the value-producing agent labor power.

But his manuscripts, and especially the first draft of the 1859 *Critique*, throw more light on the logic of derivation here; for there Marx attempts to ground circulation itself. Let us review this derivation of production.

Capital, in truth, is self-positing value "only because it is itself a constantly self-renewing circuit of exchanges."[63] But it is also clear "that the simple movement of exchange values, as it is present in pure circulation, can never realize capital."[64] This is because it has no guarantee of renewal.

The repetition of the process from both points, money and commodity, does not spring from the conditions of circulation itself. The act of exchange cannot be rekindled of itself. Circulation does not, therefore, contain within itself the principle of self-renewal. It proceeds from presupposed moments, and not from those created by itself. New commodities must be thrown into it again and again, from without, as fuel into the fire . . . . Circulation, therefore, which appears as that which is immediately present on the surface of bourgeois society, exists only in so far as it is continually mediated. Considered in itself, it is the mediation of presumed extremes. But it does not posit these extremes. Hence it must itself be mediated as the totality of mediation, as a total process. *That is why its immediate being is pure semblance* [*Schein*]. It is the *phenomenon* of a process going on behind its back. Circulation . . . now goes back into the activity that . . . produces values . . . as into its ground.[65]

This ground is "industrial capital" Marx says.[66] He sums up the trajectory of his argument as follows:

In this first section, where exchange value, money and price are considered, commodities always appear as already in existence . . . Through itself, however, [the world of commodities] points beyond itself to . . . *relations of production*. The internal structure of production therefore forms the second section . . .[67]

Thus if capital as self-valorizing value is to realize itself the movement of value must appear "in a much more complex form" than in pure circulation; it must be "the movement which simultaneously creates, produces, exchange values as its own premise."[68] The phenomenon of circulation may now be viewed in a new light; as an immediacy it is "pure semblance"; but as grounded in production it is the necessary form of appearance of capitalist relations of production.

Let us now consider the dialectical derivation as a whole. As Marx pointed out, when we derive the concept of value from exchange we must worry about whether this is just "our abstraction."[69] But, after its detailed grounding, Marx said:

In the course of our presentation, it has become evident that value, which appeared as an abstraction, is possible only as such an abstraction as soon as money is posited. On the other hand, money circulation leads to capital; and in general, it is only on the basis of capital that circulation can draw into its sphere all the moments of production.[70]

Through this argument a dialectical derivation is presented of value as the outcome of production. To sum up: value, abstractly implicit in commodity relations, becomes self-related in money, becomes its own aim in capital, and becomes self-grounded in capitalist production. The upshot is that value cannot be defined in the simple sense of either a substance preexisting exchange or as a mere phenomenal relation, but only as a moment of a totalizing process of development of internally related forms of a complex whole. Capital is the most complex value form; indeed, in a sense it is *the* value form, because only at this level of development of the concept of value can we grasp that value is a real substance, instead of a vanishing mediator in exchange. Thus it is not quite correct to say that commodity, money, and capital, are all (specifically different) value forms. For value is properly grasped only in the *comprehensive concept* of a totality whose internal moments are commodity, money and capital, which are nested within each other and enfold one another in an ever-moving mediatedness. It is quite impossible to give a simple definition of these concepts. A methodological consequence of this understanding is that the concept of capital itself (as the most highly mediated) requires, not a definition, whether nominal or real, ostensive or stipulative, but a dialectical *exposition* of its inner self-development.

Let us now try to pin down exactly how the derivation of capital from the commodity form differs from a linear development, and instead necessarily "bends back," so to speak, to re-present the beginning as a result. In fact, the starting point itself is problematic, and hence provides for movement, because it has been abstracted from the whole; and the presentation is thus impelled to reconstruct the whole precisely through "negating" the starting point.

Because Marx could not start explicitly with capitalist production as a whole, this complexity had to be reduced in form first to some simple yet characteristic aspect of itself. Many assert that, if Marx's chosen beginning, the commodity, is such a concept; then it already *presupposes* capitalist production. There is a sense in which this is true, and that reference to barter or simple commodity production (whether as historical or as a model) is quite out of place. But, regardless, there is clearly some difficulty in "presupposing" what comes *later* in the argument. Marx outlines "the circular nature of our argument" as follows:

As the elementary form of bourgeois wealth, the *commodity* was our point of departure, the prerequisite for the emergence of capital. On the other hand, *commodities* appear now as the *product of capital*.[71]

How is this circularity resolved? The commodity is really an abstraction from the reality that produced it, but it is not known as such when given immediately. However, if we observe that the commodity is the simple universal and necessary form of wealth in the bourgeois epoch then the argument gets underway by noticing how deficient in truth such a claim must be at the initially given level of analysis; in particular the claim that this social character of wealth consists in a unitary form of value is simply *ungrounded* until we have developed the argument through to the end. Then we can see why capitalism produces value, surplus value, and the capital relation itself; and in this context we can grasp the necessity of the earlier forms. As the simple element of the system the commodity, although necessary for the development of the concept of capital, lacks at the start any *necessary* existence as the general form of the product of labor. As Marx said, "only on the basis of capitalist production does the commodity become the general form of the product."[72]

Thus its concept is enriched when it is grasped as reproduced through the immanent drive of the system, infused with a determinate content under the force of valorization. A commodity is not at all the same commodity when viewed as a product, and again when viewed as a product of capital. *As a result* it is grounded in the totality and acquires the character of necessity, rather than just presented in contingent experience.

Thus the commodity that *results* from capitalist production emerges on a higher level of social being. "The commodity, as it emerges in capitalist production, is different from the commodity taken as the element, the starting point of capitalist production," said Marx.[73] But to show this requires developing the structure and law of capitalist production *from* its logical prerequisite, the form of commodity exchange.

While knowledge of the system in some sense takes the form of a circle there would be no advance at all if there was not some difference between beginning and end. Thus we have to *show* that the condition of existence of the commodity as the simple universal necessary form of the product lies precisely in the generalization of commodity production, which in turn requires capitalism to achieve full development.

The point is that only at the *end* is the commodity so *posited*. At the *beginning*, as such, it *cannot* be; for that would be to presuppose what has still to be accomplished; only through the dialectical development of the value-form can we understand just what a commodity really is, and why we had to start with it defined in the most elementary and presuppositionless fashion. The commodity cannot be *known* as what it is, and what it is grounded in, until this development is complete. To say *at the start* that the commodity as a simple universality presupposes capitalist production would be nothing but a *promissory note*—or sheer dogmatism. Certainly, Marx starts with the commodity conceived *implicitly* on the basis of capitalist production, but his argument achieves precisely the explicit *demonstration* that for the commodity in its universality and necessity to subsist this is indeed its presupposition.

While it is correct to start with the commodity, the overriding moment in the system is industrial capital, for this is the site of its reproductive drive. Although in the derivation it necessarily must appear as result, it is really the presupposition, and the starting point must be characterized in such a way as to drive us to this identification of the result as the true ground.

Furthermore, although industrial capital lies at the heart of the matter, it is important to grasp circulation as a developed totality, *before* turning to production; for the latter cannot be studied in *determinate* form, and its existing law of motion comprehended, unless the *intentionality* it is infused with, i.e., valorization, is understood as deriving from these forms. Once the value-form of capital, viz. M-C-M', is comprehended as *constituting* production as capitalist production, we can *then* see production as key in so far as it is the material potential of the productive forces to increase the productivity of labor that explains actual accumulation. The *form* of capital explains the *drive* for valorization; but it cannot in itself, i.e., as pure form, bring it about, *produce* it. Thus Marx concludes that it is best to see production as the "overriding moment";[74] but this is not production as a "factor" external to, and causally effective upon, other "factors," it is production as *mediated* by circulation whose form it internalizes. Hence, methodologically, the exposition describes a circle: commodity circulation (form of value)—circulation reflected *into* production (valorization)—circulation as a moment *of* production (realization of value).

5. Conclusion

Because in *Capital* he articulated the structure of a totality, Marx used a dialectical method; more precisely *systematic dialectic* was required. Truer to the principle of the systematic dialectical exposition of concepts than treating the starting point of *Capital* as a historical presupposition, or as a simple model, is to consider it as a provisional immature abstract moment within a complex totality; hence the exposition has to remedy the insufficiency of the starting point by showing how value, in its complete, finished form, does make good the promise of a law of value, by grounding it in the developed value-forms—first money, then capital, then productive labor, finally circulation of capital and "the movement as a whole." Such an unfolding of form, discovering deeper essential determinations at each stage, requires not a "rigid definition" of value but an *exposition* of its movement. In such an exposition, this system of forms must be grasped as a totality,[75] not as a set of independent stages.

Notes

1. The original text is available in Karl Marx, *Ökonomische Manuskripte Und Schriften 1858–61, Marx-Engels Gesamtausgabe* (hereafter *MEGA*) II 2 (Berlin: Dietz Verlag, 1980). I give page references to the Peking edition of the English translation, published as an Appendix to: Karl Marx *Preface and Introduction to "A Contribution to the Critique of Political Economy"*, 1976. For a consideration of the circumstances surrounding the publication of this review see my paper "Engels as Interpreter of Marx's Economics," in C. J. Arthur (ed.) *Engels Today: A Centenary Appreciation* (Basingstoke: Macmillan, 1996).
2. This phrase, although in general use today, e.g., R. L. Meek *Studies in the Labour Theory of Value*, (London, Lawrence & Wishart, 1956, p. 148), is not in the Engels text itself; but it is fair to it. This "logical-historical method" became so firmly established that when Meek was challenged on the question in 1975 he reacted first by pointing out that he had inherited this view of Marx's method from a long tradition of interpretation, and cited Engels's review at length as the *locus classicus* for it. *The Economic Journal*, vol. 86, June 1976, pp. 342–47. A longer version of this paper is in his *Smith, Marx and After* (London: Chapman and Hall, 1977). He had already used the Engels review in his *Economics and Ideology and Other Essays* (London and New York: Chapman and Hall, 1967) and his *Studies in the Labour Theory of Value* (1956). In all his work Meek was absolutely unself-conscious about treating Marx and Engels as one person. Throughout, he quoted freely from Engels when purporting to give Marx's views.
3. January 16, 1858; *Marx-Engels Collected Works* (London: Lawrence and Wishart, 1975) (hereafter *CW*) vol. 40, p. 249.
4. Peking ed., p. 54; *MEGA* II 2, p. 251.
5. Peking ed. p. 56; *MEGA* II 2, p. 253. T. A. Jackson, writing in 1936 (*Dialectics*, London: Lawrence and Wishart, pp. 37–38) quoted from the review. His discussion of Marx's method (p. 295 ff.) first rightly distinguished "the general dialectical movement of history (including the bourgeois epoch) from the *inner* dialectic of specific capitalist economy" (p. 298) but then tended to identify them (p. 301 ff.).
6. Peking ed., pp. 54–55.
7. See Hegel's *Elements of the Philosophy of Right* § 32 Remark & Addition; English trans. (Cambridge: Cambridge University Press) p. 61. And Marx's 1857 *Introduction . . .* Peking ed., p. 33.

8. Letter of April 2, 1858. (Meek has already drawn attention to its importance: *Smith, Marx, & After*, p. 139 n.14)
9. *MEGA* II 2, p. 252; Peking ed. p. 55.
10. *CW29*, p. 417.
11. This text is quoted, in their challenge to Meek's reliance on Engels, by M. Morishima and G. Catephores (*The Economic Journal*, vol. 85, June 1975); and very extensively in their response (vol. 86, June 1976) to Meek's reply. In his writings on Marx's method, Meek cited *both* the Engels review *and* Marx's 1857 *Introduction* . . . as authoritative; the resulting incoherence he simply ignored. (See *Studies* . . . pp. 148, 150; pp. 303, 307, n.1; *Economics and Ideology* . . . pp. 96 107, n.12.) Later he claimed Marx's *Introduction* . . . merely "qualifies" Engels's account (*Smith* . . . p. 138).
12. *CW28*, p. 43.
13. Peking ed., p. 40.
14. Letter to Marx, August 3, 1859. *CW40*, p. 478.
15. See letter to Engels October 5, 1859 (*CW40* p. 502) and letter to Lasalle November 6, 1859 (*CW40*, p. 518).
16. Quoted from M. Eldred, p. xxvi. *Critique of Competitive Freedom* (Copenhagen: Kurasje, 1984).
17. Peking ed., p. 58.
18. Tony Smith interprets Marx's *Capital* as an exercise in "systematic dialectic" influenced by Hegel's *Logic*. He has argued against the logical-historical method on three grounds: (a) that in Marx's *Capital* the historical order is clearly violated, as he shows through examples; (b) that a systematic dialectic is more congruent with Marx's effort to trace the inner relations behind the (often illusory) appearances; (c) that Marx intends to establish necessary connections, an objective for which historical observation is unsuited. (*Dialectical Social Theory and its Critics*, Chap. 3, *The Debate Regarding Dialectical Logic in Marx's Economic Writings*; Albany, NY: SUNY Press, 1993).
19. For a reading of Marx's first chapter that sharply distinguishes the determinations of form and magnitude of value see V. Pietilä, "The Logical, the Historical and the Forms of Value," in *Rethinking Marx*, ed. S. Hänninen and L. Paldán (New York: International General/IMMRC 1984), esp. pp. 64–65.
20. *CW29*, p. 300.
21. Peking ed., p. 56.
22. *Capital* III, trans. D. Fernbach (Harmondsworth: Penguin, 1981) p. 103.
23. *Capital* III, p. 1037.
24. The only occurrence of the term in the whole three volumes of *Capital* occurs in Volume 3 (p. 370), but this is in a passage given to us subsequent to Engels's editorial work; when checked against the manuscript (*MEGA* II, 4.2) itself it is clear that Engels inserted this passage.
25. In his *Anti-Dühring* (Moscow FLPH 1962, pp. 225–26) Engels claimed to have found in *Capital* a discussion of the historical transition of commodity production into capitalist production. He cited at length a passage in which Marx presupposes the worker owned his own product: *Capital*, vol. 1, trans. B. Fowkes (Harmondsworth: Penguin, 1976) pp. 729–30. He did not notice that passage is written in a hypothetical mode. I argue it is counter-factual in character in my "Negation of the Negation in Marx's *Capital*"—*Rethinking Marxism* (winter, 1993).

26. *CW28*, p. 183.
27. *CW29*, pp. 159–60.
28. *Capital III*, p. 1034; the full passage from Marx is on pp. 277–78.
29. Morishima and Catephores also have said this; *The Economic Journal*, 1975, p. 319.
30. *Studies* . . ., Introduction to the Second Edition, (1973) p. xv. Other passages quoted below are from the Appendix which was taken originally from his *Economics and Ideology* (1967).
31. Studies . . . , p. 302–03.
32. Ibid., p. xv.
33. Ibid., p. 304.
34. *Studies* . . . , p. xv. Incidentally, the "by him" in this remark is simply false, because all the quoted material is not from Marx but from Engels.
35. Ibid., p. 317.
36. See, p. 30, *The Law of Accumulation and Breakdown of the Capitalist System*, Henryk Grossman, trans. and abridged by J. Banaji (Pluto Press, London: 1992).
37. P. M. Sweezy *The Theory of Capitalist Development* (1942, reprinted New York Monthly Review Press, 1968) p. 12. It is odd that Sweezy, writing in 1942, appears unaware of Engels's 1859 review.
38. Ibid., p. 13.
39. Ibid., p. 16.
40. Ibid., p. 17.
41. Ibid., p. 23. No source is given for the words in quote marks.
42. Ibid., p. 53.
43. Ibid., p. 56.
44. For a good exposition of the problems with linear logics, see Ali Shamsavari (*Dialectics and Social Theory*, Braunton. Merlin Books, 1991); for example, Shamsavari rightly criticizes what he believes is the "standard Marxist approach" to the determination of commodity values, namely that "values are created in production and only *"realized"* in circulation" (p. 157), because it analytically separates production and circulation, and, in linear fashion, sees the latter simply as the finishing touch of the former. But production is itself formed by circulation while yet reducing circulation to a moment of itself. The linear analytical conception, common to theories of value from Marxian to neoclassical, sees circulation as "a passive moment" (p. 257) with the result that in much value theory "the very sphere in which values are formed, i.e., circulation, is ignored" (p. 259).
45. *Capital* I (Fowkes trans.), p. 125.
46. "The Commodity as 'Characteristic Form'"; Chap. 10 of *Economics as Worldly Philosophy*, eds. R. Blackwell, J. Chatha, and E. J. Nell (Basingstoke: Macmillan, 1993).
47. Jairus Banaji, "From the Commodity to Capital: Hegel's Dialectic in Marx's *Capital*," in D. Elson ed., *Value: The Representation of Labour in Capitalism* (London: CSE Books, 1979), pp. 29–30.
48. *Ibid*, p. 30.
49. The lesson for elements of the capitalist social formation that apparently existed in previous periods is drawn in my paper mentioned in note 1, where I say "the capital that preexisted capitalism is not the *same capital* that we have today."

50. An example of greater definiteness would be the re-presentation of an exchange-value to that of a product of labor once the relation of exchange to production comes into view. An example of a widening would be the shift from commodity money to other shapes of money. Another example of narrowing is the restriction introduced by Marx in the second part of Chap. 7 that "productive labor" be not only productive of use-value but of surplus-value at the same time.

51. I differ from Marx (and his exegesists such as Campbell and Banaji) in that I believe it is possible, through the power of abstraction, to push back the beginning beyond "the commodity form of the product" to the world of commodity exchange as such, because I hold that the dialectic of the "value form of the commodity" of itself reaches the required result. The "synthetic" movement, i.e., the search for the systematic grounding of value, is sufficiently powerful to derive from it the necessity of capitalist production without introducing as an initial restriction that the commodities considered at the start be products. (For my attempt at this dialectical derivation see my paper "Hegel's *Logic* and Marx's *Capital*" in F. Moseley ed. *Marx's Method in 'Capital': A Reexamination*, Atlantic Highlands, NJ: Humanities Press, 1993).

52. Results, *Capital Volume One* p. 949 (cf. also pp. 1059–60).

53. For example, in letters to Lasalle and to Engels, and in his "Index" to the *Grundrisse CW29*, p. 421.

54. Banaji, *op. cit.*, pp. 28, 36, 40.

55. *MEGA II 5*, p. 12; *Capital I* p. 90.

56. *CW29*, p. 484. "So in order to examine the further determination of form arising from the movement of circulation itself, we must keep to the side where the formal aspect, exchange value as such, is further developed . . ." (*ibid.*)

57. *CW29*, p. 490.

58. G. Reuten and M. Williams explain that in systematic dialectic "the presentation moves forward by the transcendence of contradiction and by providing ever more concrete *grounds*—the conditions of existence—of the earlier abstract determination." *Value-Form and the State* (London: Routledge, 1989), p. 22. Note also the footnote explaining the grounding relation.

59. *Capital* I, p. 154, 156, especially.

60. *CW28*, p. 388. Also *Original Text . . . CW29*, p. 441.

61. The least satisfactory of Marx's transitions in Volume 1 is that from money to capital. He simply says that empirically we find "alongside" C-M-C another movement M-C-M and then analyses the consequences of that: the movement from one to the other is treated only cursorily. (This is pointed out by M. Campbell "The Commodity as Characteristic Form" pp. 290–92.) However, in his manuscripts a more detailed treatment is provided, on which I draw. See *Grundrisse, CW28* pp. 160–62, 166–67, 182–84, 190–93; and *Original Text of CCPE, CW29*, pp. 478–79, pp. 484–500.

62. *Capital* I, p. 268.

63. *CW28*, p. 191

64. *CW28*, p. 185.

65. Composite quotation from *CW29*, p. 479 and *CW28*, p. 186.

66. *CW29*, p. 482.

67. *CW28*, p. 160.

68. *CW28*, p. 186–87.
69. Marx *Contribution* ... , *CW29*, p. 285.
70. *CW29*, p. 159.
71. *Resultäte; Capital Volume One*, p. 949.
72. *CW32*, p. 301.
73. *Ibid.*
74. *CW28*, p. 36.
75. The systematic approach need not lead to closure; for, critically presented, the logic of the capitalist system can be shown to be caught in a contradiction of positing as fully subsumed under its forms necessary conditions of its existence that 'exceed its grasp. I hope to show elsewhere that this is true of (a) its internal other, the proletariat; (b) its external other, nature.

2

Redoubled Empiricism: The Place of Social Form and Formal Causality in Marxian Theory[1]

Patrick Murray

The extraordinary importance of Karl Marx for philosophy and social theory today depends heavily on the role social form plays in his thought.[2] His understanding of social form is distinctive but deeply indebted to Aristotle and Hegel. That fact is what, unfortunately, makes Marx's thinking so inscrutable to many.[3] For Marx, like Aristotle and Hegel, is diametrically opposed to the mind-set spanning modern rationalism, British empiricism, and Kantianism, to the "purist splits"[4] that remain the backbone of our modern philosophical and scientific culture, the splits between the *conceptual* and the *empirical*, the *subjective* and the *objective*. In so doing, Marx rejects the purist philosophical underpinnings that govern classical and neoclassical economics and incapacitate them from taking the proper measure of social form.

Characteristically, "purist splits" divide their adherents into opposing philosophical camps. Following Hegel's account of the different "attitudes toward objectivity,"[5] I will separate them into modern rationalism, which I will call "purist objectivism" (or "objectivism"), and "purist subjectivism" (or "subjectivism"), which includes British empiricism and Kant's critical philosophy. Though our focus is on empiricism and, more generally, subjectivism, we will examine both branches of purism to see how each closes off the conceptual space needed to make intelligible Marx's redoubled empiricism, that is, his empirical approach to social form and his attention to formal causality. In Marx's critique of the "purist splits" and the modern philosophical alternatives that spin off from them, we find the deepest roots of his profound methodological and scientific differences with classical and neoclassical economics. To come to terms with the depth of Marx's critique of classical and neoclassical economics requires that we investigate his fundamental differences with the mind-set of the modern philosophers.

In this chapter, then, I try to get to the bottom of the distinctiveness and superiority of Marxian theory over against classical and neoclassical economics. It lies in the fact that Marx takes a radically different—philosophically and scientifically more satisfactory—approach to social form. Investigating Marx's understanding of social form opens the door to: (1) his philosophical rejection of the "purist splits," (2) his revival of Aristotelian social forms and formal causality (which means that social forms make a difference in the world), and (3) his redoubled empiricism, wherein the social forms of needs, production, distribution themselves—not just the behavior of objects already subsumed under forms—along with the powers and interconnections of these forms, are subjects for experience-based inquiry.

The six key and interrelated concepts for this chapter, then, are: "purist split," objectivism, subjectivism, social form, formal causality, and redoubled empiricism. My argument comes to this: both objectivism and subjectivism are rooted in "purist splits" between the empirical and the conceptual and between the objective and the subjective that block redoubled empiricism and any philosophically or scientifically adequate account of social form. Modern rationalism, by prizing the purely conceptual over the empirical, chokes off any possibility of redoubled empiricism. It can allow for objective social forms but not for an empirical inquiry into them. Subjectivism undercuts the notion of objective social form, for, according to it, concepts are purely subjective and what is purely subjective has no objective correlate, such as a social form. With the same stroke, subjectivism renders nonsensical both formal causality (nonexistent forms can have no effects) and redoubled empiricism (if concepts are purely subjective, there is no point to submitting them to empirical scrutiny). I claim that Marx, following Aristotle and Hegel, rejects objectivism and subjectivism and their shared purist assumptions about concepts and facts, subjectivity and objectivity, and that he thereby discloses the space for social forms, formal causality, and redoubled empiricism. This is not only philosophically more attractive, and puts Marx in the company of the most astute "post-dogmatic" empiricists,[6] it pays off scientifically.

Classical and neoclassical economics suffer scientifically, in the Marxian view, precisely because they harbor the purist assumptions of modern philosophy and, consequently, fail to advance from ordinary to redoubled empiricism: "With all later bourgeois economists, as with Adam Smith, lack of theoretical understanding needed to distinguish the different forms of economic relations remains the rule in their coarse grabbing at and interest in the empirically available material" (Marx 1862–63a, 92). Conversely, in appealing to specific social forms (e.g., value, wage-labor, capital) and their power (formal causality), Marx is able to identify, explain, and predict social phenomena that theories like classical and neoclassical economics fail to recognize, and he provides superior accounts of *aspects of* phenomena recognized by all parties (e.g., the intensification of the labor process or movements in the rate of profit).[7] The net result of Marx's integration of social form into his theory is that, as Martha Campbell starkly and rightly observes, "there are no counterparts to Marx's economic concepts in either Classical or utility theory" (Campbell 1993b, 34).[8] It is a fact much to the credit of Marxian theory.

Beyond this superior first-order explanatory power, Marx's account of social forms enables him to identify where the basic shortcomings of classical and neoclassical economics lie and to offer a historical materialist explanation of their source. These two abilities, joined to the first-order explanatory superiority of Marxian theory, add up to a powerful case for the cogency of Marx's redoubled empiricism.

1. A Brief Account of "Purist Splits" in Modern Philosophy

Subjectivism is based on two "purist splits" and their correlation: (1) separating the subjective from the objective; (2) splitting the conceptual from the empirical; and (3) correlating the conceptual with the subjective and the empirical with the objective.[9] Since the relevant purist assumptions play themselves out throughout the modern period (Bacon and Descartes through German critical philosophy), it is best to present an account of the subjectivism of modern empiricism and critical (Kantian) philosophy in the broader context of modern philosophy as a whole.

1.1 PURIST OBJECTIVISM: MODERN RATIONALISM

An earmark of modern rationalism (Descartes, Leibniz, Spinoza, Malebranche) is its "purist split" between intellect or understanding, on the one hand, and sensation and imagination on the other. In the train of that separation comes the famous doctrine of innate ideas, for innate ideas are precisely those ideas which are formed by the intellect or understanding alone. Innate ideas are radically independent of sensation and imagination; they are the autonomous ideas of the pure subject.[10] They are, accordingly, *purely* subjective but only in the sense of being purely nonempirical;[11] this does not imply that they are not objective in the sense that they do not correspond to anything in the real world. On the contrary, consider Descartes's insistence that the objective properties of material beings (their "primary qualities") are knowable only by the concepts of pure intellect. Modern rationalism, then, is purist objectivism, purist because it cleaves the conceptual and the empirical from one another and objectivist because it holds that pure concepts provide objective knowledge, that is, knowledge of things as they are in themselves.[12]

While modern rationalism and subjectivism agree in their purism that the conceptual is the subject's doing alone, they draw diametrically opposed consequences as to the objective validity of concepts. Modern rationalism holds that it is precisely these purely subjective (nonempirical), innate concepts that comprehend the nature of things in themselves and thus are objective. Whereas, for subjectivism, *because* concepts are nonempirical and purely subjective, they do not admit of objective validity. The present grip over our imaginations held by subjectivist thinking, for which subjectivity simply excludes objectivity, makes it tricky even to formulate the position of purist objectivism or the Hegelian position, which is objectivist but antipurist. For both of the latter, though they differ importantly,[13] there is a sense in which it is true that "the more subjective, the more objective." That way of thinking makes no sense to a subjectivist. In modern rationalism, the sensuous or empirical is identified with the nonobjective, with things as they seem to us, with anthropomorphism, whereas in subjectivism the purely empirical, the purely "given," is the purely objective.

1.2 THE FIRST FORM OF SUBJECTIVISM: MODERN EMPIRICISM

Modern empiricism blasted away at the rationalists' doctrine of innate ideas and their related assertion that there is an intellectual faculty, namely intellect or understanding, that is categorically distinct from sensation and imagination and yields truth about the world—from a post-subjectivist standpoint such as Hegel's or Marx's, rightly so.[14] The irony, however, was that, leaving aside certain developments stemming from Locke's revolutionary and implicitly post-subjectivist *doctrine of signs*, the modern empiricists failed to extricate themselves from the quagmires of purism. How so? Because they too insisted on the "purist split" between the conceptual and the empirical, which they lined up with the distinction between subjective and objective in opposite fashion to the rationalists.

The modern empiricist view of concepts is nominalist: concepts are purely subjective; they have no objective correlates.[15] This amounts to an attack on Aristotelian forms insofar as forms are taken to be the objective correlates of certain concepts. As Francis Bacon puts the nominalist conclusion: "forms are fictions of the human mind" (Bacon 1620, 49): forms are simply projections, like gods in Feuerbach's estimation. In the *Holy Family*, Marx calls attention to this feature of modern empiricism as found in Hobbes: "Hobbes, as Bacon's continuator, argues thus: if all human knowledge is furnished by the senses, then our concepts, notions, and ideas are but the phantoms of the real world, more or less divested of its sensual form" (Marx and Engels 1845, 128).

Similarly to Bacon and Hobbes, Locke splits the several workings of the mind (the purely conceptual and subjective) off from simple ideas (the purely empirical and objective). But, as Hegel was quick to point out, and as we will have further occasion to see, purists are prone to flip-flops and double-talk. Locke's is a highly influential—hardly unequivocal—joining of nominalism with the subjectivist critique of Aristotelian "real essences" or forms. Locke seems to be talking out of both sides of his mouth in his theory of "nominal essences" in the third book of the *Essay Concerning Human Understanding*. Sounding like a razor-sharp nominalist, Locke writes that "general and universal belong not to the real existence of things; but are the inventions and creatures of the understanding, made by it for its own use" (Locke 1690a, 414). Only two sections later, however, we find Locke hedging this stark nominalism, supplementing the subjectivist contention that nominal essences are "*the workmanship of the understanding*" with the proviso that they "*have their foundation in the similitude of things*."[16] Here we see Locke's subjectivism being buffeted about: he cannot help but want it both ways: concepts (nominal essences), with their generality and universality, are *purely* the work of the subjective understanding, Baconian "fictions of the human mind"—and they are not: they are "also" determined by the objective similarities of things.

Redoubled empiricism, i.e., the empirical scrutiny and fixing of concepts in relation to other concepts, makes no sense if we stand by the subjectivist tenet that concepts are purely the work of the understanding. If that were so, experience could not play any role in the determination of concepts. Locke's anti-subjectivist—and contradictory—proviso, however, opens the space for redoubling empiricism, by allowing objective properties ("*the similitude of things*") to enter into the constitution of concepts.

We find the "purist splits" of empiricism ready, once again, to hand in David Hume's seminal critique of causality. For Hume accepts the data of sense perception as perfectly objective, but he is unable to find the impression of necessary connection anywhere in that objective world of sense. When he eventually does locate the impression of necessary connection, he identifies it as a *purely subjective* feeling implicated in a habit or custom of mind, which we unwittingly *project* onto the objective world.[17] Hume's identification of the purely subjective with the strictly nonobjective makes this a shocking refutation of objective claims about causal connections. But this shock value relies on a dubious phenomenology in which "purely subjective" items crop up. Whenever we come across talk of the "purely subjective"—we will hear it prominently in neoclassical economics' notion of utility—we should look to see where a "distinction of reason,"[18] notably, the one between the subjective and objective, has been hypostatized into a supposed separation. So, for all its bold and well-meaning forays against modern rationalism, modern empiricism missed the deeper issue of purism and yoked itself to the vain abstractions of the subjectivist mind-set.

1.3   THE SECOND FORM OF SUBJECTIVISM: CRITICAL (KANTIAN) PHILOSOPHY

In one sense, little needs to be said about critical philosophy and subjectivism, as it was Kant who crystallized the doctrine in his "Copernican Revolution"; however, we want to see how this second type of subjectivism distinguishes itself from the first (modern empiricism). Following up on Hume's assertion that sense perception taken strictly can provide no warrant for universality or necessity, Kant reasoned— implicitly accepting Hume's presupposed identification of sense perception with objectivity (of one sort, at least)[19]—that, since in fact we have experience of universality, it must come from the subject, the knower, and from the knower alone. In the *Critique of Pure Reason* Kant identifies space and time as nonempirical,[20] *purely subjective* forms of sensibility and the twelve categories of the understanding as nonempirical, *purely subjective* functions necessary for the synthesis that is experience. Where Kant's critical philosophy differs from empiricism is: (1) in the assertion that what is given, the purely empirical, cannot be determined in utter abstraction from the concepts of the understanding and the forms of sensibility: intuitions without concepts are blind.[21] (2) Rather, the phenomenal world is co-constituted by what is given in intuition and by the purely subjective forms of intuition in conjunction with the categories of the understanding as they are schematized by the (transcendental) imagination. Hence, these purely subjective forms and categories have a sort of objectivity. That counts as a half step away from modern empiricism's stance that subjective forms and concepts are not objective at all, and a half step back in the direction of modern rationalism's doctrine that pure thought discovered the objective nature of the world. But it is only a half step, because the objectivity Kant allows purely subjective forms and categories is of Hegel's second type, not his third. "Critical" objectivity is compromised by the skeptical qualification that it pertains only to things as they appear to us (phenomena), not things as they are in themselves (noumena).

Despite its differences with modern empiricism, is Kant's critical philosophy a type of subjectivism? It is, first, the now familiar claim to have identified *purely* nonempirical, *purely* subjective forms.[22] Second, it is the fact that, despite Kant's half measures of granting *phenomenal* objectivity to purely subjective forms and categories, in the end Kant denies their objectivity in Hegel's third, and ultimate, sense.[23] These half measures inevitably (and rightly) raise the suspicions of both traditional empiricists and "post-dogmatic" empiricists that Kant's critical philosophy is really no more licit than either the modern rationalism or empiricism it was meant to supersede.[24] Kant is at once *too dogmatic*—in putting the forms of sensibility and the concepts of the understanding beyond the pale of any empirical criticism (out of bounds for redoubled empiricism) and *too skeptical*, for insisting on the impassable gulf between phenomena and things in themselves. This conjuncture of countervailing excesses is a telling concomitant of "purist splits."

2. Critiques of Subjectivism

2.1 THE ARISTOTELIAN CONCEPTIONS OF FORM AND SOCIAL FORM

Form is that in reality which answers to a concept that says *what* a thing is. Form involves *necessity, universality* (kind), and *quality*. For example, in Marx's theory, value is the social form of the product of labor in capitalism; this social form is an actual feature of the world that answers to Marx's concept of value. Value is qualitative in that *socially necessary abstract* labor constitutes it; it involves universality as it is the social form that all products tend to take in capitalism; and it involves necessity in a number of ways, one being the necessary connection between value and money.[25]

Subjectivism supposes that a thing can *be* even without any determination of *what it is*. Kant's "thing-in-itself" is the epitome of this supposition. The Aristotelian tradition—I locate Hegel and Marx in this tradition—rejects this blank ontology. Making just such an Aristotelian criticism, Elizabeth Anscombe writes: "Such views are based on the unconscious assumption—which we have seen in Locke—that one can identify a *thing* without identifying it as a such-and-such—or that if one cannot do this, this is because *we* are incapable of conceiving substance except as having some qualities. The thing, then, that is taken to be postulated becomes a thoroughly mysterious entity which *in itself* has no characteristics: a 'somewhat we know not what' which is postulated as *underlying* the characteristics that it is said to 'have' and which alone enable us to conceive it" (Anscombe 1961, 10–11). The subjectivist separation of what a thing is "in itself" (the objective) from what it is as determined "for us" (the subjective) is a vain abstraction.[26] What is truly absolute—where the buck always stops—is the inextricability of "in itself" and "for us."

Hegel insists on this absolute: "The tendency of all man's endeavors is to understand the world, to appropriate and subdue it to himself: and to this end the positive reality of the world must be as it were crushed and pounded, in other words, idealized. At the same time we must note that it is not the mere act of *our* personal self-consciousness which introduces an absolute unity into the variety of sense. Rather, this identity is itself the absolute" (Hegel 1817, 69). Reasoning again along Aristotelian lines, Hegel concludes that the "what it is" of a thing cannot be severed from the "that it is," as subjectivism would have it. And a thing's form is what answers to the "what it is" question. Hegel writes: "But neither we nor the objects would have anything to gain by the mere fact that they possess being. The main point is not *that* they are, but *what* they are ... Laying aside therefore as unimportant this distinction between subjective and objective, we are chiefly interested in knowing what a thing is: i.e., its content, which is no more objective than it is subjective" (Hegel 1817, 71; my emphasis in bold). This plain, but not innocent, conclusion that in knowing we want to know what things are, is echoed in Donald Davidson's stunning finale to his unraveling of the subjectivist mind-set: "In giving up the dualism of scheme and world, we do not give up the world, but re-establish unmediated touch with the familiar objects whose antics make our sentences and opinions true or false" (Davidson 1974, 198). Our contact with the world is "unmediated" only in that the "purist split" between "in itself" and "for us" proves idle; their nexus is absolute.

Aristotle recognized that the "what is it" question bears on society as well as nature: for this Marx praises him as "the great investigator who was the first to analyze the value-form, like so many other forms of thought, society and nature" (Marx 1867, 151). Aristotle's *Politics*, among others of his writings, is a seminal inquiry into social and political forms, their content, consequences, and relationships with other such forms—in short, an ancient yet instructive case of redoubled empiricism. Marx's pivotal observation that "All production is appropriation of nature on the part of an individual within and through a specific form of society" (Marx 1857–58, 87; my emphasis) is a profoundly Aristotelian one. Furthermore, being a careful, experience-based study of the social forms constitutive of capitalist societies, *Capital* is an Aristotelian work.[27]

There is an important terminological point to be made in connection with this brief exposition of the Aristotelian conceptions of form and social form. It is a caution about the use of the terms "determine" and "modify." It is easy to slide over the conceptual distinction between the two. "Determine" pertains to what makes a thing what it is; something indeterminate, for example "need," "wealth," "labor," lacks form—and therefore, on Aristotelian principles, actuality. "Modify" operates at a different metaphysical and conceptual level; here we are dealing with something actual, something that is determinate, has form, and is undergoing some alteration. In this case the issue is not: What is it? but, assuming we already know that, How does it behave?[28] Ordinary empiricism targets this latter sort of question; redoubled empiricism takes on both.

2.2 PRAGMATISM AND "POST-DOGMATIC" EMPIRICISM

Pragmatists and "post-dogmatic" empiricists such as William James, Friedrich Waismann, W. V. O. Quine, and Donald Davidson make common cause with Aristotelians against subjectivism around these fundamental points: (1) they recognize that the subjectivist position turns on the purist claims that the objective can be filleted from the subjective, the empirical from the conceptual, and (2) they find these claims untenable, if even intelligible.[29] A clear statement of this second point is found in William James's lecture "Pragmatism and Humanism." "Humanism," to which James gives the pragmatist endorsement, turns out to be precisely the rejection of the subjectivist split between the subjective and the objective. James defines "humanism" as "the doctrine that to an unascertainable extent our truths are man-made products" (James 1907, 116–117). The crucial phrase for present purposes is "to an unascertainable extent," for it rules out the subjectivist separation of subjective from objective, conceptual from empirical. For the subjectivist image of human contributions as extractable weeds in the garden of knowledge (122), James exchanges that of a river and its banks: "Does the river make its banks, or do the banks make the river? . . .

Just as impossible may it be to separate the real from the human factors in the growth of our cognitive experience" (120).[30] James's critique of subjectivism is a phenomenological one.

Contemporary "post-dogmatic" empiricists are thinking along much the same lines. In his renowned article "Two Dogmas of Empiricism," W. V. O. Quine concludes: "My present suggestion is that it is nonsense, and the root of much nonsense, to speak of a linguistic component and a factual component in the truth of any statement. Taken collectively, science has its double dependence upon language and experience; but this duality is not significantly traceable into the statements of science taken one by one.... The unit of empirical significance is the whole of science" (Quine 1951, 64–65).[31] Quine's rejection of separable "components" disqualifies subjectivism at the starting blocks, and his final statement economically expresses the outlook of redoubled empiricism.

Donald Davidson (sounding much like Hegel—or Marx) provides a yet more thorough excavation of the subjectivist terrain: "there is the idea that *any* language distorts reality, which implies that it is only wordlessly if at all that the mind comes to grips with things as they really are. This is to conceive language as an inert (though necessarily distorting) medium independent of the human agencies that employ it; a view of language that surely cannot be maintained. Yet if the mind can grapple without distortion with the real, the mind itself must be without categories and concepts. This featureless self is familiar from theories in quite different parts of the philosophical landscape. There are, for example, theories that make freedom consist in decisions taken apart from all desires, habits, and dispositions of the agent; and theories of knowledge that suggest that the mind can observe the totality of its own perceptions and ideas. In each case, the mind is divorced from the traits that constitute it; an inescapable conclusion from certain lines of reasoning, as I said, but one that should always persuade us to reject the premises" (Davidson 1974, 185–186).

These pragmatists and "post-dogmatic" empiricists do not disagree with subjectivism that there is a human or subjective ingredient in cognition as well as an empirical or objective one; they just think that all attempts to separate one ingredient from another are in vain: as Hume recognized with his "distinctions of reason," what can be distinguished cannot always be separated.

Marx concurs on both points. He loudly applauds the tradition of German idealism, which itself famously builds upon insights of modern empiricism (and rationalism for that matter), precisely for recognizing the constitutive role of human activity in knowing; at the same moment he criticizes its purist conception of that activity. That is the unmistakable message of the "Theses on Feuerbach," whose first thesis begins: "The chief defect of all hitherto existing materialism (that of Feuerbach included) is that things [*Gegenstand*], reality, sensuousness are conceived only in the form of the *object or of contemplation*, but not as *sensuous human activity, practice*, not subjectively. Hence, in contradistinction to materialism, the *active* side was set forth abstractly by idealism—which, of course, does not know real, sensuous activity as such" (Marx 1845, 3). This critique of subjectivism and its purist premises puts Marx at the philosophical cutting edge, among the "post-dogmatic" empiricists.

3. Assessing the Marxian Theory of Redoubled Empiricism, Social Form, and Formal Causality

The strength of the Marxian approach to social form rests first in its definite[32] and sound underlying philosophy: Marx was a self-conscious and highly sophisticated "post-dogmatic" empiricist long before logical positivism ever reared its head. Now I want to consider further strengths of Marxian theory. (1) Once our eyes are opened to how central social form and scientific explanation in terms of formal cause are to Marxian theory, we begin to appreciate the tremendous range of phenomena that the Marxian theory of capitalism explains and successfully predicts: phenomena which, as indicated by Martha Campbell's point noted earlier, classical and neoclassical economics fail to acknowledge and are methodologically—not to mention politically—debarred even from recognizing. (2) Marxian theory discloses exactly *what* is wrong with its competitors (classical and neoclassical economics) and *where* they have gone wrong. This disclosive power must count heavily in its favor when it comes to any comparison of the merits of competing research programs. Marxian theory provides a historical materialist explanation of *why* classical and neoclassical economics go wrong—something always appropriate and to be welcomed in dealing with inadequate theories. The case for this is too involved to be made in this chapter.[33]

3.1 MARXIAN THEORY'S EXPLANATORY POWER

I do not attempt here a thorough, much less a thoroughly comparative, assessment of the explanatory strength of the Marxian theory of capitalism. My affirmation of Martha Campbell's statement about the lack of counterparts to Marx's concepts in classical or utility theory suggests that comparative assessment is, in one sense, not an easy-matter; yet once the Marxian theory of social form has been appropriated, it is easy enough to see what perfect nonstarters are those two competitors to Marxian theory. And for this simple reason: if there always is a determinate social form of production, distribution, needs, etc., it will always have its effects (formal causality). To fail to theorize social form, then, is to fail to grasp the movements of the actual society under scrutiny and their causes.[34] Here, I will limit myself to some observations on how the considerations of this paper bear on the evaluation of Marxian theory's explanatory power. I'll do that in the form of a few comments on two recent papers by Fred Moseley (Moseley 1993b and Moseley 1995), in which he contributes to the comparative assessment of Marxian theory by defending its explanatory power against criticisms by Daniel Hausman and Mark Blaug, respectively.

The tendency in Moseley's defenses is to make the comparisons as if the theories operated on the same playing field. That misses the significance of Campbell's observation: there is a sense in which Marxian theory is not talking about the same sorts of things as classical or utility theory. Which is good news for Marxian theory since it talks about determinate realities whereas the other two rattle on about hypostatized abstractions (notably "labor" and "utility"). When, for example, Moseley concludes: "Neoclassical theory provides much less empirical content than Marx's theory" (1993b, 12), he supposes that the domain conditions for the two theories are well established and identical. The difference is that in this ballpark Marxian theory drives in more runs. While I agree with Moseley's affirmation of the explanatory superiority of Marxian theory, the considerations of this chapter suggest that the presuppositions framing the judgment need reexamination.

The domains of the competing theories are radically different; Marxian theory deals with actual social life in its definite forms while classical and neoclassical theory, by neglecting social forms, do not come to grips with actual social life; at best they deal with *aspects of* phenomena. Marxian theory contrasts with them not as apples to oranges but as apples to the color red. In Marxian social theory specific social forms *determine* (not modify) the phenomena to be identified, explained, and predicted. The subjectivist underpinnings of neoclassical theory bar it from thematizing the phenomena in this way. A much stronger case for Marxian theory's empirical superiority (now in a more comprehensive sense) results from these considerations.

Moseley's presentation of the case for the empirical superiority of Marxian theory underplays the crucial dimension of social form and

formal causality.[35] Consider this text Moseley cites in making his case
that, contra Hausman, Marx has a good explanation for why the rate
of profit doesn't drop to zero: "The law of capitalist accumulation,
mystified by the economists into a supposed law of nature, in fact expresses the situation that the very nature of accumulation excludes
every diminution in the degree of exploitation of labor, and every rise
in the price of labor, which could seriously imperil the continual reproduction, on an ever larger scale, of the capital-relation" (Marx 1867,
771–771). I take this appeal to "the very nature" of (capital) accumulation to involve explanation by formal causality: the most fundamental law of capitalist accumulation is that it is *capital* that is accumulated,
that is, wealth in determinate social form (hence the law of capitalist
accumulation is no "law of nature"), and that the specific kind of social relation between capitalists and wage laborers is reproduced in
the process. Setting aside periods of crises or collapse, the Marxian
theory of capital accumulation predicts that the "capital-relation," that
determinate form of social relation between capitalists and wage-laborers, will persist and be extended. Surely this is a terrifically successful
prediction, but, due to the ascendancy of subjectivism with its blind
eye to social form, one seldom noticed.

In surveying the empirical superiority of Marxian over neoclassical
theory, Moseley draws attention to inherent technological change and
inherent conflict between capitalists and workers over the length of
the working day. These two are expressions of capital's drive to increase relative surplus-value and absolute surplus-value, respectively.[36]
Attention to the role of social form and formal causality should not be
set aside or ignored here. This is so in two ways. First, *that* technological change, an *aspect of* the phenomenon of capitalist production recognizable to all, is inherent to capitalism depends, in Marx's account
(I don't supply the account here), upon the causal role of the value
form of social production. *That* there are the described conflicts between capitalists and wage-laborers, an *aspect of* capitalist work relations recognizable to all, is likewise explained in terms of formal causality;
the conflict proceeds from the determinate social form of the relationship. Second, it is not just that Marx successfully predicts "technological change," where neoclassical theory does not; Marx identifies
and predicts the social form of that changing technology. For the new
technology is not just new "instruments of production" (a general,
indeterminate concept). No, the "instruments of production" always
have a determinate social form; Marx identifies that social form, capital, and accurately predicts that the new "instruments of production"
will be *determined* by it.

Similarly, the struggle to increase absolute surplus-value is a struggle governed by the specific capitalist forms: the point of the capitalist drive to lengthen and/or intensify the work day is not adequately characterized by saying that it is about increasing "surplus product." It *is* about increasing "surplus product," but a surplus product must have a determinate social form, and in capitalism that form is value. Marx does not simply predict that capitalists will constantly war with wage laborers to pump out more surplus; he shows that the surplus will have the form of surplus-*value*. What reinforces these points (concerning inherent technological change and conflict in the workplace) is that Marx explicitly conceptualizes capital's inherent drive to increase relative and absolute surplus-value as the real and the formal subsumptions of technology and labor under the social form of capital, respectively.[37] When we set aside the determinate social form of "technology" or "labor," we fail to come to grips with the pertinent "what is it" questions and overlook the whole domain of formal causality, i.e., the power of social forms. Therein lies the terrible, *empirical failure* of classical and neoclassical economics. Marxian theory's success at addressing these questions is its triumph.[38]

3.2 WHERE CLASSICAL AND NEOCLASSICAL THEORIES GO WRONG

Marxian theory discloses how debilitating are the purist underpinnings of classical and neoclassical economics. First, in a general way, they preclude any honest, clear-headed, and experiential approach to social form. This is a serious defect if Marx is right both that "All production is appropriation of nature on the part of an individual within and through a specific form of society" (Marx 1857–58, 87) and that social forms affect what happens in the world (formal causality).[39] Second, "purist splits" (mis)shape the constitution of the foundational concepts of labor and utility themselves. Purism, especially in its classical empiricist form, undergirds and encourages a methodological attitude of neglect where matters of form arise: within the orbit of classical empiricism "what is it" questions get faint and slurred responses. That's where this second, more specific, disabling feature of (unredoubled) empiricism comes into play. For as Hegel observed, scientific empiricism is only kidding itself to think that it gets along without concepts and forms, or to think that they play no constitutive role in science.[40] Science never has done without "metaphysics," that is, without drawing on the necessary and universal character of its concepts, on "the content of its concepts"—nor can it. (Of course it is possible to try to hide this reality from oneself, to engage in self-deception, as scientific empiricism does.) So we can expect purist prejudices to come through in the stumbling self-clarifications by classical and neoclassical economists of their concepts, notably their respective foundation stones, labor and utility. And they do.

(1) CLASSICAL ECONOMICS

Classical political economy is known for its labor theory of value: *labor is the source of all value.* What is anything but clear in this simple statement is *what* either labor or value is. Those are just the type of questions that the assumptions of subjectivism impede its adherents from attending to. All the same they rear their heads. And, in their own mixed-up ways, thinkers in the hold of the classical mind-set run upon them. We will see what a muddle they sink into and what roles their subjectivism and purism play in making that condition an inescapable sand pit, first, by smudging the distinction between wealth (and wealth-producing labor) and value (and value-producing labor), and second, by leading to an abstract (idealistic) conception of labor.

For several reasons, I would like to proceed in a somewhat off-centered manner and take up a passage from Locke's *Second Treatise.* Locke's *philosophy* (at least the official version) is well nigh definitive of the subjectivistic field within which classical political economy operates,[41] and we are interested in the connections between the purism of modern philosophy and the purism of classical economics. On this score, Locke is particularly appropriate because both Locke and classical political economy hitch purist *objectivism* in their ontologies (of matter and value) to the purist *subjectivism* of empiricist epistemology. Locke's labor theory of property (not value) may be seen as one of Marx's primary targets in the first volume of *Capital.*[42] In his thinking on *economics* Locke is commonly, and not without reason, seen in company with Petty, Berkeley, and Hume as a forerunner of the classical labor theory. Fair enough, but Locke was a great mind, and the great minds often feel something fishy is fishy, even when they can't put their fingers on what stinks. With the hindsight provided by the Marxian theory of value, I believe that we can see that Locke did not adopt a strict, classical labor theory of value, not because he was born too soon or because he lacked the penetration of a Ricardo or Mill, but *because he was thinking more deeply:* he sensed the confusions afflicting the classical labor theory even though he was tossed around by them himself. There is greater virtue in his resistance to the classical labor theory than in the theory itself.

Locke's text reads: "An Acre of Land that bears here Twenty Bushels of Wheat, and another in America, which, with the same Husbandry, would do the like, are, without doubt, of the same natural, intrinsick

Value. But yet the benefit Mankind receives from the one, in a Year, is worth 5 L. [British pounds] and from the other possibly not worth a Penny, if all the Profit an Indian received from it were to be valued, and sold here; at least, I may truly say, not 1/1000. 'Tis Labour then which puts the greatest part of Value upon Land, without which it would scarcely be worth any thing: 'tis to that we owe the greatest part of all its useful Products" (Locke 1690b, 316). The muddles Locke finds himself in here are characteristic of classical political economy; they turn on confusions over the concepts of wealth and value. Wealth is a *general*, universally applicable but indeterminate concept, whereas value is the concept of the *determinate* social form of wealth in capitalism. Thus, while uncultivated land is intrinsically a source of wealth, it is given *value* only within certain (commercial) social forms. Neither Locke nor the classical political economists properly register this distinction or the correlative one between wealth-producing labor and value-producing labor, these two distinctions being the fountainheads of Marx's critique of classical political economy.

Following this lead we can detect these fundamental problems with classical economics stirring in Locke's words: (1) the failure to fix the distinction between value and wealth (Locke wanders from value and price to usefulness and worth); (2) the correlative failure to distinguish between wealth-producing labor and value-producing labor (the text falsely suggests that all wealth-producing labor is value-producing); (3) the then unavoidable failure to recognize that value and wealth, value-producing labor and wealth-producing labor, are of two different logical types (in each pair the former is a determinate, the latter a general, abstraction); (4) the consequent tendency to reify "wealth," i.e., to treat it as if it really were something actual, when in fact it is not—not when abstracted from any and every determinate social form (such as value):[43] the "what is it" question concerning *any actual* wealth demands an answer, and any adequate answer must identify it by a determinate social form; (5) the tendency simply to identify wealth and value, wealth-producing labor and value-producing labor; (6) the misconception that value is intrinsic to objects in the same way as are those properties that make them useful to us; (7) the failure, then, to recognize the internal relation between value and money,[44] that value must appear as something other than itself, namely as a use-value—there being no such connection between wealth and money— and that there can be no manifest, invariable measure of value;[45] and (8) the faulty presumption—it comes with slurring the difference between wealth and value—that wealth may be summed, as can value's necessary form of appearance, money.

Though he makes no clear distinction between wealth and value, I think it is Locke's sense of the difference that is one thing that keeps him from affirming the strict labor theory of value. Petty's famous line about labor being the father of material wealth and the earth its mother (cited by Marx in *Capital* I, 134) may be nagging at Locke.[46] There is no place for Petty's observation within the purist horizon of the classical theory of value, according to which it is labor pure and simple that is the source of value. Which is so much the worse for it—and for Ricardian socialists, as Marx bitingly observed in the *Critique of the Gotha Programme*: "labor is *not the source* of all wealth. *Nature* is just as much the source of use-values (and it is surely of such that material wealth still consists!) as is labor" (Marx 1875, 3). Though Locke does not toe the Ricardian line, his own thinking about wealth is nonetheless stuck within a subjectivist conceptualization of labor, according to which the "value-added" by (pure) labor may be distilled and its proportion mathematically ascertained,[47] and an objectivist conception of value as an intrinsic property of goods. Still, in his stumbling way, Locke does not cave in unreservedly to the purist conceptions of labor and value, to the "unalloyed abstractions" (to borrow a phrase from Hegel), definitive of the strict classical approach.

To sum up: (1) the ordinary empiricist horizon of classical economics blinds it to the reality of social form; no wonder then that it fails to make the all-important distinctions between value and wealth, value-producing labor and wealth-producing labor, or any of the crucial points that depend upon these distinctions; (2) operating in the grip of purist assumptions, classical political economy comes up with a suitably purist conception of labor that attributes "supernatural creative power" to (pure) labor: it is the source of all wealth; (3) like Locke, who is an empiricist in epistemology but a purist objectivist (Cartesian) when it comes to matter, classical political economy is empiricist in epistemology but purist objectivist in its theory of value as "intrinsic" to goods; (4) though Locke can sensibly be read as a forerunner of classical political economy, it turns out that several of his differences with the classical theory harbor intimations of Marx's critique of the classical theories of labor, value, and wealth.

(2) NEOCLASSICAL ECONOMICS

The ordinary empiricist and (more broadly) the subjectivist horizons of neoclassical economics lead it into the same two sorts of problems found in classical political economy: failures stemming from inattention to social form and a subjectivist conceptualization of its foundational category (utility). Where classical political economy failed to fix the distinction between wealth and value, neoclassical economics fails to distinguish between use-value and utility. And where the classical conception of labor is of *pure* labor, the "supernatural creative" source of all wealth, neoclassical economics prides itself on its "purely subjective" conception of utility.

A full treatment of the Marxian claim that neoclassical economics rests on a failure to distinguish between use-value and utility, the former a general abstraction, the latter a determinate one, cannot be given here.[48] Marx refers to utility as an "apparently metaphysical abstraction" (Marx and Engels 1845–46, 409): "metaphysical" (here in the bad sense) because it purports to stand for some single, qualitatively homogeneous and measured actuality and "apparently" because this bad abstraction does point to the reality of the practices of generalized commodity exchange. As opposed to utility, the general concept of use-value makes no assumptions about the commensurability of all use-values. Utility is a concept with ties to societies having a specific social form, namely those in which commodity exchange has been generalized.[49] Hobbled by the ordinary empiricist prejudices against social form, neoclassical economics fails to recognize the difference between use-value and utility and the connections between utility and the social form of generalized commodity exchange.

In the circles of neoclassical economics, Marx's contention that use-value is a property of useful objects counts as a piece of old-fashioned, metaphysical (=bad) objectivism, a real "howler." In reality, what is humorous is to observe as neoclassical authors play out the inexorable and irredeemable perplexities of their subjectivist fancies. When neoclassical authors bother to try to pin down what it is they pretend to be talking about, utility, they necessarily end up ceaselessly equivocating. I say "necessarily" because they are hung up by their subjectivist prejudices. C. E. Ferguson writes: "if one sought a single criterion to distinguish modern microeconomic theory from its classical antecedents, he would probably decide it is to be found in the introduction of *subjective value theory*" (Ferguson 1972, 20–21). Similarly, Antonietta Campus, writing in the *New Palgrave* dictionary of economics, pithily characterizes utility as use-value "reinterpreted in subjective terms" (Campus 1987, 320). What manner of "reinterpretation" is this? What is this "*subjective value theory*"? It is the concept of use-value nailed to the cross of subjectivism's vain dualisms. Watch what happens when you try to make sense of this supposed "reinterpretation."

Ferguson states: "Economists define 'utility' as that quality which makes a commodity desired" (Ferguson 1972, 20). *That quality of what?* Of the commodity? But a quality of a commodity is *its* quality, not one of a subject, and therefore is something *objective* in an intelligible sense of that word. Yet we also find Ferguson heedlessly identifying utility with satisfaction (18) and saying "any good or service deliberately consumed by a household provides utility" (21). One sees how consuming a good can provide satisfaction to members of a household, but if the satisfaction is *what utility is,* how is *that* a quality of the commodity? Flip-flop; flip-flop.

Of the early marginal utility theorists Gossen, Jevons, and Walras, Ferguson writes that they regarded utility "as a measurable quality of any commodity" (21), implying that utility is a property of a commodity, not of a subject. Consider, then, just how well Ferguson's statement fits in with his or Campus's pronouncements about "*subjective value theory*" being the pivotal innovation of neoclassical microeconomics! C. Welch pushes these shenanigans to an even higher pitch in his contribution to the *New Palgrave* when he writes that the early marginalists held the "notion of pleasure as a quality inherent in a good" (Welch 1987, 772), a proposition that suggests that the pioneers of neoclassical theory went altogether through the looking glass into a topsy-turvy world where pleasure is a property of things!

In his contribution to the *New Palgrave,* R. D. Collison Black displays the (bad) abstractive proclivities of the subjectivist mind-set in action: "Utility in the sense of desiredness is a purely subjective concept, clearly distinct from usefulness or fitness for a purpose" (Black 1987, 776). Black possesses the wit to call attention to confusions among utility theorists over this distinction. But evidently the distinction is not so well fixed in Black's own mind as to keep him from writing in the sentence before the one quoted that "desiredness" is "the capacity of a good or service to satisfy a want, of whatever kind" (that being a sensible definition of use-value, more or less identical to Marx's definition on the first page of *Capital!*). Are such *capacities of goods* to serve the purpose of our satisfaction "purely subjective"? So Black is no more consistent than the utility theorists he chides. Nor is he in any position to be, since he is equally hung up by the subjectivist assumption that "purely subjective" is a phrase that picks out something actual.[50] Give up that prejudice and the neoclassical idea of a "subjective value theory" loses its point.[51] Out with that goes the misconception that neoclassical economics has a leg to stand on.

4. Conclusion

In this chapter we have explored the deep philosophical differences that set Marx off from the mainstream of modern philosophy and from those scientific research traditions, such as classical and neoclassical economics, which rely on the purist assumptions of their modern philosophical underlaborers, especially the empiricists. We found that Marx's rejection of the modern "purist splits" between the conceptual and the empirical and between the subjective and objective opens the space for redoubled empiricism and for a conscious, realistic, and experiential approach to social forms and their powers (formal causality). This enabled us to situate his thought in the company of Aristotle and Hegel, looking backward, and pragmatists and "post-dogmatic" empiricists, looking forward. The latter part of the chapter investigated the significance of these abstruse philosophical matters for assessing the cogency of Marxian theory as a scientific research program in comparison to classical and neoclassical economics. By highlighting its attention to social form and formal causality, we found reasons to judge Marxian theory vastly superior to those two scientific competitors in its explanatory power, and we saw how the Marxian critique of purism uncovers where they go wrong to begin with. All of these considerations point up the philosophical and scientific vitality of Marxian theory.[52]

Notes

1. The phrase "redoubled empiricism" (which replaces "empiricism in second intension," used in my *Marx's Theory of Scientific Knowledge*) requires some preliminary comments. First, to "redouble" empiricism simply means to double, not quadruple it; the phrase carries the connotation of a renewal and intensification of the efforts of empiricism. The redoubling I have in mind pertains to the *concepts* employed in empirical studies. Ordinary empiricism takes these for granted and to that extent handles them in an unselfconscious, nonempirical, and consequently dogmatic manner. Why it falls into this trap will be examined in the chapter. Redoubled empiricism steers away from this dogmatism by consciously and empirically reflecting on the fixation of concepts in their relations to one another. *How* this is done will not be the subject of this chapter.

    It is a fair question as to whether or not such non-dogmatic empiricism should be called empiricism at all. Donald Davidson, who criticizes the "very idea of a conceptual scheme" as the third dogma of empiricism— W. V. O. Quine having criticized two others—wonders whether it makes sense to extend the term "empiricism" to what remains once the dogmas have been eliminated (Davidson 1974, 189). I choose to keep the term and risk confusions for this reason: the criticisms of ordinary empiricism on the part of redoubled empiricism are internal to the original empiricist project, which was to avoid unexamined and empirically unsupported assumptions in order to combat dogmatism. Redoubled empiricism is truer to the empiricist project.

2. Among the growing number of interpreters of Marxian theory who are

particularly attentive to the role of social form let me mention these: Georg Lukács, Karl Korsch, I. I. Rubin, Roman Rosdolsky, Furio Cerutti, David Harvey, Derek Sayer, Simon Clarke, George McCarthy, Moishe Postone, and the contributors to this volume and its predecessor, *Marx's Method in "Capital": A Reexamination.*

3. This is a point Scott Meikle makes in no uncertain terms. See his *Essentialism in the Thought of Karl Marx.*

4. I borrow this term from James Collins's *Interpreting Modern Philosophy* (Collins 1972, 14ff.).

5. See Hegel 1817, 47–112.

6. Compare Bernstein 1971, 72.

7. The significance of speaking here of "aspects of" phenomena will come clearer later in the chapter.

8. This is so precisely because Marx conceives of production as a social relation having a determinate form.

9. As we will see, this is true of Kantian philosophy only with qualifications.

10. This dual assertion about innate ideas does not hold for Leibniz, since he classifies all ideas, including those of sensation and imagination, as innate.

11. Thus Descartes, in his famous study of the bit-turned-blob of wax in the second meditation, reaches the conclusion: "We must therefore agree that I cannot even conceive what this bit of wax is by means of the imagination, and that there is nothing but my understanding alone which does conceive it" (Descartes 1641, 88).

12. Hegel praises this objectivism of rationalist metaphysics: "This metaphysical system took the laws and forms of thought to be the fundamental laws and forms of things. It assumed that to think a thing was the means of finding its very self and nature: and to that extent it occupied higher ground than the Critical Philosophy which succeeded it" (Hegel 1817, 48).

13. Hegel makes this criticism of rationalism: its "purist split" between the conceptual and the empirical closes off the space for "redoubled empiricism"—which calls for empirical scrutiny of concepts—and thereby leaves its concepts empirically inadequate and dogmatic (Hegel 1817, 60).

14. Caution must be taken with categories like "modern rationalist" and "modern empiricist." These are philosophical "ideal types," and the modern philosophers do not fit neatly under one or the other type. (See Loeb 1981 and Collins 1972).

John Locke, for example, comes quickly to mind as an empiricist. Indeed he famously attacked the rationalist doctrine of innate ideas, yet Berkeley heartily criticized his Cartesian materialism. From Marx's point of view this is an important observation, for a pair of reasons: he identified Locke as the chief philosophical underlaborer for classical political economy, and Marx conceived of the classical labor theory of value along the lines of the purist objectivism of Descartes's theory of matter. (See Murray 1988, 149, and Postone 1993, 142.) Classical political economy, like Locke, claims to follow an empiricist epistemology but defends an objectivistic theory of value as "intrinsic worth," much as the empiricist Locke defends a largely Cartesian and objectivistic theory of matter.

15. In the *Holy Family* Marx observes: "Nominalism is a main component of English materialism and is in general the first expression of materialism" (Marx and Engels 1845, 127).

16. These phrases come from Locke's title to Book III, section 13 (Locke 1690a, 30).

17. For a recent and powerful challenge to Hume's subjectivist employment of this rhetoric of projection, see Stroud 1993.

18. Hume sets forth the important notion of a "distinction of reason" in two pages at the beginning of his *Treatise of Human Nature* (Hume 1739–40, 24–25). "Distinctions of reason" enter in when we can distinguish but not separate, as, to use Hume's example, between the whiteness and the roundness of a marble globe.

19. Of Hegel's three meanings of objectivity this is the first: "First it means what has external existence, in distinction from which the subjective is what is only supposed, dreamed, etc. Secondly, it has the meaning, attached to it by Kant, of the universal and necessary, as distinguished from the particular, subjective and occasional element which belongs to our sensations. Thirdly, ... it means the thought-apprehended essence of the existing thing, in contradistinction from what is merely *our* thought" (Hegel 1817, 68).

20. By "nonempirical" I mean that they are not arrived at empirically, not that they have no place in experience; on the contrary, Kant insists that neither the forms of intuition nor the categories of the understanding directly yield any knowledge apart from experience.

21. This comes very close to a rejection of the "purist split" between the conceptual and the empirical. For it is not evident what is the difference between saying, on the one hand, that you can split the conceptual and the empirical but once you do you have nothing to say about either and, on the other hand, saying that the conceptual and the empirical are inseparable.

22. Marx reacted strongly against this dualism of form and matter as early as the letter he wrote as a nineteen-year-old to his father. There he criticized his own "Kantian-Fichtean" sketch of a science of jurisprudence: "The mistake lay in my belief that matter and form can and must develop separately from each other, and so I obtained not a real form, but something like a desk with drawers into which I then poured sand" (Marx 1837, 15). Getting at "real forms" is what redoubling empiricism is all about. For an excellent study of the topic of form in Kant see Pippin 1982.

23. Hegel comments: "But after all, objectivity of thought, in Kant's sense, is again to a certain extent subjective. Thoughts, according to Kant, although universal and necessary categories, are *only* our thoughts—separated by an impassable gulf from the thing, as it exists apart from our knowledge" (Hegel 1817, 67).

24. For the more traditional empiricists, see Hans Reichenbach 1951. For the "post-dogmatic" empiricist view, see Waismann's critique of Kant (Waismann 1945, 48ff.)

25. On this, see Murray 1993a.

26. It is the *separation* of the two that is objectionable; a "distinction of reason" can be made.

27. This claim is examined in detail in the second of two excellent studies of Marx's relationships to Aristotle by George E. McCarthy, *Marx and the Ancients* and *Dialectics and Decadence: Echoes of Antiquity in Marx and Nietzsche*.

28. Compare this conceptual distinction to the Lakatosian one between propo-

sitions in the core and those in the periphery as discussed in Tony Smith's chapter in this volume.

29. This means that pragmatism and "post-dogmatic" empiricism involve more than a criticism of empiricism or even subjectivism; they address the underlying "purist splits" that cut across modern philosophy.

30. This illustrates Hume's point regarding "distinctions of reason."

31. Compare Friedrich Waismann's comment: "People are inclined to think that there is a world of facts as opposed to a world of words which describe these facts. I am not too happy about that" (Waismann 1945, 54).

32. As opposed, say, to Simmel's wild swings between subjective and objective accounts of social form, as depicted by David Frisby in his Introduction to Simmel's *Philosophy of Money*. Given the neo-Kantian horizon of Simmel's thought, such swings might be expected.

33. The thrust of the argument is that the peculiarly abstract social forms of capitalism promote the abstract understandings of labor and thought that characterize classical political economy and modern philosophy, respectively.

34. For Aristotle change of (social) form is a type of movement, the sort Marx thematizes with his concept of *formal subsumption*.

35. I say "underplays" because Moseley also invokes points that turn on social form, for example, Marx's account of the necessary connection between value and money.

36. According to Marx the work day is divided into two parts, necessary labor time and surplus labor time. The necessary labor time is that part of the work day spent in producing an amount of value equivalent to the value of the worker's labor power; this is the source of the worker's wages. The surplus labor time is the remainder of the work day, and it is the source of surplus-value (distributed as profits, interest, and rent). The concepts of absolute and relative surplus-value pertain to the two ways surplus-value can be increased: shortening the part of the work day devoted to necessary labor (usually through increased productivity in the production of those commodities that enter into the value of labor power)—relative surplus-value—or by increasing the part of the work day devoted to surplus labor, while leaving the other part unchanged—absolute surplus-value. Marx further distinguished between increasing absolute surplus-value by lengthening the work day and by intensifying it.

37. *Formal* subsumption of a labor process under capital means that the distinctive capitalist/wage laborer relationship obtains and that the process aims at the production of surplus-value. *Real* subsumption means that the labor process undergoes a technical transformation in order better to pump out surplus-value. See Marx 1863–66, 1019 ff.

38. It should not be thought that Marxian theory has a corner on the market where careful observation and articulation of social forms or explanation through formal causality are concerned. Brilliant contributions come from many corners. See Murray (ed.) 1997.

39. Notice the contrast between Adam Smith's talk of the "wealth" of nations, which remains silent on the question of the form of that wealth, and the sentence with which Marx begins *Capital*: "The wealth of societies in which the capitalist mode of production prevails appears as an 'immense collection of commodities'; the individual commodity appears as its elementary

form" (Marx 1867, 125). For more on the significance of this opening, see Paul Mattick Jr.'s chapter in the present volume.

40. "The fundamental illusion in scientific empiricism is always this, that it uses the metaphysical categories of matter, force, those of one, many, universality, also infinity, etc. Furthermore, [it] extends *implications* along the thread of such categories, whereby [it] presupposes and applies syllogistic forms, and in all this [it] does not know that it itself carries on and contains metaphysics and uses those categories and their connections in a fully uncritical and unconscious manner" (Hegel 1817, 62).

41. Compare Marx's observation: "On the whole . . . the early English economists sided with Bacon and Hobbes as their philosophers, while, at a later period, Locke became 'the philosopher' *par excellence* of political economy in England, France and Italy" (Marx 1867, 513).

42. See Marx 1867, especially 733–734.

43. On this tendency to reify general abstractions, see Derek Sayer's excellent book *The Violence of Abstraction*.

44. With this in mind there is something to be said for Locke's own nonclassical theory of value, which is geared to the market considerations of supply and demand. Locke rightly sees that the market conditions play a *constitutive* role in the determination of value, so the (indeterminate) classical notion of "labor" as the source of value won't work (as it doesn't). Thus Marx observes that the Ricardians could make no convincing reply to Samuel Bailey's attack on Ricardo's "absolute" theory of value "because they are unable to find in Ricardo's own works any elucidation of the inner connection between value and the form of value, or exchange-value" (Marx 1867, 177, n. 38).

45. Compare Martha Campbell's treatment of the invariable measure of value, in Ricardo, in her chapter in the present volume.

46. Cross-referencing that comment of Petty's with Locke's proportions may reveal something about the gender politics in play here.

47. The purism that persists in Locke's view may be accented by contrasting his talk of numerically identifying the proportion of (pure) labor's contribution to wealth with James's antipurist defense of "humanism," according to which the portion of the subjective ingredient in knowing is "unascertainable." Locke's view of wealth may usefully be likened to Kant's theory of knowledge: knowledge always involves both intuition (Nature) and the work of the transcendental ego (labor), and the critique of pure reason ascertains exactly what that contribution of the knowing subject is.

48. I treat this topic at length in my unpublished paper "The Difference between Use-Value and Utility and the Difference it Makes: Grounds for a Marxian Critique of Neoclassical Theories of Value and Price."

49. Marx further argues that it is only with the dominance of capital as a social form that this generalization takes place.

50. Marx explicitly attacks this subjectivist assumption when he writes at the beginning of the first chapter of *Capital*: "The usefulness of a thing makes it a use-value. But this usefulness does not dangle in mid-air. It is conditioned by the physical properties of the commodity, and has no existence apart from the latter" (Marx 1867, 126). Utility theories want to make usefulness "dangle in mid-air"; they want to abstract from the notion of usefulness all properties of the object—precisely by relying on the bad

abstraction of the "purely subjective." Marx means to confute the very idea of a usefulness that is "purely subjective." And he polishes off the first chapter of *Capital* by yoking the "purist objectivism" of classical value theory (value is an intrinsic property of objects) with the "purist subjectivism" of utility theory (use-value is independent of an object's properties): "So far no chemist has ever discovered exchange-value either in a pearl or a diamond. The economists who have discovered this chemical substance, and who lay special claim to critical acumen, nevertheless find that the use-value of material objects belongs to them independently of their material properties, while their value, on the other hand, forms a part of them as objects" (177). The point of the present chapter has been to uncover the deepest conceptual sources of these erroneous beliefs.

51. This Marxian critique pulls utility theories up by the root: the neoclassical innovation of "marginal" utilities is useless, as is the later neoclassical abandonment of intersubjective utilities.

52. I would like to thank for their patient, diverse, and very helpful comments: Chris Arthur, Martha Campbell, Peter Fuss, Paul Mattick Jr., Fred Moseley, Geert Reuten, Jeanne Schuler, and Tony Smith.

References

Anscombe 1961. G. E. M. Anscombe, "Aristotle," in *Three Philosophers* by G. E. M. Anscombe and Peter Geach (Ithaca, NY: Cornell University Press, 1961).

Aristotle. Aristotle, *The Politics of Aristotle*, trans. Ernest Barker (Oxford: Oxford University Press, 1946).

Bacon 1620. Francis Bacon, *Novum organum*, trans. and ed. Peter Urbach and John Gibson (Chicago: Open Court, 1994).

Bernstein 1971. Richard Bernstein, *Praxis and Action* (Philadelphia: University of Pennsylvania Press, 1971).

Black 1987. R. D. Collison Black, "Utility," in Eatwell et al. 1987, vol. 4, 776–779.

Campbell 1993a. Martha Campbell, "The Commodity as Necessary Form of Product," in *Economics as Worldly Philosophy: Essays in Political and Historical Economics in Honor of Robert L. Heilbroner*, ed. Ron Blackwell et al. (New York: St. Martin's Press, 1993).

Campbell 1993b. Martha Campbell, "Marx's Concept of Economic Relations and the Method of *Capital*," in Moseley 1993a, 135–155.

Campus 1987. Antonietta Campus, "Marginalist Economics," in Eatwell et al. 1987, vol. 3, 320–322.

Cerutti 1984. Furio Cerutti, "The 'Living' and the 'Dead' in Karl Marx's Theory," in Sakari Haenninen and Leena Paldan (eds.), *Rethinking Marx* (Berlin: Argument-Verlag, ARGUMENT-SONDERBAND AS 109 and New York & Bagnolet, France: INTERNATIONAL GENERAL/IMMRC., 1984.

Clarke 1982. Simon Clarke, *Marx, Marginalism and Modern Sociology* (Basingstoke: Macmillan, 1982).

Collins 1972. James Collins, *Interpreting Modern Philosophy* (Princeton, NJ: Princeton University Press, 1972).

Davidson 1974. Donald Davidson, "The Very Idea of a Conceptual Scheme," in Donald Davidson, *Inquiries into Truth and Interpretation* (New York: Oxford University Press, 1984).

Descartes 1641. René Descartes, *The Meditations Concerning First Philosophy*, in René Descartes, *Discourse on Method and Meditations*, trans. Laurence J. Lafleur (Indianapolis: The Bobbs-Merrill Company, 1960).

Eatwell et al. 1987. John Eatwell, Murray Milgate, and Peter Newman (eds.), *The New Palgrave: A Dictionary of Economics* in four vols. (London: Macmillan, 1987).

Ferguson 1972. C. E. Ferguson, *Microeconomic Theory* (third edition) (Homewood, IL: Richard D. Irwin, Inc., 1972).

Frisby 1978. David Frisby, "Introduction," in Georg Simmel, *The Philosophy of Money*, trans. Tom Bottomore and David Frisby (London: Routledge & Kegan Paul, 1978).

Harvey 1982. David Harvey, *The Limits to Capital* (Oxford: Basil Blackwell, 1982.)

Hegel 1817. G. W. F. Hegel, *Hegel's Logic*, trans. William Wallace (Oxford: Clarendon Press, 1975).

Hume 1739–40. David Hume, *A Treatise of Human Nature*, ed. P. H. Nidditch (Oxford: Clarendon Press, 1989).

James 1907. William James, *Pragmatism*, ed. Bruce Kuklick (Indianapolis: Hackett Publishing Company, 1981).

Jevons 1871; 1879. William Stanley Jevons, *The Theory of Political Economy*, ed. R. D. Collison Black (Harmondsworth: Penguin Books, 1970).

Kant 1781; 1787. Immanuel Kant, *The Critique of Pure Reason*, trans. N. Kemp Smith (Atlantic Highlands, NJ: Humanities Press).

Korsch 1923. Karl Korsch, *Marxism and Philosophy*, trans. Fred Halliday (New York: Monthly Review Press, 1970).

Locke 1690a. John Locke, *An Essay Concerning Human Understanding*, ed. P. H. Nidditch (Oxford: Oxford University Press, 1975).

Locke 1690b. John Locke, *Second Treatise of Government*, in *Two Treatises of Government*, ed. Peter Laslett (Cambridge: Cambridge University Press, 1960).

Loeb 1981. Louis E. Loeb, *From Descartes to Hume* (Ithaca, NY: Cornell University Press, 1981).

Lukács 1922. Georg Lukács, *History and Class Consciousness*, trans. Rodney Livingstone (Cambridge, MA: The MIT Press, 1971).

MacIntyre 1981; 1984. Alasdair MacIntyre, *After Virtue* (second edition) (Notre Dame, IN: University of Notre Dame Press, 1984).

Marx 1867. Karl Marx, *Capital*, vol. I, trans. Ben Fowkes (Harmondsworth: Penguin Books, 1976).

Marx 1875. Karl Marx, *Critique of the Gotha Programme* (New York: International Publishers, 1938, 1966).

Marx 1857–58. Karl Marx, *Grundrisse*, trans. Martin Nicolaus (Harmondsworth: Penguin Books, in association with *New Left Review*, 1973).

Marx 1837. Karl Marx, "Letter from Marx to His Father," in *Karl Marx, Frederick Engels: Collected Works*, vol. 1: *Karl Marx: 1835-1843* (New York: International Publishers, 1975).

Marx 1879–80. Karl Marx, "Notes (1879–80) on Adolph Wagner," in *Karl Marx: Texts on Method*, trans. and ed. by Terrell Carver (New York: Harper and Row Publishers, 1975).

Marx 1863–66. Karl Marx, *Results of the Immediate Production Process*, trans. Rodney Livingstone, in *Capital*, vol. I.

Marx 1862–63. Karl Marx, *Theories of Surplus-Value*, Part I, trans. Emile Burns and ed. S. Ryazanskaya (Moscow: Progress Publishers, 1963).

Marx 1862–63. Karl Marx, *Theories of Surplus-Value*, Part III, trans. Jack Cohen and S. W. Ryazanskaya, ed. S. W. Ryazanskaya and Richard Dixon (Moscow: Progress Publishers, 1971).

Marx 1845. Karl Marx, "Theses on Feuerbach," in *Karl Marx, Frederick Engels: Collected Works*, vol. 5: *Marx and Engels: 1845–1847* (New York: International Publishers, 1976).

Marx and Engels 1845. Karl Marx and Friedrich Engels, *The Holy Family*, in *Karl Marx, Frederick Engels: Collected Works*, vol. 4: *Marx and Engels: 1845–1847* (New York: International Publishers, 1976).

Marx and Engels 1845–46. Karl Marx and Friedrich Engels, *The German Ideology*, in *Karl Marx, Frederick Engels: Collected Works*, vol. 5: *Marx and Engels: 1845–1847* (New York: International Publishers, 1976).

McCarthy 1990. George McCarthy, *Marx and the Ancients: Classical Ethics, Social Justice, and Nineteenth-Century Political Economy* (Savage, MD: Rowman & Littlefield, 1990).

McCarthy 1994. George McCarthy, *Dialectics and Decadence: Echoes of Antiquity in Marx and Nietzsche* (Savage, MD: Rowman & Littlefield, 1994).

Meikle 1985. Scott Meikle, *Essentialism in the Thought of Karl Marx* (La Salle, IL: Open Court, 1985).

Moseley 1993a. Fred Moseley (ed.), *Marx's Method in "Capital"*: A *Reexamination* (Atlantic Highlands, NJ: Humanities Press, 1993).

Moseley 1993b. Fred Moseley, "Explanatory Progress or Retrogression in Economics? A Marxian Response to Hausman," unpublished paper presented at Mt. Holyoke College, June 1993.

Moseley 1995. Fred Moseley, "Marx's Economic Theory: True or False? A Marxian Response to Blaug's Appraisal," in Fred Moseley (ed.), *Heterodox Economic Theories: True or False?* (Brookfield, VT: Edward Elgar Publishing, 1995).

Murray 1988. Patrick Murray, *Marx's Theory of Scientific Knowledge* (Atlantic Highlands, NJ: Humanities Press, 1988).

Murray 1993a. Patrick Murray, "The Necessity of Money: How Hegel Helped Marx Surpass Ricardo's Theory of Value," in Moseley 1993a.

Murray 1993b. Patrick Murray, "The Difference Between Use-Value and Utility and the Difference it Makes: Grounds for a Marxian Critique of Neoclassical Theories of Value and Price," unpublished paper presented at Mt. Holyoke College, June 1993.

Murray 1997. Patrick Murray (ed.), *Reflections on Commercial Life: An Anthology of Classic Texts from Plato to the Present* (New York: Routledge, 1997).

Pippin 1982. Robert Pippin, *Kant's Theory of Form* (New Haven: Yale University Press, 1982).

Postone 1993. Moishe Postone, *Time, Labor, and Social Domination: A Reinterpretation of Marx's Critical Theory* (Cambridge: Cambridge University Press, 1993).

Quine 1951. W. V. O. Quine, "Two Dogmas of Empiricism," in W. V. O. Quine, *From a Logical Point of View* (New York: Harper Torchbooks, 1953).

Reichenbach 1951. Hans Reichenbach, *The Rise of Scientific Philosophy* (Berkeley: University of California Press, 1951).

Rosdolsky 1968. Roman Rosdolsky, *The Making of Marx's 'Capital,'* trans. Pete Burgess (London: Pluto Press, 1977).

Rubin 1928. I. I. Rubin, *Essays on Marx's Theory of Value*, trans. Milos Samardzija and Fredy Perlman (Detroit: Black & Red, 1972).

Sayer 1987. Derek Sayer, *The Violence of Abstraction* (Oxford: Basil Blackwell, 1987).

Smith 1990. Tony Smith, *The Logic of Marx's "Capital": Replies to Hegelian Criticisms* (Albany: State University of New York Press, 1990).

Stroud 1993. Barry Stroud, "'Guilding and Staining' the World with 'Sentiments' and 'Phantasms,'" *Hume Studies*, 19:2, 253–272.

Waismann 1945. Friedrich Waismann, "Verifiability," in *The Theory of Meaning*, ed. G. H. R. Parkinson (Oxford: Oxford University Press, 1968).

Welch 1987. C. Welch, "utilitarianism," in Eatwell et al. 1987, vol. 4, 770–776.

Williams 1985. Bernard Williams, *Ethics and the Limits of Philosophy* (Cambridge, MA: Harvard University Press, 1985).

Williams 1973. Bernard Williams, "A Critique of Utilitarianism," in J. J. C. Smart and Bernard Williams, *Utilitarianism for and against* (Cambridge: Cambridge University Press, 1973).

3

Theory as Critique:
On the Argument in *Capital*

Paul Mattick Jr.

Although *Capital* is recognized to be a critique of political economy, this is generally not taken to have important implications for the structure of Marx's argument. Commentators tend to understand Marx's theory of capitalist society, in relation to its bourgeois predecessors (and contemporaries), on the model of rival theories of the same basic sort. Extended to the present this conception underlies the idea of "Marxist economics," as a school of economic theory contending with others. From this point of view—the dominant one, I believe—*Capital* presents a critique of political economy in the same sense as that in which general relativity may be taken as a critique of classical mechanics. This is all the more true when Marx is thought of, and again I think this is the dominant view, as having adopted, from his theoretical forbears, the labor theory of value. From this viewpoint, Marx's version of this theory may be an improvement over Ricardo's, and it may be deployed in a scientifically superior manner, but its fundamental place in his system makes him an heir of classical economics, in the same way that Einstein can be seen as an heir of classical physics.

It is only natural, then, for discussions of the structure of Marx's argument in *Capital*, what he called the "method of presentation" of his theory, to explain that structure primarily in terms of various logics of theory construction; for example, by searching for analogies to the progression of concepts in Hegel's logic or, more plausibly, by noting such features as a movement from relatively abstract to relatively concrete descriptions. I will argue that the architectonic of Marx's work cannot be adequately understood without direct reference to its character as critique not just of rival theories but of what I will call economic discourse.

1. Political Economy as Text and Discourse

Writing to Lassalle in 1858, Marx described the manuscript he was completing as "a *Critique of Economic Categories* or, if you like, the system of bourgeois economy in a critical description. It is both a description of the system and, in describing it, a critique of the same." He goes on to say that "in general the critique and the history of political economy and of socialism should form the subject of another book."[1] It is clear that "economy" is meant differently in these two sentences. In the first, Marx speaks of a critique directed at a system of social relations, in the second of a critique of economic theory. And yet, the ambiguity of *Ökonomie* appears also in the reference to *Kategorien* as objects of critique. It is in fact essential to Marx's whole conception of his theoretical project that economic categories be both what Durkheim would call "social facts" and what some later French thinkers would call "mentalités." Cultural, embodied in language as well as in action, these categories exist both as structures of social activity and as symbolic representations of those structures. Thus, speaking of historically variable "forms of social life" in the first volume of *Capital,* Marx wrote that "The categories of bourgeois economics consist precisely of forms of this kind. They are forms of thought which are socially valid and therefore objective, for the relations of production belonging to this historically determined mode of social production, i.e., commodity production" (Marx 1867, 91).

The economists' category of "value" was produced in the attempt to understand commodity exchange, which had long since developed as a social practice. It corresponds to the vernacular concept of value invoked when it is asked what some good is "worth" or if payment for it will receive "value for money." What makes it appropriate to describe features of that practice themselves as categories is, in Marx's conception, that they amount to a historically specific mode—what Marx calls a "social form"—of organizing the nature-imposed task of production. They embody, so to speak, a view of the labor process. In the exchange of commodities the kinds of labor that have produced them are, necessarily, treated as interchangeable. Exchange establishes their interchangeability. This involves a different way of classifying, dealing with, and thinking about labor than one in which the products of different kinds of labor are not treated as interchangeable.

Further: interchangeability of products makes the labor that has produced them *social.* In capitalism, it is the exchange process that by realizing the social character of commodity-producing labor signifies this mode of sociality. Other kinds of labor can have a social character as well, of course—for instance, much of the work performed in the household. But this can be explicitly recognized as social, by the use of such categories as "chores." Commodity-producing labor has a special status in capitalism society (namely, it is "productive" labor, productive of surplus value). It is a special kind of social labor, and this character also needs to be signalled in some way. It is the act of exchange against money that in this case classifies the labor performed as social labor. As Marx explains it in the *Grundrisse*, money as "sign of exchange value" is a "symbol" that "represents" the social labor contained in a particular commodity (Marx 1857–58a, 144). The vocabulary of value—the equation of a commodity to a sum of money in answer to the question, how much is it worth?—provides a signifier for this particular type of social labor.

There are thus two levels of representation to be distinguished under the heading of economic categories. First, commodity exchange "transforms every product of labor into a social hieroglyphic." In the exchange process, each of two commodities exchanged represents the labor that has gone into the making of the other product, and by doing so marks that labor as social. Because equation to a sum of money is the only form in which labor is so marked, "value" as an expression in everyday language is used to refer to an (apparent) property of commodities.

On the second level, that of economic theory, "value" so used is a phenomenon to be explained; it is asked what determines the value of a commodity, or in what the value of commodities consists. "Later on, men try to decipher the hieroglyphic, to get behind the secret of their own social product: for the characteristic which objects of utility have of being values is as much men's social product as is their language" (Marx 1867, 167). According to Marx, the classical economists were not able finally to "decipher the hieroglyphic," specifically because they were unable to recognize the representational—in today's jargon one would say, socially constructed—character of value.

To recognize this character, as Marx did, is to transform the conditions of theorization. From his point of view (though not in his words), to understand value is to understand a social practice and the discourse that is part of it. "Political economy," Marx wrote, "has indeed analyzed value and its magnitude, however incompletely, and has uncovered the content concealed within these forms. But it has never once asked the question why this content has assumed that particular form, that is to say, why labor is expressed in value . . ." (ibid., 174)[2] To ask this is to ask a social-historical question, one not answerable within economics: under what conditions did people come to represent social labor in the form of exchange value? It is to ask a question about the historical conditions of economic discourse, about the circumstances under which the categories of economics have a use. If we understand "critique" in its Kantian use, as a demonstration of the limits of applicability of some theory or, more broadly, some discourse, an historical critique of economic theory is thus at once a historical critique of the social practice in relation to which economic discourse exists.[3]

Capital is, in accord with the intentions expressed in Marx's letter to Lassalle, not a study of political economy as a set of texts ("the critique and the history of political economy," which was to come later). It is an investigation of economic discourse—the field of categories defining a mode of conceptualization and discussion of social experience. For this reason, Marx refers to specific texts in *Capital* for the most part in footnotes, as illustrations of his analysis. Because social experience itself has a discursive aspect—because the categories fundamental to economic theory are (relative) theorizations of categories describing, as they have a part in, structures of social practice—the critique of the categories deployed in political economy raises questions about the society reproduced by way of that social practice. This is why *Capital* is a critique of economic categories, as determinants of social practice, by way of an investigation of the conditions of applicability of economic theory.

2. Representation and Reality

In the "General Introduction" that heads the *Grundrisse* manuscripts, Marx concludes a discussion of the sequence in which topics should be taken up in a critical study of capitalist economics by declaring that

> The order obviously has to be (1) the general, abstract determinations which obtain in more or less all forms of society... (2) The categories which make up the inner structure of bourgeois society and on which the fundamental classes rest. Capital, wage labor, landed property. Their interrelation.... (3) Concentration of bourgeois society in the form of the state.... (4) The international relation of production.... (5) The world market and crises (Marx 1857–58a, 108).

The preface to the *Contribution to the Critique of Political Economy*, the first published work to emerge from these manuscripts, restates this plan as the series of topics "*capital, landed property, wage-labor; the State, foreign trade, world market*" (Marx 1859, 261). This evidently corresponds

to the contents of (2)–(5) in the *Grundrisse* plan (which in this form
Marx never changed).[4] Abandoned is what had earlier seemed the
"obviously" proper beginning with a treatment of "the general, abstract
determinations which obtain in more or less all forms of society." The
general introduction is omitted since, Marx says, "it seems to me
confusing to anticipate results which still have to be substantiated"
(Marx 1859, 261).

A glance at the *Grundrisse* introduction shows the nature of these
"results." They fall into two main groups. The first Marx describes under
the headings "1) Production in General; 2) General Relationship Between Production, Distribution, Exchange and Consumption; 3) The
Method of Political Economy." The second falls under the heading "4)
The Means (Forces) of Production and Production Relations; Production Relations and Relations of Intercourse, etc."[5] Sections (1) and (2)
concern general categories of the discourse of political economy. In
the first Marx emphasizes the social and historical nature of the human relation to nature called "production," thereby criticizing the economists' attempt "to present production . . . as encased in eternal natural
laws independent of history, at which opportunity *bourgeois* relations
are then quietly smuggled in as the inviolable natural laws on which
society in the abstract is founded" (Marx 1857–58a, 87). In the second
section he focuses on "the various categories which the economists
line up next to" that of production (ibid., 88). Arguing both against
bourgeois economists and radical critics of capitalism (notably Proudhon)
Marx insists on the analytical primacy of the category of production
for social analysis. Finally, his discussion of method emphasizes again
that "even the most abstract categories . . . are . . . themselves a product of historic relations, and possess their full validity only for and
within those relations" (ibid., 105).

The first group of topics, then, develop a critique of fundamental
categories of bourgeois political economy. Presumably the "results which
still have to be substantiated," therefore, concern the limits and inadequacies of bourgeois theory. Their substantiation would be the Marxian
critique as a whole, and in fact Marx returns to "Relations of Distribution and Relations of Production" at the end of the materials published posthumously as Volume 3 of *Capital.* On the other hand, Marx
judged it appropriate to give, in the preface to the *Contribution,* a précis
of his conception of the dynamic relation between "production relations and relations of intercourse," in the form of "brief remarks regarding the course of my study of political economy" (Marx 1859, 261).

These "remarks," removed from their context, as they are in countless anthologies, constitute one the best known passages in Marx's oeuvre,

the most concise statement of what has come to be called "historical materialism." It is worth remembering that they represent a highly abbreviated residue of (the last part of) Marx's projected introduction to his critique of economic categories when we ask, as is rarely done, what is the significance of their presence at the head of the *Contribution*, beyond their announced purpose of demonstrating that Marx's views "are the outcome of conscientious research carried on over many years" (ibid., 265).

The central point of Marx's remarks is made in his statement that "It is not the consciousness of men that determines their existence but their social existence that determines their consciousness" (ibid., 263). It was his conviction on this point that led Marx in the early 1840s away from philosophy and to the study of political economy. In particular he became convinced that a study of "relations of production" was required if the prospects for social revolution were to be comprehended.

> In studying such transformations it is always necessary to distinguish between the material transformation of the economic conditions of production, which can be determined with the precision of natural science, and the legal, political, religious, artistic, or philosophical—in short, ideological forms in which men become conscious of this conflict and fight it out. Just as one does not judge an individual by what he thinks about himself, so one cannot judge such a period of transformation by its consciousness, but, on the contrary, this consciousness must be explained from the contradictions of material life, from the conflict existing between the social forces of production and the relations of production (ibid.).

At the time when he wrote these words Marx seems to have believed that he was living at least near such a period of social transformation. He wished his work to contribute to the coming social revolution by clarifying the issues at stake. We may remember here the intention stated in Marx's February 22, 1858 letter to Lassalle, that "another book" (in addition to the six called for by the plan of his critique) should address the critique and history of socialism along with that of political economy. But just as the discourse of political economy is criticized in advance of detailed examination of the history of economic theory, so socialist ideologies fall already under the same critique insofar as they submit to the rule of that discourse. Thus Marx wrote Weydemeyer, in reference to the chapters on commodities and money in the *Contribution*, that "In these two chapters, the basis of Proudhonist socialism, now fashionable in France, which leaves private production alone *but organizes* the exchange of private products, which wants the *commodity* but not the *money*, will be run into the ground. Communism must above all dispose of this 'false brother.'"[6] This was all the more important in Marx's eyes as he had come, since his move to England, to understand that such ideas, far from being peculiar to Proudhon, were widespread in the English workers' movement.[7]

Essential to Marx's project, then, was a distinction between people's understanding of their social activities and the actual processes underway (particularly in a "period of transformation"). Such a distinction implies, first, the need for a redescription of those activities, in terms systematically different from those in use. Second, it suggests that, in place of the usual procedure of analyzing society by means of the categories in current use, the normal understanding of social life is itself to be explained by reference to features of that life as redescribed.[8] In the case of Marx's critique, the normal terms are those furnished by economic discourse, taken for granted by political economy. The workings of this discourse must itself be explained by reference to the categories of a newly produced social description.

3. The Starting Point

Marx takes his distance from the economists' representation of the social world in the first sentence of his text. "The wealth of bourgeois society," the *Contribution* begins, "at first sight, presents itself as an immense accumulation of commodities, its unit being a single commodity" (Marx 1859, 269). *Capital* only reformulates this with more elegance, quoting the earlier version to emphasize the continuity of thought: "The wealth of societies in which the capitalist mode of production prevails appears as an 'immense accumulation of commodities'; the individual commodity appears as its elementary form" (Marx 1867, 125). Translation obscures the fact that Marx uses the same verb in both texts: *erscheint*, which refers, through Hegel's particular treatment of it, to the oldest of philosophical and scientific distinctions, that between appearance and reality. "Appearance" here indicates the terrain of economic discourse.

The object of study is that identified by the "father of political economy," Adam Smith: the wealth of nations, "the necessaries and conveniences of life" (Smith 1776, 10). To begin with the analysis of commodities is to begin on the terrain of the science of political economy Smith initiated, which defined itself in opposition to mercantilism's equation of wealth with money. From the viewpoint of political economy, as J. S. Mill explained in his *Principles* of 1848, money "is rightly regarded as wealth" but so also is "everything else which serves any human purpose." Thus wealth may be defined as "all useful or agreeable things which possess exchangeable value" (Mill 1848, 7, 10)—i.e., as commodities. In his restatement of Mill's definition, however, Marx specifies the wealth under discussion by reference to a specific type of "nation," bourgeois society. This sentence, then, contains *in nuce* the program of the Marxian critique as a whole. The appearance of wealth in the commodity form is to be explained, in the manner suggested by the preface to the *Contribution,* by reference to the system of social relations constituting the capitalist mode of society.

If the mention of social wealth calls Smith to mind, Marx's initial theme—use-value and exchange-value as complementary properties of the commodity—evokes the *Principles of Political Economy,* by the author Marx considered the greatest of all economists. Ricardo's first chapter, "On Value," opens with the distinction between value in use and value in exchange; it is echoed by the second sentence of the *Contribution's* Chapter 1, and is the main topic of the version of this chapter in *Capital* as well. In this Marx is choosing the path of Ricardo as against that of, say, Mill. Thus he insists in the *Grundrisse* that "To develop the concept of capital it is necessary to begin not with labor but with value, and, precisely, with exchange value in an already developed movement of circulation. It is just as impossible to make the transition directly from labor to capital"—as Mill does, in the first four chapters of the *Principles,* discussing value only in Book III, on Exchange—"as it is to go from the different human races directly to the banker, or from nature to the steam engine" (Marx 1857–58a, 259).[9] The reason is that "labor," which can be used as a transhistorical concept, does not then pick out an element specific to capitalist society, any more than "means of production" does; only specified as the production of value can the category of labor serve in an explanation of the nature of capital, accumulated surplus value.

Thus it is that the index to the *Grundrisse* manuscripts which Marx prepared as preliminary to producing a publishable text begins with the heading, "I) VALUE" (followed by "II) MONEY" and "III) CAPITAL IN GENERAL") (Marx 1857–58b, 421–423). When he began to prepare that text, Marx still called his first chapter "Value." But he opened with a sentence recognizably the ancestor of the initial sentences of the *Contribution* and *Capital:* "The first category in which bourgeois wealth presents itself is that of the *commodity*" (Marx 1857–58a, 881). "Commodity," strikingly, is not among the "simplest determinations"— the thinnest abstractions to be reached through analysis of the concrete phenomena of economic life, such as "division of labor, money, value, . . . exchange value"—listed in the "General Introduction" to the

Grundrisse (ibid., 100). The analogous passage in the preface to the first edition of *Capital* speaks of "the power of abstraction" as revealing "the commodity form of the product of labor, or the value-form of the commodity" as "the economic cell-form" of bourgeois society (Marx 1867, 90). This idea led, as we know, to the writing of the chapter on the commodity, which replaced value as the starting-point of his study of capital,[10] or rather which provided the theme in relation to which the theory of value is developed.

This might seem to be a minor point. Yet in his notes on Adolph Wagner, written 1879–80, Marx stressed that "neither 'value' nor 'exchange-value' are my subjects, but *the commodity*."[11] One significance of this change is suggested by a passage in the *Grundrisse* written before it was made. Discussing the exchange relation, in the "Chapter on Capital," Marx calls the "pure form" of exchange "the economic side of this relation," contrasting it with "the content" which "falls entirely outside economics," and is "the different use values of the commodities being exchanged (Marx 1857–58a, 241–242). This is the same contrast made in *Capital* by distinguishing the value form of the commodity from its use value, "the material content of wealth, whatever its social form may be" (Marx 1867, 125). To begin with value as such would have been to begin inside the discourse of economics; to begin with the commodity is implicitly to set the society in which that discourse has its place against other forms of society in which it does not. Transhistorical content must exist always in one form or another, but there is no reason why it must eternally exist in *this* form.[12]

There is a further aspect of this matter. What is peculiar to capitalism is not the phenomenon of exchange-value, but the fact that the commodity is the dominant form of product, so that wealth appears as an "immense collection of commodities." This is only the case (as Marx argues in *Capital*) when the ability to perform labor is itself a commodity. "The capitalist epoch is therefore characterized by the fact that labor-power, in the eyes of the worker himself, takes on the form of a commodity which is his property; his labor consequently takes on the form of wage-labor. On the other hand, it is only from this moment that the commodity-form of the products of labor becomes universal" (Marx 1867, 274). The condition of this is the separation of the producers from the means of production, including land, which makes it impossible for them either to produce goods either for their own consumption or for exchange. The generalization of the commodity form, that is, is an index of the class relation between capital and wage labor, the relation that makes possible the exploitation of the working class by the owners of capital. Its key point is the appearance of labor power as a commodity.[13]

Derek Sayer is therefore mistaken in holding that capital "in no sense" remains "the starting point as well as the finishing point" of Marx's investigation. According to Sayer,

> The hidden exegetical structure of *Capital* is that of a hierarchy of conditions of possibility. Thus the commodity is analyzed before money, and money before capital, the first form in either pair being a condition of the second; the concept of value is developed before that of surplus-value, and that of surplus-value before those of its transmuted forms (profit, rent, interest) for the same reason (Sayer 1979).

The hierarchy Sayer has in mind is one of logical conditions, a structure that gives *Capital* a "quasi-deductive" form with good reason reminiscent of the deductive chain of categories in Hegel's logic. This is not the place to enter on a discussion of the thorny question of the relation of Marx's argument to Hegelian dialectics, invoked by many to explain the structure of that argument.[14] It can, however, be pointed out that Sayer's purported logical chain of categories in *Capital* does not exist.

While Marx indeed defines capital—at least, initially—in terms of money and, obviously, surplus-value in terms of value, the commodity cannot be "analyzed before money" since the analysis of money is part of that of the commodity. Under capitalist conditions money and commodities exist together as elements of market exchange. As Marx argues, even if we imagine the simplest exchange of good against good, each must function, if the other is to be a commodity, as the value equivalent of the other—and thus functionally as already money. The commodity is discussed before money not because it is a condition of the latter's existence but because, as a unity of use-value and exchange-value, it represents the double character of capitalism, as a particular form of the general imperative of production, whose historically specific aspect is exhibited in money.

Further, as this suggests, capital is the condition for the dominance of the commodity form, Marx's starting point: in the words of the draft "sixth chapter" of *Capital*, "Only on the basis of capitalist production does the commodity actually become the *universal elementary form of wealth*," (Marx 1863–66, 951) the cell form. The initial discussion of the commodity is thus already—as the opening sentence suggests—a discussion of capital. Finally, the concept of surplus-value, as we shall see, is developed "before those of its transmuted forms" not because it is logically prior but because it is epistemically posterior. It constitutes Marx's theoretical explanation of the phenomena of profit, rent, and interest which, as well-established elements of economic practice and discourse, occupy a radically different epistemological status than their

Marxian explanation. Here, too, it is the relation of reality (surplus-value) to appearance (profit *et al.*), the relation of social-theoretical explanation to ideological form, that is represented by the structure of the argument.

4. The Argument in *Capital*

This structure is fully visible, within the limits set by its place within the argument of *Capital* as a whole, in Chapter 1. Beginning with the commodity as the historical form in which wealth appears in capitalist society, Marx proceeds to describe exchange-value as it "appears" in the exchange ratio between two commodities. "Value" is then defined as the reality, which thus appears, although Marx is quick to emphasize that it can *only* appear in this form. "We may twist and turn a single commodity as we wish; it remains impossible to grasp it as a thing possessing value." This is because value is a "purely social" property, a relation between people engaged in commodity exchange, and therefore "can only appear in the social relation between commodity and commodity" (Marx 1867, 138–9). This reference to a "social relation" between things is at once ironic, hinting at the topsy-turvy character of a world in which people represent their mutual relations by relations between things, and literally true, for as exchange is a social act exchange relations are social relations. It becomes ironic when the actual exchangers are left out of the depiction of the act (and the irony is doubled when, in Chapter 2, the exchangers appear as the "bearers" of commodity relations, as persons who "exist for one another merely as representatives and hence owners, of commodities" [ibid., 178–9]).

Irony is the appropriate rhetorical mode here, for it is the particular set of social practices that go under the name of exchange that the discursive representation of those practices as an exchange of commodities conceals (ibid., 169).[15] Capitalism, like any other mode of society, must, whatever else it does, organize the labor process by which human life is maintained. It is clear that, in the absence of any other mechanism for doing this, it is—as the classical economists already realized—the practice of market exchange that regulates the production and distribution of goods. For this reason "the private producer's brain reflects [the] . . . social character of his labor only in the forms which appear in practical intercourse, in the exchange of products" (ibid., 166). This is what Marx calls the "fetishism" of commodities, the treatment of the historical peculiarities of capitalist society, in everyday life and economic theory alike, as though they were "as much a self-evident and nature-imposed necessity as productive labor itself" (ibid., 175). Ending with the discussion of this "fetishism," Marx's chapter has begun with a set of appearances—the phenomena of commodity exchange—which are then redescribed in terms of a novel theoretical vocabulary (notably, the distinction between abstract and concrete labor) that makes possible a social-historical explanation of the appearances and their place in economic discourse.

Marx is at pains in his chapter on the commodity to demonstrate the oddness, even the "absurdity" of economic discourse. But the demonstration of its inability to account for fundamental aspects of capitalism comes only in Part II of the first volume of *Capital*, which explicitly introduces the concept of capital. Capital is money advanced to make money. Considered "in the form in which it appears (*erscheint*) directly in the sphere of circulation," (ibid., 257) its existence is inexplicable, for acts of exchange, as Marx argues, cannot produce an increment of value. As we know, the solution to this riddle is the existence of the commodity labor-power, embodied in a class of propertyless producers. It is the purchase and use of this commodity by capitalists that makes possible the production of value in excess of its own value. "The consumption of labor-power is completed, as in the case of every other commodity, outside the market or the sphere of circulation." To understand the production of surplus-value, therefore, we must leave the realm of appearances, "this noisy sphere, where everything takes place on the surface and in full view of everyone," for "the hidden abode of production" (ibid., 279).

This represents a further break with the Ricardian model, of course. From Ricardo's point of view, "the principal problem in Political Economy" is "to determine the laws which regulate [the] distribution" of "the produce of the earth ... among three classes of the community ..." (Ricardo 1817, 5). The second section of the *Grundrisse* introduction had such a view in mind, in considering the relation between production and "the various categories which the economists line up next to it":

> Production is determined by general natural laws, distribution by social accident, and the latter may therefore promote production to a greater or lesser extent... When one examines the usual works of economics, it is immediately striking that everything in them is posited doubly. For example, ground rent, wages, interest and profit figure under distribution, while land, labor and capital figure here under production as agents of production. ... [E]conomists such as Ricardo ... have defined distribution as the exclusive object of economics, because they have instinctively conceived the forms of

distribution as the most specific expression into which the agents of production of a given society are cast (Marx 1857–58, 94–96).

Because of its double nature, the commodity form obscures the class relation on which its social dominance rests. For when the ability to work appears as a commodity, its exchange against money seems no different from any other act of market exchange. (In Ricardo's words, "Labor, like all other things which are purchased and sold, and which may be increased or diminished in quantity, has its natural and its market price" [Ricardo 1917, 93].) Thus

> The sphere of circulation or commodity exchange, within whose boundaries the sale and purchase of labor-power goes on, is in fact a very Eden of the innate rights of man. It is the exclusive realm of Freedom, Equality, Property, and Bentham. Freedom, because both buyer and seller of a commodity, let us say of labor-power, are determined only by their own free will. They contract as free persons, who are equal before the law. . . . Equality, because each enters into relation with the other, as with a simple owner of commodities, and they exchange equivalent for equivalent. Property, because each disposes only of what is his own. And Bentham, because each looks only to his own advantage. The only force bringing them together [as in Smith's description of the market] . . . is the selfishness, the gain, and the private interest of each. . . . And precisely for that reason, either in accordance with the pre-established harmony of things, or under the auspices of an omniscient providence, they all work together to their mutual advantage, for the common weal, and in the common interest (Marx 1867, 280).

These ideological categories—in their socialist as well as in their bourgeois-economist use—must be distinguished from the actual "economic conditions of production" by reference to which the fact that they appear to the common and the educated sense of bourgeois society as appropriate for the description of economic life must be explained. A passage in the *Grundrisse* makes clear that this is an application of the "guiding principle" of Marx's studies explained in the preface to the *Contribution*: "Equality and freedom are thus not only respected in exchange based on exchange values but, also, the exchange of exchange values is the productive real basis of all *equality* and *freedom*. As pure ideas they are merely the idealized expressions of this basis; as developed in juridical, political, social relations, they are merely this basis to a higher power" (Marx 1857–58a, 245).[16] The centrality of economic discourse to capitalist social life, which itself reflects the dominance of the commodity form as the general form of labor product, shapes the vocabulary of politics, along with other systems of representation, such as philosophy. It is for this reason that "the anatomy of . . . civil society . . . has to be sought in political economy" (Marx 1859, 262). The inadequacies of political economy, however, will point the way to a radically new understanding of society.

The domain of production provides the solution to the problem of the origin of surplus-value precisely because it does not share the essential features of the marketplace, the domain of circulation. Freedom and equality are gone: the exchange of labor-power for wage concluded, "the worker works under the control of the capitalist to whom his labor belongs . . ." (Marx 1867, 291–2). The nature of capital becomes clear: what from the point of view of economics is alternatively a sum of money invested in production or the means of production purchased with part of that sum is visible, in the activities constituting the production process, as a social power relation between employer and employee. Later in Volume 1 this redescription of capital is deepened, in the course of Marx's explanation of capital accumulation. Looked at over time, a capitalist in the present hires workers with surplus value produced by workers in the past. "The relation of exchange between capitalist and worker becomes a mere semblance belonging only to the process of circulation, it becomes a mere form, which is alien to the content of the transaction itself, and merely mystifies it" (ibid., 729–30).

In this way the labor theory of value itself, the great theoretical conquest of classical political economy (and generally reputed the foundation of "Marxist economics") is revealed to belong to the appearances of economic discourse. In the discussion of commodity exchange, "the rights of property seemed to us to be grounded in a man's own labor" since "the means of appropriating the commodities of others was the alienation of a man's own commodities, . . . produced by labor."

> Now, however, property turns out to be the right, on the part of the capitalist, to appropriate the unpaid labor of others or its product, and the impossibility, on the part of the worker, of appropriating his own product. The separation of property from labor thus becomes the necessary consequence of a law that apparently originated in their identity (ibid., 730).[17]

As the last sentence suggests, this is not an injustice to be corrected by political enforcement of the rights of labor, but is essential to the existence of a social system in which "labor" is the name of a factor of production, and in which market exchange is an act involving for all practical purposes "only the mutually independent buyer and seller" (ibid., 733). Were we to examine the exchange process as one taking place between social classes, rather than between individuals, "we should be applying standards entirely foreign to commodity production" (ibid., 732) and its style of self-representation. From the viewpoint implied by those standards, however, value can be recognized to be a social form for the exploitation of one part of society by another, in the guise of a principle of equality in exchange.

While the exchange relation is a "mere form" when it is a matter of explaining the origin of surplus-value, according to Marx actual modes of social life are determined by such forms. In another variation on the basis/superstructure theme, Marx explains in Volume 3 of *Capital* that "the specific economic form in which unpaid surplus labor is pumped out of the direct producers determines the relationship of domination and servitude" that differentiates one form of class society from another, so that "On this is based the entire configuration of the economic community arising from the actual relations of production, and hence also its specific political form" (Marx 1894, 927). Therefore *Capital* must return, as it does in the second volume, to the circulation process with which the argument began.

The commodity remains the cell form of the specifically capitalist mode of exploitation. Wealth is not, as it appears, an accumulation of commodities. Wealth is the accumulation of *capital*, and capital "is not only the command over labor, as Adam Smith thought. It is essentially the command over unpaid labor" (Marx 1867, 672). But capital operates only through the commodity form; it is the commodification of labor power that makes possible the control over others' labor in the specific form of surplus-value. "Capital, as self-valorizing value, does not just comprise class relations, a definite social character that depends on the existence of labor as wage-labor. It is a movement, a circulatory process through different stages, which itself in turn includes three different forms of the circulatory process" (Marx 1885, 185). Hence the material contained in Volume 2, while covering a range of topics, above all demonstrates that the category of the market—in economic terms, demand—represents the social form of the reconstitution and growth of capital as a surplus labor-extracting system.[18]

This understanding, however, is only available on the basis of the critique of economic categories effected in the first volume. Indeed, according to Marx, a reexamination of the circulation process explains why to those whose experience is defined by its forms in action "the conditions of the original production of value fall completely into the background. . . . Both the restoration of the values advanced in production, and particularly the surplus-value contained in the commodities, seem not just to be realized only in circulation but actually to arise from it" (Marx 1894, 966). The third volume of *Capital*, synthesizing the class relation at the heart of capitalist production with the specific forms in which capitals interact with one another, in explaining the forms taken by surplus-value in circulation—profit, interest, and rent—accounts more thoroughly for "the everyday consciousness of the agents of production themselves" and for the economists' theorizations of that consciousness (ibid., 117).

Volume 3 concludes, accordingly, with a discussion of the way in which the workings of the economy obscures from view the nature of value, which seems to be, not a representation of social labor under the control of capital, but a method for the fair division of the social product among those who have contributed in different ways to its production. The portion of the social product necessary for the reproduction of the working class appears as wages, the price of labor, just as the labor required to reproduce the means of production appears as a portion of the price of the product. The labor performed beyond that required for reproduction—the surplus labor—appears in the various categories into which its money-representation ("surplus-value") is divided: profit, interest, rent, commercial profit, each the payment for a "service" rendered by an owner of property. It must so appear, for in real economic life the various claimants to portions of the social product must be satisfied, at least in proportion to their ability to make their claims count for others, if that life is to continue.

Only at this point in the argument is commodity-exchange, with which Marx began, fully theorized (at least on the relatively abstract level of analysis, disregarding the various particular forms of competition at work in the market, undertaken by *Capital*). As Marx observes in the *Theories of Surplus Value*, "to be produced, to be brought to the market, the commodity must at least fetch [a] market price" yielding a satisfactory rate of profit to its capitalist producer, "whether its own value be greater or smaller than that [price]" (1861–63c, 273). Since, as was established in the first volume of *Capital*, value provides the social form of the product of labor only when production is dominated by capital,

> values are defined for products that are exchanged as products of capitals, not just as products of "social labor." Though the labor input to the product of a given firm counts as socially necessary only to the extent that the exchange *makes* it a part of social labor time, the commodity is exchanged as part of the social product only as the private property of the firm. Its price must therefore yield, to its owner-producer, a rate of profit at least as high as that received by any other firm (Mattick Jr., 1981, 39).

As a result, according to Marx, "just *because* the value of the commodity is determined by *labor time*, the average price of the commodities . . . can *never* be equal to their value although this determination of the average price is only derived from the value which is based on labor time" (Marx 1861–63b, 269). Value, which regulates capitalist society as a system of class exploitation, is invisible at the level of market exchange. Here it appears only in the form of the exchange value, in money terms, of commodities, determined for all practical purposes by relations of supply and demand, in which the various divisions of surplus-value appear as so many elements of a commodity's price.[19]

It is quite natural, Marx concluded, "that the actual agents of production feel themselves completely at home in these estranged and irrational forms . . . for these are precisely the configurations of appearance in which they move, and with which they are daily involved." It is equally natural that those he called "vulgar economists"—the ancestors of today's neoclassical writers—whose theory is "nothing more than a . . . more or less doctrinaire translation of the everyday notions of the actual agents of production" elaborate the same points of view, while even the classical economists "remained more or less trapped in the world of illusion" their theorizing had attempted to penetrate (Marx 1894, 969). Thus, at the end of the third volume of his work, Marx returns to his starting point: the capitalist economy as it is represented in economic discourse—both the "religion of everyday life" and the theology erected by economists—as a set of institutions, structured by exchange relations, for the production of goods satisfying human desires: wealth as an accumulation of commodities.

On the other hand, the consciousness of capitalism's critics must also be explained, and even the understanding, however limited, of the system's structural difficulties represented by the political economists' conception of a tendency of the rate of profit to fall. The discussion of the process of capital accumulation in the first volume of *Capital* concludes with a consideration of "the influence of the growth of capital on the fate of the working class" (Marx 1867, 762). Discovering the consequences of accumulation in the tendential replacement of living labor by means of production, on the one hand, and the cycle of expansion and contraction produced by the need to reorganize the social structure of capital in response to changing conditions of accumulation, on the other, Marx argues that "in proportion as capital accumulates, the situation of the worker, be his payment high or low, must grow worse." In bad times, unemployment rises, wages fall, and working conditions worsen, but even in good times "all methods for raising the social productivity of labor are put into effect at the cost of the individual worker . . . so that they become means of domination and exploitation of the producers . . ." (ibid., 799). It was in these terms that Marx accounted for the workers' movements of the nineteenth century, arguing that the growth of "the mass of misery, oppression, slavery, degradation, and exploitation" brought with it "the revolt of the working class . . . trained, united, and organized by the very mechanism of the capitalist mode of production" (ibid., 929).

As the first volume of *Capital* progresses from an analysis of appearances—capitalism's economic representation as a system of commodity exchanges between individuals—to a redescription of the system as one of class exploitation, it ends appropriately with the effects of the working of this system on the working class and the promise of "the expropriation of a few usurpers by the mass of the people" (ibid., 930). In the third volume, which examines the operation of the economic categories that obscure the actual class structure of society, the same subject is reexamined, this time as it appears in the vicissitudes of the category of profit.

Profit is defined, in the first two parts of the volume, as surplus-value considered as the "return" to capital invested in labor-power and means of production. This is to look at surplus-value from what one may call the viewpoint of a schematic capitalist; as experienced by actual capitalists, surplus-value appears under different rubrics—as interest and rent, as well as profit—depending on the particular nature of the claim made to it. In Part 3 Marx presents his law of the tendential fall of the rate of profit "before depicting the decomposition of profit into various categories which have become mutually autonomous" in order to show "how the law in its generality is independent of that division and of the mutual relationships of the categories of profit deriving from it" (Marx 1894, 320).

In a letter written to Engels, after publication of the first volume of *Capital,* Marx listed as the first of the "fundamentally new elements of the book" that "in contrast to all former political economy, which *from the very outset* treats the particular fragments of surplus value with their fixed forms of rent, profit, and interest as already given, I first deal with the general form of surplus value, in which all these fragments are still undifferentiated . . ."[20] Given the result established in the second part of Volume 1, that the expansion of value definitive of capital cannot be explained on the basis of exchange relations but only in terms of the expropriation of (unpaid) labor time—that is, in terms of the class relation between workers and capitalists—"surplus-value" is the explanatorily illuminating name for the revenue known to the agents of production (and distribution) as profit, rent, etc.

As Marx observed to Engels in another letter, the treatment of the struggle over the length of the working day which follows the analysis of surplus-value in *Capital* "shows how very well Mister Bourgeois is enlightened *practically* on the source and essence of his profit."[21] Were economic theory to employ the concept of surplus-value, however, it would have to give up the idea that capitalism is completely describable as a system of market exchanges, for this concept involves understanding labor-power as unique among commodities in its capacity to produce, when consumed, more value than it represents. It is for this reason, Marx argues in Volume 3, that the economists, while they perceived the phenomenon of the tendency of the profit rate to fall—most spectacularly visible in the periodic crises that afflicted capitalism during the nineteenth century—"tortured themselves with their contradictory attempts to explain it." In Marx's view, this law, given its importance for the life of the social system, "forms the mystery around whose solution the whole of political economy since Adam Smith revolves and that the difference between the various schools since Adam Smith consists of the different attempts made to solve it" (Marx 1894, 319).

The unsolvability of this mystery arose from the internal structure of the discourse of economics: the impossibility of understanding the functioning of capitalism in terms of economic concepts, which nevertheless are experienced as "natural" and fundamental categories of social life by those who employ them. A theory capable of explaining both capitalist accumulation and its crisis tendency required a redescription of economic relationships as relations of class exploitation. It is for this very reason that, once having solved the mystery, Marx devotes the remainder of Volume 3 to the explanation of economic appearances. Having worked out the forms taken by surplus-value (more correctly: the phenomena redescribed in terms of surplus-value), Marx can then examine economic reality as it appears in "vulgar" economic theory, as the production of wealth by the three factors of production, capital, land, and labor, to which revenue accordingly (and justly) flows as profit (plus interest), rent, and wages. The entire text of his work to this point has exposed the reality experienced in the form of these categories; here Marx is in a position to explain their power. For the trinity of economic factors actually are the sources of their specific revenues "in the sense that capital for the capitalist is a perpetual pumping machine for surplus labor, land for the landowner a permanent magnet for attracting a part of the surplus labor pumped out by capital and finally labor the constantly self-renewing condition and means for the worker to obtain a part of the value he has produced and hence a part of the social product measured by this portion of value, under the heading of wages" (ibid., 961).

The viability of economic discourse is in this way shown to depend on the fact that "the capitalist mode of production, like every other, constantly reproduces not only the material product but also the socio-economic relations, the formal economic determinants of its formation." Economic theory gains its plausibility from the conformity of its conceptual apparatus to the assumptions embodied in commercial calculations and contracts, and these assumptions maintain their power because people naturally attempt to carry on their lives within the social relations they find themselves caught up in, of which the assumptions provide the structural terms. As Marx put it, in a concise statement of the culturally-constructed character of social reality, "The specific shape in which the value components [of social wealth] confront one another is presupposed because it is constantly reproduced, and it is constantly reproduced because it is constantly presupposed" (ibid., 1012).

On the other hand, Marx has argued that the reproduction of capitalist social relations involves a tendency to economic crisis, and that this, given the massive degradation of working-class life it entails, contains the possibility of social crisis. Marx emphasized the historically specific, and so in principle transitory, nature of economic categories in the postface to the second edition of *Capital*'s first volume, asserting that "the fact that the movement of capitalist society is full of contradictions impresses itself most strikingly on the practical bourgeois in the changes of the periodic cycle through which modern industry passes, the summit of which is the general crisis" (Marx 1867, 103). This remark gives a particular content to the general proposition in the preface to the *Contribution* that "an era of social revolution" begins when "the material productive forces of society come into conflict with the existing relations of production" (Marx 1859, 263). Marx uses nearly the same words at the end of Volume 3 of *Capital* when he criticizes the notion, particularly associated with J. S. Mill but shared with political economy generally, that only the relations of distribution are historical, and not the relations of production. In reality, says Marx—and this can stand as a summary of *Capital*'s critique of economics—production is only ever carried on within the social framework represented by particular relations of distribution, or claims to the social product. That a "contradiction and antithesis between, on the one hand, the relations of distribution, hence also the specific form of relations of production corresponding to them, and, on the other hand, the productive forces, productivity, and the development of its agents, gains in breadth and depth" is the sign that a moment of social crisis has arrived, in which the construction of new forms of social life is possible (Marx 1894, 1024).

Marx explained the timid criticism of capitalism he saw in Mill's differentiation between distribution and production as a reaction to the evidence of the system's tendency to such crisis. His own work, as a thorough critique of the categories of life and thought in which economists like Mill were caught alongside the "actual agents of production," was made possible by his engagement with the working-class movements that Marx believed were working out new categories of social action. A positive critique of economics, *Capital* was also, one might say, a negative theory of socialism, clarifying the social relations that needed to be abolished for a fundamental break with capitalism to be accomplished. Consciousness, both that embodied in economic discourse and that capable of imagining a new mode of social life, is thus "explained from the contradictions of material life," as the preface to the *Contribution* demanded and promised.

Notes

1. Marx to Lasalle, February 22, 1858, in Karl Marx and Frederick Engels, *Letters on 'Capital'*, trans. Andrew Drummond (London: New Park Publications, 1983), 51–52.
2. See also the manuscript later published as *Theories of Surplus Value* (Marx 1861–63a, 389–90): ". . . *Ricardo* does not *examine* the form—the peculiar characteristic of labor that creates exchange value or manifests itself in exchange values—the *nature* of this labor. Hence he does not grasp the connection of *this labor* with *money* or that it must assume the form of money."
3. My thinking about this question was long ago stimulated by Johannes Witt-Hansen, *Historical Materialism: The Method, the Theories*, Book I (Copenhagen: Munksgaard, 1960).
4. For a discussion of Marx's evolving writing plan, see Maximilian Rubel, "Plan et méthode de l'Économie," in *Marx critique du marxisme* (Paris: Payot, 1974), 369–401.
5. Quoted in Karl Marx, Frederick Engels, *Collected Works*, vol. 28 (New York: International Publishers, 1986), 542 n. 6.
6. Marx to Weydemeyer, February 1, 1859, in *Letters on 'Capital'*, 65.
7. See the discussion in Fred E. Schrader, *Restauration und Revolution. Die Vorarbeiten zum "Kapital" von Karl Marx in seinen Studienheften 1850–1858* (Hildesheim: Gerstenberg, 1980), 210 ff.
8. For a discussion of epistemological issues raised by this project, see Paul Mattick Jr., *Social Knowledge* (Armonk: M. E. Sharpe, 1986).
9. The passage is repeated in the Economic Manuscripts of 1861–63; see Marx 1861–63a, 20.

10. See Marx to Engels, November 29, 1858, in *Letters*, p. 63. For a detailed and illuminating discussion of this transformation of Marx's plan, see Fred Schrader, *Restauration*, 196 ff.

11. Karl Marx, "Notes on Adolph Wagner," in *Texts on Method*, trans. and ed. Terrell Carver (Oxford: Basil Blackwell, 1975), 183.

12. For a related argument about Marx's choice of the commodity as his starting point see Martha Campbell, "Marx's Concept of Economic Relations," in Moseley 1993, 135–155, especially 144 ff.

13. For the relation between the focus on the commodity and Marx's discovery of the twofold nature of commodity-producing labor, on the one hand, and his abandonment of an Hegelian mode of conceptual development in the exposition of his ideas, on the other, see Schrader, *Restauration und Revolution*, 204–213.

14. I have gone into this matter in some detail—arguing that, whether or not there is such a thing as a dialectical logic to be found in Hegel, Marx does not employ one in *Capital*—in "Marx's Dialectic," Moseley 1993, 115–133.

15. For a stimulating discussion of irony in Marx's deconstruction of economic discourse, see Robert Paul Wolff, *Moneybags Must Be So Lucky. On the Literary Structure of* "Capital" (Amherst: University of Massachusetts Press, 1988). Despite its excesses and errors this is an interesting little book. Its treatment of Marx's critique of economics is all the more remarkable given its description of *Capital* as "a work of theoretical economics" and its author's own insistence, in an earlier book, on a neo-Ricardian reconstruction of Marxian theory—a project quite incompatible with the picture of that theory given in this volume.

16. The last phrase is a striking variant on the concept of "superstructure," suggesting the error involved in over-literal readings of Marx's architectural metaphor.

17. The idea is developed in the manuscript, "Results of the Immediate Process of Production": while "Capitalist production is the first to make the commodity into the general form of all produce," this system "destroys the basis of commodity production in so far as the latter involves independent individual production and exchange of commodities between owners or the exchange of equivalents" (Marx 1863–66, 951).

18. "In so far as the capitalist simply personifies industrial capital, his own demand consists simply in the demand for means of production and labor-power. . . . In so far as the worker converts his wages almost wholly into means of subsistence, . . . the capitalist's demand for labor-power is indirectly also a demand for the means of consumption that enter into the consumption of the working class" (Marx 1885, 197).

19. For a discussion of the implications of Marx's treatment of value for the solution of the "value-price transformation problem" to which the Ricardian labor theory of value gave rise (but which has come, curiously, to be discussed as a difficulty of Marxian theory), see Mattick, Jr., 1981.

20. January 8, 1868, in Karl Marx and Frederick Engels, *Selected Correspondence* (Moscow: Foreign Languages Publishing House, n.d.), p. 238. The same point is stressed in a letter to Engels of August 24, 1867; see ibid., 232.

21. August 16, 1867, in ibid., 231.

References

Marx 1857–58a. Karl Marx, *Grundrisse*, trans. Martin Nicolaus (Harmondsworth: Penguin, 1973).

Marx 1857–58b. Karl Marx, "Index to the 7 Notebooks," in Karl Marx, Frederick Engels, *Collected Works*, vol. 29 (New York: International Publishers, 1987).

Marx 1859. Karl Marx, *A Contribution to the Critique of Political Economy*, in Karl Marx, Frederick Engels, *Collected Works*, vol. 29 (New York: International Publishers, 1987).

Marx 1861–63a. Karl Marx, "Economic Manuscript of 1861–63," in Karl Marx, Frederick Engels, *Collected Works*, vol. 31 (New York: International Publishers, 1989).

Marx 1861–63b. Karl Marx, "Economic Manuscript of 1861–63," in Karl Marx, Frederick Engels, *Collected Works*, vol. 32 (New York: International Publishers, 1989).

Marx 1861–63c. Karl Marx, "Economic Manuscript of 1861–63," in Karl Marx, Frederick Engels, *Collected Works*, vol. 33 (New York: International Publishers, 1991).

Marx 1863–66, Karl Marx, "Results of the Immediate Process of Production," in Marx 1867.

Marx 1867. Karl Marx, *Capital*, vol. I, trans. Ben Fowkes (Harmondsworth: Penguin, 1976).

Marx 1885. Karl Marx, *Capital*, vol. II, trans. David Fernbach (Harmondsworth: Penguin, 1978).

Marx 1894. Karl Marx, *Capital*, vol. III, trans. David Fernbach (Harmondsworth: Penguin, 1981).

Mattick Jr. 1981. Paul Mattick Jr., "Some Aspects of the Value-Price Problem," in *International Journal of Political Economy*, 21:4 (1991–2), 9–66.

Mill 1848. John Stuart Mill, *Principles of Political Economy* (Toronto: University of Toronto Press, 1965).

Moseley 1993. Fred Moseley (ed.), *Marx's Method in "Capital"* (Atlantic Highlands: Humanities Press, 1993).

Ricardo 1817. David Ricardo, *On the Principles of Political Economy and Taxation*, ed. Piero Sraffa (Cambridge: Cambridge University Press, 1966).

Sayer 1979. Derek Sayer, *Marx's Method. Ideology, Science and Critique in "Capital"* (London: Harvester, 1979).

Smith 1776. Adam Smith, *An Inquiry into the Nature and Causes of the Wealth of Nations*, ed. R. H. Campbell et al., vol. I (Oxford: Clerandon Press, 1976).

4

Marx's Theory of Money: A Defense

Martha Campbell

Even sympathetic interpreters of Marx consider the actual disassociation of money from gold to have left his theory of money in "considerable embarrassment" (Foley 1983, 17). This would be true if the theory depended on money being a commodity, which, as I will argue, it does not. Marx poses his explanation in terms of commodity money because it is the simplest form of money. Because it presupposes fewer other characteristics of capitalism than any other form of money, Marx can use it to establish what money is in the earliest stages of his presentation. Everything the theory claims to demonstrate, however, applies to money of any form. Further, it proposes to explain why money is necessary, which is both a fundamental question and one that economics has had little success in answering. While, for Marx, commodity money is a device, his interpreters have made it the focus of their attention. In the preoccupation with money being a commodity, what Marx sought to demonstrate by means of this device—the real purpose of the theory—is overlooked. Responding to Marx's critics is a way of revealing it.

The critics chosen here, Levine and Ong, are exceptional in that, like Marx, they argue that money is essential. In addition, their criticisms pertain to the argument of the early chapters of *Capital* in which Marx presents the theory of the universal equivalent. Both reject the very idea of commodity money, maintaining that it reduces money to a commodity. They regard the commodity character of money as an essential feature of Marx's theory and as the theory's fatal flaw. Their misgivings are undoubtedly shared by others. Hence their criticisms provide an occasion to clear up a variety of misconceptions about what the universal equivalent is. Before turning to the details of their arguments, I will present an overview of their positions, their criticisms of Marx, and my response to them.

1. An Overview

The significance of money for Levine consists in its implications for need. In a monetary economy, need can develop in infinitely varied ways free of the limits imposed by tradition. Money is required for this kind of need to be realized in practice because it gives a tangible and objective form to abstract wealth—to the means of satisfying needs, apart from any particular need or way of satisfying it. The existence of money means that abstract wealth can be the motive of production. When it is, production generates the variegated and ever changing array of products typical of capitalism. This is Levine's alternative to the neo-classical explanation of money as the solution to the double coincidence of wants problem. The error Levine sees in the neoclassical account, therefore, is that it takes needs to be determined apart from the market and monetary exchange.

Ong shares Levine's idea of the interdependence of money and need, but emphasizes that money is constituted by social recognition. He stresses also that the needs of capital accumulation require an endogenously determined money supply. Joining the two, Ong argues that bank credit supported by a central bank both gains recognition because of its stability and adjusts to the needs of trade. On this basis, he concludes that money is in principle "the highest quality debt" (Ong 1983, 50).

Levine and Ong oppose Marx on essentially two counts. First, both believe that Marx begins *Capital* with barter and is obliged to present money as commodity money as a result. Further, beginning with barter presupposes that money is not among the "fundamental determinants of circulation" (Levine 1983, 27). This means that the market is conceived to serve a "technical purpose"—allocating given resources among given needs—rather than the social purpose of sustaining the "development of needs and wealth," which according to Levine is the purpose it really serves (ibid.).

Second, Levine, and Ong argue that money cannot be a commodity. Both maintain that money cannot have a value of its own because it *is* value over and against commodities. For Levine, this follows from the nature of value. For Ong, the defect that makes commodity money impossible is that its supply is exogenously determined.

Regarding the first criticism, Levine and Ong are right that beginning with barter trivializes money but wrong to attribute this way of beginning to *Capital*. They do so because they do not recognize the methodological principles on which its first chapter is based. As a result, on the one hand they attribute Ricardo's concept of value to Marx.

On the other, to avoid Ricardo's triviallization of exchange (which Marx also criticizes), they propose that value and money be conceived entirely in terms of exchange. The opposite of Ricardo, this is the position espoused by Bailey. Marx explicitly and intentionally avoids both these alternatives, arguing that value is based on the interdependence of production and exchange. According to Marx, the first defect to emerge in Bailey's position is that by disconnecting exchange from production, Bailey loses the objectivity of value. The same criticism applies to the proposals advanced by Levine and Ong.

Regarding the second set of criticisms, Marx's claim that money must be a commodity applies at most to its function as measure of value. Since this function does not require the presence of any actual money, his explanation does not involve special assumptions about the quantity of the money commodity. Moreover, Marx indicates the path by which a noncommodity could replace commodity money even in its measure of value function. This imples that commodity money is meant to be a temporary assumption rather than an essential feature of money. Levine and Ong take Marx to mean that money must be a commodity in all its functions. In particular, the modern debate over the endogenous determination of the money supply concerns money's function as medium of exchange. Marx explains why this function cannot be performed by the money commodity and, following Steuart, conceives the quantity of means of circulation to be endogenously determined.

2. Marx's Barter Starting Point

2.1 MARX'S ARGUMENT ON THE VALUE FORM

The most devasting charge Levine and Ong have to make is that the idea of commodity money, and so Marx's theory, transforms monetary exchange into barter. As evidence for it, they claim that Marx begins with a "barter system" and so assumes "the fundamental idea of valuation . . . to be contained within . . . the immediate relation between two particular commodities" (Levine 1983, 28).[1]

The preliminary evidence that the charge is false is that Marx shares Levine's view of the attempt to derive money from barter and of the resulting opinion that money overcomes the "technical inconveniences" of barter (Marx 1859, 51).

The source of the problem is the simple value form; it is the nonmonetary commodity relation that Ong and Levine regard as Marx's starting point. They take it to contain Marx's "fundamental idea of valuation" because he speaks of value being expressed within this relation and says that it contains "the whole mystery of the form of value" (Marx 1867, 139). The simple value form, however, neither is barter nor expresses value. These misconceptions arise from treating Marx's discussion of the value form (Section 3 of Chapter 1 of *Capital*) as an independent argument. It is instead the third and final part of the argument prior to it.

In the first part (Section 1), Marx derives value from exchange value (as I will show in a moment, the relation that originally yields value is money price or the exchange relation between an ordinary commodity and money). In the second, he considers "the nature of value independently of its form of appearance" (ibid., 128), but based entirely on the fact that value does appear in money. With this, Marx returns to the form of value in Section 3, to explain why value requires money to appear. This involves identifying each aspect of the money price relation together with its contribution to the expression of value. To consider one aspect at a time (there are four), Marx treats each of the "value forms" as potential expressions of value. Each has the capacity to bring out some aspect of value, but also, until the money form, each one fails to express value in some respect. The premise of the value-form argument, which drives it forward from one form to the next, is that we know what the value form has to express (i.e., "the nature of value" just cited). Because this is given, we can recognize the one form that is capable of expressing value, namely, money.

It is only because the relation of two ordinary commodities is considered as a potential expression of value that this relation is the simple value form and, as such, that it expresses, not value, but one aspect of value. Further, because it expresses value (however, inadequately), the simple value form is completely different from barter, even though both involve the relation of two commodities. When Marx does describe barter, or as he calls it "direct exchange," he states that "the articles exchanged do not acquire a value form independent of their own use value" (ibid., 182). To justify this interpretation, the derivation of value (in Section 1) and the form of value in Section 3 will be considered in greater detail.

The derivation of value contains the same sequence of relations as the value-form argument. The difference in perspective is immediately apparent. The first relation is exchange value conceived as the relation of two use values. This relation not only fails to express value but belies any notion of it (which is why it is the relation of use values rather than commodities).[2] The same would be true of the simple value form if the form of value section were an independent argument and value were not taken as given. The second relation, the equivalence of one commodity to various others does not manifest the presence of value either since here, the first commodity "has many exchange values instead of one." In the expanded value form, which is the same relation considered as an expression of value, this would be the commodity whose value is expressed. Next, Marx reverses the two sides of the second relation to obtain the third; a step he justifies by the observation that the various quantities of different commodities that are equivalent to one commodity "must . . . be mutually replaceable or of identical magnitude." Since commodities appear as "identical magnitudes" and so as magnitudes of the same thing, only when they are all set equal in exchange to the same one commodity, it is only with the third relation that value emerges as the "something equal" expressed in exchange value (ibid., 127).[3]

The third relation evidently corresponds to the general form of value; between it and the money form, Marx claims, there is no fundamental difference (ibid., 162). In the derivation of value, there is nothing to drive the argument forward from one relation to the next (as the nature of value does in the argument on the value form). Hence it is evident that the third relation is not implicit in and cannot be derived from the first. Evidently, then, the third relation, like the other two, is one way of characterizing the commodity's price or its relation to money. Thus, as Rubin (1927, 130–31) says:

> Marx does not set out from the contrived example of a random comparison of two commodities, nor from a purely logical analysis of all the characteristics which they may have in common, but from the real form of the exchange of products which is characteristic of commodity production,"

namely, the money form.

Because value is revealed only by money price (rather than by any of the other exchange value relations), Marx assumes that value requires money to appear. Money, however, is complex and Marx does not identify its component aspects until the argument on the value form. At this point in his presentation, therefore, we do not know what money involves, hence, what it means that value requires money. Clearly, it means that value cannot be labor, as Ricardo implies, since then a commodity's value could be expressed as a quantity of labor time rather than as money price. Beyond this, the explanation Marx proposes in place of Ricardo's will simply be cited for the moment; why value, in Marx's sense, requires money will emerge as the characteristics of money are considered in the argument on the value form. In brief, value is social labor of a definite kind, "private and independent," which exists as the objective property of its products because their exchange relation is the means by which labor activities are associated.[4] This is merely another way of describing production for sale.

Turning to the value forms, the simple value form is the most abstract version of money price. The one feature it captures is that money price is an exchange relation in which one commodity expresses the value of another. Considering money price in this way abstracts from necessary features of money. (As the later forms will show, it abstracts from money's all-inclusiveness, its uniqueness, and the selection of the object that serves as money by convention.) It is sufficient, however, to pose what Marx calls the "riddle of money" (alternatively, since the other features of money are disregarded, the "riddle of the equivalent form" [ibid., 139, 150]), namely, "how does the equivalent express value?"

There is more to the question than first appears. First, to say that value is expressed by the equivalent means that value is not the equivalent itself, but something non-phenomenal revealed by the equivalent. Second, the equivalent is one of the poles of a relation and gets its character from the role it plays in that relation. Last, and the reason why the question is not just difficult, but a riddle, the same characteristics that the equivalent has because it expresses value, create the "false semblance" or "inversion" that the equivalent (in its finished form, money) *is* (rather than expresses) value (ibid., 187, 150). This is Bailey's position.

According to Bailey, value (in the sense of a property expressed through but not reducible to exchange value) is a delusion that Ricardo derives from money: commodities only seem to have a common property because they appear as various quantities of one thing, money. Since Bailey sees value as a misconception arising from money's uniqueness, he seeks to dispel it by appealing to relative price. For Bailey, the demonstration that a commodity has "as many kinds of value as there are commodities . . . with which it is compared," proves that there is no underlying property expressed in exchange value (Marx 1867, 155 n. 25). Rather, value is simply exchange value. The argument on the simple value form is Marx's response to Bailey. It is meant to explain not only why Bailey's view is false but also how it is supported both by the inadequacy of Ricardo's explanation of value and by the way money appears.

The virtue of the simple value form is that it allows Bailey's position to be characterized precisely. Bailey's claim is that value is price. He is not concerned with the difference between relative and money price (except to explain Ricardo's delusion by the latter). Rather his point is that value is *constituted* by the exchange relation of commodities (see Marx 1863b, 139). When Marx presents his objections in terms of value, he says that Bailey's view implies that there is no continuity of value, either among the different exchange relations of one commodity to various others or over time, that it eliminates the distinction between use value and exchange value (ushering in the utility theory of price) and for both these reasons, precludes the concept of capital.[5] In simpler terms, Bailey's position means that exchange stands on its own, unconnected to production. Its eventual triumph has made its implications familiar as the neoclassical theory of exchange of endowments.

No explanation of exchange prior to Marx's formulates the alternative to Bailey's position. Aristotle argues that exchange presupposes the "essential identity" of commodities (their underlying qualitative equivalence), but cannot find any "common substance" on which it could be based (ibid., 151). Ricardo (who exemplifies the "usual" procedure of considering value only in quantitative terms [ibid., 140]) assumes that labor is this common substance but does not explain why labor would be expressed in the exchange of its products. To account for this, Ricardo would have to explain why exchange is the normal way of distributing products. In other words, he would have to identify the feature of production that makes exchange necessary. Since he presupposes that products are exchanged instead of explaining why they must be, he lacks the grounds to deny Bailey's claim that exchange is independent of production.[6]

In Marx's explanation, cited earlier, value is the result, not of labor, but of production being carried out privately and independently.[7] Exchange is necessary because it is the sole means of associating the activities that make up the total labor of society. As such, it accomplishes the transformation of private labor that is intended to be social (or ideally social labor) into actually social labor (see Marx, 1863b, 131, 136). Exchange, therefore, allows these opposites to coexist; it allows independently directed labor activity to be a form of social labor. The exchange of an ordinary commodity for money accomplishes this transformation because the former, being a privately produced product intended for sale, is the product of individual labor whose social character is yet to be established (or has an ideal value) and the latter represents social labor (or value). Ultimately, Marx will argue that this transformation can be accomplished only by monetary exchange; the necessity for the transformation then establishes the necessity of money. His first step, the argument on the simple value form, is to show how value is expressed in exchange value, given, by prior argument, that value results from private and independent production. This is also the first half of Marx's refutation of Bailey's claim that exchange is self-contained or independent of production.

The second half is the demonstration that Bailey's view is a misinterpretation of money price arising from the combination of the peculiarities of the equivalent form and the objective character of value. As Marx illustrates by the example of weight, a non-phenomenal property, such as value, is expressed through the relation between two things that possess it, when one (the equivalent) serves as the embodiment of that property and shows how much of (and therefore also that) it is present in the other. Because the concrete object that serves as the equivalent stands for the abstract common property within this relation, it acquires the characteristics of that property. These characteristics are its "peculiarities" (with exchange value, the particular use value that serves as equivalent represents value, hence also the concrete and private labor that produced it represents abstract and directly social labor).

The "peculiarities" are not deceptive in the case of weight. We know that iron has the characteristics of weight because it expresses weight, not because it is weight. This is because we are aware of the existence of weight independently of the relation by which we measure it and establish this relation (i.e., set objects in a balance) intentionally, in order to measure it. Intentionality and awareness are absent in the case of value. Exchange relations between commodities are not established in the awareness that they are values and for the sake of measuring their value (see ibid., 166–7). Production and exchange involve intentional action, but do not require that agents formulate their intentions in terms of value. The value of a commodity expresses that it is a component of the total social product and that it embodies some fraction of the total labor of society. A commodity's value, in other words, reflects that it is part of a whole. One of the principal characteristics of a price system, however, is that the actions of individual agents are coordinated without any of them having a concept of the whole. From the standpoint of economic agents (also "vulgar" economics), value does not exist. Marx compensates for this lack of awareness by his derivation of value. Hence he can appeal to value to explain the role and peculiarities of the equivalent. The equivalent appears entirely differently to Bailey, who adopts the standpoint of economic agents. (To use Marx's analogy, it appears the way iron would if we had no independent experience of weight). This reverses every element of Marx's account.

Based on his prior explanation of value, Marx argues that the equivalent commodity has the characteristics of value because it represents value in relation to other commodities. It follows that its character as equivalent arises from its relation to other commodities (meaning from the private and independent character of production which makes commodities values). In the absence of a concept of value, by contrast, the equivalent commodity "appears to have the equivalent form independently of this relation" (ibid., 187). As far as Marx is concerned, it does not matter whether the equivalent is thought to be "endowed with . . . its property of direct exchangeability by nature" or by convention (ibid., 149). If the direct exchangeability of the equivalent is attributed to any source but private and independent production, the equivalent is conceived to be (rather than to express) value. Last, its relation to other commodities seems to be the result of its being value rather than the source of its peculiarities. If the equivalent is value, then value refers to a characteristic of exchange relations rather than to a property expressed through them. Hence it is what Marx calls exchange value. As these inversions demonstrate, money is not transparent; it does not reveal value, which underlies it. Rather, the concept of value had to be established independently in order to interpret money correctly.[10] This is the purpose underlying the sequence of Marx's argument (see Marx 1863b, 134, 161).

To summarize the value form argument so far: the simple value form is concerned with the expression of value in exchange value (alternatively, of production relations in exchange relations) and with the inversions that prevent the connection between them from being recognized. Neither Bailey (neoclassical theory) nor Ricardo (classical theory) do recognize it; hence Marx rejects features of both their theories. While Marx explicitly opposes Bailey's identification of value with exchange value, he also discards Ricardo's identification of value with labor and explains value by the specific relations of production that require products to be exchanged. Because the distinction between relative and money price is irrelevant to this issue, Marx abstracts from it. When he says that the simple value form contains "the whole mystery" of the value form he does not mean that it is able to express value. Rather, he means that the remaining development into a form that does have this ability does not involve any further "inversions" to obscure the expression of value in exchange value.

This development consists of alterations in the structure and arrangement of the relation between the two poles. In brief, the value form must be all-inclusive if it is to present "the total labor power of society . . . as one homogeneous mass of human labor power" (Marx 1867, 129). This requires that the value form equate each commodity to every other and, by this means, each product to every other; it is the contribution of the expanded form.[11] Further, the value form must express the value of all commodities in the same unit if it is to express their values as quantitatively comparable magnitudes. This requires that every commodity in the relative form of value be related to the same equivalent commodity and is the contribution of the general form. It is the first form to express the continuity of value throughout all its exchange-value expressions, thus the first form to show, as Marx says in the derivation of value, that "the valid exchange values of a particular commodity express something equal" (ibid., 127). Hence (with one minor addition) it is the form from which value was originally derived and the only form that is capable of expressing value.[12] Marx could explain the role of the equivalent in terms of the simple value form, but the equivalent is really the embodiment of value only when it is directly exchangeable for all other commodities, that is, in the general value form. Last, the one concession Marx makes in all of Chapter 1 of *Capital* to commodity exchange being exchange among commodity owners, the general equivalent becomes money when it is "restricted to a specific kind of commodity" "by social custom" (ibid., 162). This identifies the role of convention, or arbitrary stipulation, in the determination of money. Its insignificance reflects the lack of social control inherent in production for sale (in Marx's terminology, private and independent production). All the other aspects of money are dictated by the way production is organized. These are: that exchange is necessary, that it encompasses all products and that it presents each one as a fraction of the total social product. All that is left to the intentional and conscious control of society is to choose which commodity the general equivalent will be.

To review the features of Marx's method that have emerged from this account, first, the derivation of value together with the form of value argument describes a circle in which exchange value as the nearly completed money form allows value and its source to be identified and, reversing directions, the nature of value guides the development of money. This circle reflects the relation of value to money as that between underlying mechanism (and in this sense, substance) and phenomenal form or surface.[13] The reason to present them in this way is that the underlying mechanism is not directly visible from the surface but is obscured by inversions (in this case, the equivalent could not be interpreted without value).[14]

Second, the value-form argument itself traces the "development of the expression of value," as Marx says, in that it reconstructs the concept of money from its component aspects. These aspects (that value is objective, all encompassing, and unified, and that the money commodity is conventional) are revealed, one from each exchange value relation, starting with the simplest and revising it in light of its defects until a relation capable of expressing value is attained. This exemplifies the progression from simple to complex, which Marx claims is the correct way to reproduce a complex real entity in thought (see Marx 1858, 101). The reason to reconstruct money in this way is to identify its components and to establish why each one is necessary by showing the purpose it serves. Marx's "point of departure in reality" and the real entity to which the argument on the value form refers, is the fully constituted money form (Marx 1858, 100). When, at the end of the argument, Marx presents money as the combined result of the features revealed in the previous forms, he also reverses directions to show how each form can be analyzed into the previous one.[15] The simple value form is derived by this process of analysis; it is not a real entity but an aspect of the money form.

Third, in Chapter 1 of *Capital*, Marx describes exchange as exchange value — as the relation of commodities—and even speaks of it as *their* social relation. Social relations in the normal sense appear only in Chapter 2, where they are derived from the exchange relation of commodities. Judging by Marx's discussion of commodity fetishism, which comes between the two, this reflects the objective character of value. This means that although value results from the human relations through which production is carried out, it is not a result intended by economic agents. Hence its social origin is not apparent, but has to be deduced from examining the commodity form. The unintentional nature of value means also that economic activity is not subject to human control. Rather, the law of value, operating through relations among commodities, dominates individuals. Presenting money as a commodity, set apart by "the social action of all other commodities," makes the point that money is objective in this sense (Marx 1867, 180). This is at least one reason to present money as a commodity.

2.2 DIGRESSION ON BARTER

One last way of showing that the simple value form is not barter is to consider Marx's view of barter. From Marx's perspective, a "barter economy" is a chimera. Barter has never been and cannot be the normal way of distributing products within one economy (or mode of production). It is true that in nonmonetary economies, the products of different activities within the social division of labor are transferred among their producers. Because the producers do not confront each other as independent traders, however, this transfer is not barter. Barter, in other words, presupposes the independence of individual producers relative to each other, which can only exist within one society in the presence of money. Thus, according to Marx, barter is always external to society, occuring either in external trade or accidentally—in the sense that it is not the typical or normal way of distributing products—between two individuals. This is why barter does not express anything about the nature of social production.

The idea that money solves the double coincidence of wants problem presupposes that members of one society determine their own needs in the absence of money. Marx sees the individual determination of need as one of the effects of commodity production (see 1867, 178–180). The mistaken idea that money overcomes technical difficulties, he argues, originates, first, from supposing the characteristics of a monetary economy (such as the individual determination of need) to exist without money, and then, introducing money to solve difficulties (such as the double coincidence of wants) that would arise from these characteristics if money were absent (see Marx 1859, 50–51).

2.3 MISINTERPRETING THE VALUE FORM ARGUMENT AND ITS EFFECTS

Marx does not derive money from a nonmonetary context, as Levine and Ong maintain. Obviously, Marx begins with the commodity form. He cannot be appealing to a nonmonetary setting, however, since he argues that the commodity's value character presupposes money. Although Marx never regards exchange value as anything but money price, he does not specify that it is until he shows what money price involves. Since its features arise from the nature of value (in other words, from social production being private and independent), Marx must postpone this demonstration until he has identified the origin of value. The alternative, conceptualizing money without value, results in Bailey's position. Levine and Ong see his argument differently because they do not notice any of the methodological principles on which it is based.

First, because they do not recognize the circle from exchange value to value and back, they see no difference between Marx's first description of exchange value in Section 1 and the simple value form in Section 3. Hence they miss the point Marx makes in terms of the simple value form, namely, that exchange value expresses value, rather than exchange value being value (Bailey) or labor time expressing value (Ricardo).[16] Then, because they do not see that Marx is focusing on this one aspect of the expression of value in money price, and because Marx speaks of value being expressed in the simple value form, they conclude that he regards it as an adequate expression of value. It follows that, for Marx as for Ricardo, money is not necessary to express value and, in its place, "the unit of labor time acts as the unit of value measurement" (Levine 1983, 26). In other words, Ricardo's concept of value is attributed to Marx. Marx, however, criticizes Ricardo precisely for conceiving value so that it has no connection to money, for regarding money as a "ceremonial form," for failing to see value as the result of the specific kind of labor that becomes social only once its products are exchanged for money, and for overlooking the need to transform independent into social labor (Marx 1859, 331).[17]

Second, Levine and Ong show no sign of recognizing the principle underlying the sequence of value forms in Section 3. Levine sees the value-form argument as a series of "wholly unintelligible . . . artificial constructs of commodity to commodity relations" that Marx "posits" (1983, 28) instead of the development, based on the nature of value, towards a progressively more adequate expression of value.

Last, Levine and Ong do not mention the objectivity of value in their interpretations of Marx. That it is also absent from their alternatives to the universal equivalent, suggests that they are unaware of it. As will be illustrated shortly by Ong's argument that money cannot be a product, this means that Levine and Ong do not see that Marx *has* presented money as the result of a social process. Nor do they see his point that this process is not social in the normal sense (i.e., directly social), but is instead carried out through the relation of all commodities to money. This is the major reason to present money as a commodity.

2.3.1 MONEY CANNOT BE A PRODUCT

To simplify reference to Ong's argument, it will be quoted directly. His reasons for maintaining that money cannot be a product are:

1. Since money is the "social standard of value" the process that makes some object money "can only be imposed in an *exclusive* manner" so that this object "cannot readily be produced as money by private individual wills. In other words"
2. If money is to be a privately produced commodity, "its supply must be easily monopolized by the monetary authority."
3. In fact, "individuals are forced to produce useful commodities for society at large because they cannot privately produce money as they do commodities."

Undermining the whole argument (but pertaining most directly to points (1) and (3)) is the assumption that the money-commodity becomes money by the process of its production. As De Brunhoff (1973, 65, see also, 70) points out, Marx does not attribute "the monetary character of gold as 'general equivalent'" to "the particular character of its production as a commodity." Rather a commodity becomes money, according to Marx, through the process of its exclusion from the relative form of value by the relation of all other commodities to it as equivalent. This is a social process; as Marx says, "only the action of society can turn a particular commodity into the universal equivalent" (1867, 180). Because the members of society act independently of each other, this social action is carried out through commodity relations ("the social action of all other commodities . . . sets apart the particular commodity in which they all represent their values" [ibid.]). Since its being indirectly social does not make it nonsocial, money is not just a privately produced commodity (point 3).[18]

With point (2), Ong substitutes a different basis for money's uniqueness: the control of the money supply by the monetary authority. To maintain that money cannot be a commodity, Ong must explain why certain commodities could have served as money. He argues that because the precious metals are scarce and durable, their supply consists primarily of inventories that increase gradually. He concludes from this that the feature responsible for their success as money is the ease with which their supply can be controlled by a monetary authority. This is, in Ong's view, the significant feature of money, which precious metal shares with credit money.

The scarcity of the precious metals is significant to Marx for the entirely different and minor reason that a small quantity has a substantial value. This is convenient because it makes value easy to transport (see Marx 1953, 166), but it does not make the scarcity of precious metals the basis of their existence as money. (It is a condition for their having value, but this does not distinguish them from any other commodity.) The precious metals are naturally suited to be money, according to Marx, not because they are scarce, but because they have the same features as value, which, as money, they express. They are uniform, which makes them "capable of purely quantitative differentiation," and they can be easily divided and reassembled (Marx 1867, 184).[19]

On the one hand, Ong's opposition to money being a product is based on the misconception that Marx attributes gold's character as money to its production. This is the source of countless criticisms of Marx, all resembling the claim, to use one of Marx's metaphors, that the pope cannot be a catholic because he is not a catholic like any other. On the other hand, the basis Ong supplies for money, illustrates why Marx presents money as a commodity. Attributing the special properties of money to the capacity of a central bank to control its supply, implies that money is the intentional creation of the central bank. This is one form of the "false semblance" (or "inversion") that money acquires the equivalent form from some other source than its value relation to other commodities. The meaning of Marx's insistence to the contrary—that the equivalent's peculiarities come from its relation to other commodities, that *their* action excludes it from the relative form—is that the social process that makes money, money is not an intentional and conscious collective action by the members of society ("they have . . . already acted before thinking" he says [1867, 180]). It follows also that the extent to which money can be controlled is limited. This is the effect of production being private and independent, which is the real reason why Marx ties money to production. To the extent that the replacement of gold by paper money does not abolish the law of value, the limits to social control imposed by this law apply to money of either form.

Ong's alternative, bank money, is more apparently social because it is directly social. As it illustrates, money conceived as the result of a directly social process does not express the unintentional nature of value. Insofar as commodity production is, in reality, indirectly social and not subject to social control, gold money is not merely a convenient way of expressing the objectivity of value, but a truer form of money.[20]

3. Money as a Commodity

Apart from their misinterpretations of Marx, Levine and Ong present two sets of arguments based on their own concepts of money claiming that money cannot be a commodity. One set concerns the intrinsic value of money and denies that money can (Levine) or must (Ong) have intrinsic value. The other concerns the quantity of money and contends that the supply of precious metal money is inadequate to meet the needs of circulation.

3.1 Intrinsic Value

3.1.1 MONEY CANNOT HAVE INTRINSIC VALUE

Levine summarizes his difference from Marx, by saying that in his view "money is value," while in Marx's, "money has value" (1983, 26).[21] Levine's view of money is, in turn, based on his concept of value. As noted earlier, Levine maintains that money is essential in a market economy because it institutes a particular kind of need: need emancipated from all "naturally and historically fixed forms" with the potential for infinite diversity and variation (ibid., 23). Need acquires this character because money "is the idea of wealth given a unitary and abstract form" (ibid.). The relation between a particular commodity and money *is* that commodity's value and measures the "portion of social wealth it embodies" (ibid., 23). Since value consists in the relationship of commodity to money, money itself cannot have value.

Levine's view of value resembles Bailey's in that value "only really exists in and through the external relations into which the commodity enters" (ibid., 24). Not only does money not *have* value, but neither do commodities, meaning that their relationship is not the expression of anything else (social labor). By contrast, Marx's claim that exchange value expresses (rather than is) value, means that exchange is the necessary consequence of private and independent social production. Products produced for sale (or commodities) have value, according to Marx, in the sense that they have an intended (or as Marx calls it, ideal) value which may or may not be realized in exchange. The strongest claim that can be made about commodity money is that, unlike other commodities, its value is real even before exchange.[22]

Unlike Bailey (or, at least, all that Marx reveals of Bailey), Levine argues that money is necessary because of its implications for need. Like Marx, Levine sees the significance of the specific form of economic relations.[23] Whereas Marx traces the origin of exchange (and its forms, commodities and money) to the private and independent character of production, however, Levine explains exchange in terms of its consequences. The immediate effect of this difference is that value, as Levine conceives it, lacks the objectivity Marx attributes to it. For Levine, economic relations appear to be transparent and intentionally established. Money seems to be instituted deliberately in order to "set in motion the development of need" and this "in turn creates a many-sided system of commodity relations" (ibid., 23). From Marx's perspective, this is another example of Bailey's "inversion" since Levine attributes the characteristics of the equivalent to a different source than its value relation to other commodities, thus, to a different source than the relations in which commodities are produced. Marx's case that the necessity for exchange is instead inherent in private and independent production, means that exchange and its forms are the unintended consequences of carrying out social production in this way. This is the reason why Marx insists that exchange value expresses (rather than is) value. It is also why he confines the institutionally determined aspect of money to deciding which commodity will function as universal equivalent; this means that once social production is arranged along private and independent lines, engaging in monetary exchange is not a matter of choice. In short, it is the point, at least in Chapter 1 of *Capital*, of connecting exchange to production.

Two points may be noted as an addendum to this comparison of Levine and Marx. First, although neither mentions it explicitly, the ultimate source of their differences over money and value is a disagreement over private property. While Levine regards private property as the basis of the individual determination of need, Marx adds to this, the implications of private property for production (that is, of the means of production being private property), the simplest of which are that production is private and independent and that products are commodities.[24] Second, Marx does recognize that the market system has implications for need, including the characteristics Levine cites.[25] Because he considers the implications of private ownership for production, and includes among them the relation of wage labor to capital, he conceives need to be restricted by the conditions for generating surplus value.[26]

3.1.2 CREDIT MONEY: INTRINSIC VALUE IS IRRELEVANT TO MONEY

As suggested earlier, Ong attributes money to a different source than the private and independent character of production. This source is social recognition.[27] On the grounds that it constitutes money, Ong argues that money need not have intrinsic value.[28]

This proposal preserves the formal structure of a society composed of individuals (i.e., the structure of unity combined with independence, which Marx explains by the sequence from the expanded to the money form). It lacks the indirectly social character of private and independent production, however, which is the source of value's objectivity. While Marx attributes the universal equivalent to the exclusion by all other commodities of the money commodity from the relative form (by which he means that the same relations that make products commodities, make one commodity money), Ong attributes the universal equivalent to social recognition. This substitution involves the tacit assumption that production is directly social.

According to Ong (1983, 43), money originates in the "social judgment" by a creditor (banker, or financial capitalist) that a particular borrower (industrial capitalist) is credit worthy. For the individual creditor's recognition to gain general acceptance throughout society, banks must be stable and safeguards must be instituted to make them so. Ong lists the usual safeguards: individual banks specialize in evaluating credit worthiness, at a second level, the system of banks supports individual banks, and, at a third level, a monetary authority safeguards "the viability of the system as a whole" (ibid., 48).

The contradiction between private and social cannot be transcended so easily. Careful evaluation of credit worthiness is not a guarantee against bad loans. A bad loan indicates a difference between the banker's and society's judgment of the "socially usefulness" of a given project.

In other words, it indicates that the leap from private to social product failed, in spite of the expertise of the banker, who thought it would succeed. The addition of another level of social recognition does not change the nature of the situation. By its lender of last resort function, a central bank can prevent one bank from collapsing because of its bad loans, or it can prevent the collapse of one bank from generating a chain reaction of bank failures. It does both, not by eliminating the loss but by spreading it to preserve the banking system (see Reuten and Williams, 1989, 86–87). If the central bank cannot preclude losses (transform bad loans into money), but only forestall or generalize them, its recognition is not the origin of money. As long as production is private and independent, there is no creditor whose "recognition" could guarantee that credit (representing the ideal value of as yet unsold products) is money (realized value, representing a definite portion of the total social product). Alternatively, the central bank could guarantee that credit is money, only if it is a planning board controlling production directly or if it serves a purely technical record keeping function in a system that coordinates production directly by some other means.[29] In that case, however, production would not be private and independent, the economy would not be a monetary economy and money would not be a universal equivalent.

Since the introduction of paper money would not abolish the law of value, the objectivity of value does not require that money have intrinsic value. There are, however, few other properties that are objective in the same way as value and their explanation poses its own difficulties.[30] Hence the simplest way to capture value's objectivity is to present money as a commodity. In this respect, commodity money is a heuristic assumption.

3.1.3 MARX: INTRINSIC VALUE AND MONEY AS MEASURE OF VALUE

Marx does claim that money must be a commodity in order to measure value.[31] This, however, appears to be the only reason why he maintains that money has to be a commodity. As I will show in a moment, he argues that the medium of circulation function cannot be performed by the money commodity and that the functions he classifies under the heading "money" do not have to be. Thus, money has to be a commodity, according to Marx, for the same reason that only a commodity can measure value. The straightforward reason follows from the general principle of measurement, that a measure must possess the quality it measures. Hence the claim that the measure of value must be a commodity means that value is exclusively a property of commodities.

This makes the same point as Marx's earlier argument that exchange value expresses value. The commodity, as a product that is produced for sale, contains the interconnection of production and exchange. This connection is absent in the alternatives to Marx's position: Bailey's claim that value is a property of exchange relations and Ricardo's claim that value is a property of labor. The evidence that this is Marx's point, is that he refers to both alternatives at the beginning of his discussion of the measure of value. In opposition to Bailey, Marx maintains that commodities are "in themselves commensurable" and, for this reason, one of them can measure the value of the others (1867, 188). In opposition to Ricardo, Marx maintains that value must be expressed in money, since labor time is only "the measure of value that is immanent in commodities," meaning that before exchange, the value of commodities is only ideal or intended (ibid.).[32]

Having made this point, in the section on the measure of value itself, Marx opens up the possibility of a money that has no value. He indicates that external and immanent value may diverge from each other in two ways. First, there may be "quantitative incongruities" between them, or price may diverge from the magnitude of value because of "circumstances," or market conditions (1867, 196). Second, the "price form . . . may also harbor a qualitative contradiction," meaning that things that are not commodities may have prices. Such prices may be either purely imaginary or derived from real value relations. Marx illustrates the second by the price of uncultivated land. As he will argue in Volume III of *Capital*, this price is derived from a capitalized rent, and rent itself, from the division of surplus value. The point must be relevant to money as measure of value or Marx would not have introduced it in this context. Hence the implication is that money can assume forms in which it has no value (like uncultivated land) but either represents value based on a similar transformation of value or has a purely imaginary value.[33]

Such transformations cannot be considered at this stage in the argument of *Capital*, since Marx has not even developed the concept of surplus value. Their only effect on the issues that are considered at this stage, however, is that they make the determination of money's value more complicated. One of the advantages of supposing that money is commodity money is that the value of money can be handled very simply. As Foley (1983, 19) observes, commodity money "remove[s] the value of money from center stage." In other words, Marx is not concerned with the value of money at this stage in his argument except to establish that it is expressed in rather than constituted by exchange relations. The commodity money assumption implies a way of determining the value of money which fulfills this requirement. Any features of the explanation of money's value that apply only to commodity money will be discarded with the commodity money assumption.

This function of the commodity money assumption may be illustrated by working out one of the important implications of Marx's case against Bailey, namely, that the quantity theory of money is false. The theory presupposes that "commodities enter circulation without prices and money without value" and claims that the prices of one and the value of the other are determined within circulation by the relative quantities of the two (Marx 1867, 220). This is an implication of Bailey's claim that "money... renders commodities commensurable" (ibid., 188).[34] By contrast, Marx's case that commodities are already commensurable before exchange implies that the means of circulation adjusts to the needs of trade by changes in the quantity of money that remains in circulation rather than by changes in its value. Posing the argument in terms of commodity money for the moment, money enters circulation with a given value (whether the circulating medium is supposed to be the money commodity itself or is recognized as a symbol of it) and commodities enter circulation with given ideal prices (their intended values expressed in the money commodity). This yields the rule that governs money as means of circulation. In its simplest version, the quantity of money required for circulation is determined by the given commodity prices, the value of money and the velocity of money while the actual amount of circulating medium adjusts to this required amount through changes in hoards (see Marx ibid., 219). Marx modifies this rule by incorporating additional factors, but adheres to it throughout his theory.[35] Especially important in this context, the assumption that money has intrinsic value can be dropped. Even if the value of money were derived (like the price of land) from the division of surplus value or were imaginary, it would still not be determined within simple circulation in the manner supposed by the quantity theory.

Turning to money's other functions, Marx argues that money is necessarily a symbol in its function as medium of circulation because coins cannot circulate without losing their metal (and so their value). Even in a full value coinage system, coins that enter circulation for the first time with the quantity of precious metal they are supposed to contain (hence with the value of that quantity) become symbols of that quantity of metal (and so symbols of its value). That the money commodity is reduced to a symbol of itself by its circulation, shows that this function cannot depend on the intrinsic value of the object that circulates. Hence it need not be performed by the money commodity (see Marx 1867, 222–3).

As for the functions Marx lists under the heading of "money," these, he states, can be performed either by the money commodity "in person or by a representative" (ibid., 227). Evidently, the term "money," does not refer solely to the money commodity. The distinguishing characteristic of these functions is that money acts as the adequate form of value over and against either commodities or credit. Leaving aside world money, this does not require that money be the money commodity. Coin (meaning the circulating medium, whether it consists of metal or paper) acquires the capacity to perform these additional functions just by being the medium of circulation. Its function as means of circulation makes it the means of purchase of commodities, hence the adequate form of value relative to them. The same holds for the means of payment function, in which capacity money is the adequate form of value relative to credit (see ibid., 232 and 236–7). Last, while coin is a symbol of the money commodity in its function as means of circulation (because it realizes commodity prices established in terms of the money commodity as measure of value), the same coin accumulated as a reserve fund or used to pay a debt is not a symbol of the money commodity but the adequate form of value.[36]

To summarize Marx's views on the need for money to have intrinsic value, he makes this claim only in connection with the measure of value function and because of the nature of value (that it is constituted neither by labor by itself nor by exchange by itself, but by their interconnection, that is, by production for sale). His argument is compatible with a demonstration at a later stage that money may either have no value or represent value by way of transformations resulting from the division of surplus value. Since no actual money has to be present to measure value, the quantity of money is irrelevant to this function. On the other hand, since money does not need to be a commodity in its other functions, the existing quantity of the money commodity would not in principle impose limits on that commodity's ability to function as money. With this, it can be shown that many of the problems Levine and Ong associate with the intrinsic value of money (and that are, very likely, typically associated with it) are in fact misconceptions arising from the conflation of different functions of money.

For example, as evidence that money does not have an intrinsic value, Levine (1983, 25) observes that:

When we calculate the magnitude of social wealth, we do not add the total amount of money to the value of commodities. Instead we add up the money required to purchase those commodities. Historically, when a particular commodity such as gold also acts as money, this complicates the problem. But in no case would we consider the issuing of bank notes to directly constitute a net addition to the amount of wealth in circulation.

This argument runs together two functions. Calculating the magnitude of social wealth involves money's function as measure of value. No actual money is required to perform this function (bank notes do not need to be issued). The circulating medium, gold or bank notes, does need to be present but need not have value. Whether or not the circulating medium has value (and so forms part of social wealth) has no bearing on Marx's case that money as measure must have intrinsic value.

Similarly, Ong repeatedly conflates the measure of value and medium of circulation functions, arguing that the symbolic nature of coin (the fact that it wears away) proves that money need not have intrinsic value. He claims, for example, that "Marx holds that commodity-money has an intrinsic value which is independent of (but also less than) that posited by its money role" (Ong 1983, 39). The "commodity-money" in question is presumably a worn coin (and its "money role," the medium of circulation), which contains less precious metal than it is supposed to. Hence it only symbolizes the quantity of precious metal it is meant to contain or has a nominal value, by virtue of its imprint, greater than the value of the actual metal it contains. Not only is this Marx's own argument, but it is his evidence for the case that money in its function as medium of circulation need not be a commodity. In a second instance, to show that money cannot be a product Ong (ibid., 37) states:

> The necessity of [a] ... social process of sanctification in the production of the commodity-money as money explains why its social value can be higher than and cannot be accounted for by its value as a privately produced commodity.

The "social process of sanctification" is presumably the process of stamping metal into coin. The reason why money's "social value"—the nominal value of the coin—is higher than "its value as a privately produced commodity"—the value of the metal the coin contains—is that coins wear away in circulation; as Marx puts it "the road from the mint is also the path to the melting pot" (1867, 222)." Ong means to establish something else entirely: in accordance with his claim that money is constituted by recognition, that the value of the money commodity is determined by being stamped into coin and, this being the case, money might just as well not be a commodity. This again supposes that the function in which money cannot retain an intrinsic value is the function in which its intrinsic value matters.[37]

To take one final example, Ong (1983, 34) conceives the store of value (hoard) function of money to rest on the intrinsic value of the money commodity and so on the constancy of that commodity's value:

> Since Marx holds that the commodity-money has an intrinsic value . . . the commodity-money's ability to carry value forward in time does not depend in any way on its quality as money.

Based on this interpretation, Ong charges that Marx has overlooked the possibility of changes in the value of money. On the contrary, Marx addresses precisely this question in his discussion of hoarding: "It is true that the value of money varies" but this does not prevent money from being hoarded, amongst other reasons, because it "does not prevent the metallic natural form of this object from continuing to be the universal equivalent form of all other commodities" (Marx 1867, 230).[38]

3.2   THE MONEY SUPPLY

Ong's principal objection to commodity money, however, is that its supply is limited by the supply of precious metals, imposing an external constraint on the process of capital accumulation. He charges that Marx dismisses this constraint based on the unrealistic assumption that the stock of precious metals is always adequate and that, having dismissed it, Marx is oblivious to the detrimental effects of an exogenously fixed money supply. The effects Ong has in mind are: (1) that the value of money would be subject to violent changes, and (2) "because there is a lack of the necessary medium of circulation" the circulation of commodities—reciprocal sales among individual producers—would come to a halt (Ong 1983, 37, 39). These problems, Ong claims, demonstrate that commodity money is unsuitable for an expanding capitalist economy, and that Marx's theory of money is inadequate. For Ong "the responsive elasticity of bank money clinches the superiority" of noncommodity over commodity money, establishing that Marx's theory of money should be replaced with a theory of credit money (Ong ibid., 50). These are not problems for Marx's theory, however.

The first problem appears to presuppose that the value of money is determined within circulation, as the quantity theory maintains. The second presupposes that trade would be halted for the lack of circulating medium before symbols or certificates of debt would be introduced to replace metal coin as medium of circulation. Both are dealt with by the argument against the quantity theory Marx (1859, 166–7) cites from Steuart:

The standard price of every thing . . . bear[s] no determined proportion whatsoever to the quantity of gold and silver in the country. . . . The circulation of every country . . . must ever be in proportion to the industry of the inhabitants producing the commodities which come to market . . . If the coin of a country, therefore, falls below the proportion of the produce of industry offered to sale . . . inventions such as symbolical money, . . . mutual prestations, and a thousand other inventions . . . will be fallen upon to provide an equivalent for it. But if the specie be found above the proportion of the industry, it will have no effect in raising prices, nor will it enter into circulation: it will be hoarded up in treasures.

In other words, first, prices (the value of money) are not determined by the quantity of means of circulation but rather determine the quantity required. This is the same as the case against the quantity theory implied by Marx's critique of Bailey. Second, the stock of precious metal does not restrict circulation (or cause prices to rise) because symbolic currency and other "inventions" such as certificates of debt ("prestations") compensate for any shortfall of coin in periods of expansion. Although the former circulate, Marx insists on calling them credit rather than "real money" (1867, 238 n. 54).[39] This gives his explanation of money as means of circulation considerably more flexibility than Ong recognizes. Thus Marx even agrees with Ong that capitalist production "would come up against the limited scale of precious-metal production . . . with a merely metallic circulation" (1885, 420). Whereas Ong takes this to demonstrate that money must be conceptualized as credit money, however, Marx takes it to establish that "capitalist production on its present scale would [not] be possible without credit" (ibid.). With the addition of credit, Marx's "coin" or commodity money as means of circulation is as endogenous or flexible as modern credit money.

Marx refuses to equate money with credit, however, maintaining that the distinction between them asserts its reality in times of crisis (Marx 1867, 236–7). Evidently, then, he does not make this distinction simply because he regards money as commodity money. If credit can collapse into money (of whatever form), then credit and money are essentially distinct. The distinction between them does not rule out credit money, rather it still applies when money becomes credit money with the development of the credit system. While Marx clearly recognizes the existence of credit money, he does not pose his initial explanation in terms of it because he regards the credit system, of which credit money is a part, as the logical outgrowth of the monetary system. His account of the development of one from the other spans all three volumes of *Capital*. Only its main features will be outlined here.

Two features of this development appear in Volume 1. First, Marx locates the origin of credit in money's function as means of payment and argues that money performs this function because commodities that are used in each other's production are produced in different amounts of time (Marx 1859, 143; 1894, 525). The second feature is hoards which, from the standpoint of simple circulation, are accumulated to protect producers from market fluctuations (1867, 228) and serve the additional purpose of enabling the quantity of means of circulation to adjust as required by the needs of trade (ibid., 231). To these Marx adds in Volume 2, various kinds of hoards that are required for the reproduction process of capital to proceed continuously. Taken together, these hoards form the basis of the credit system. Deposited with banks to capture interest income, they are the funds the banking system collects and redistributes. Thus, although capitalist production could not develop on the same scale without the credit system, the system develops, not to meet the need for means of circulation (as Ong's argument suggests) but because capitalists use the hoards, which they must accumulate anyway, to claim a share of surplus value. Marx first treats financial capital as an independent kind of capital in Volume 3, where he considers the interaction among different kinds of capital. Only at this point can he introduce credit in its specifically capitalist form, as it results from loans to industrial capitalists by financial capitalists.

In Marx's account, therefore, credit money presupposes all the features identified up to this point (i.e., the interaction between different kinds of capital, the circulation process of capital, and the relation of capital to wage labor). Commodity money, by contrast, does not even presuppose capital. The transition from one to the other, while incomplete, is evidently another instance of the movement from simple to complex.[40] For Marx, therefore, commodity money is not money itself but one form of money. It is the proper initial conception of money because it is the simplest form (see Marx 1885, 554).

4. Conclusion

Presenting money as a commodity allows Marx to explain money as the outcome of the "social action" of commodities. By this Marx means that the exchange relations of commodities, which are necessarily relations of monetary exchange, arise from the relations in which commodities are produced. This removes money from the "consensual domain occupied by symbols" (Ganssmann 1988, 309). It is the alternative, in other words, to regarding money as the intentional creation of society and subject to its control.

The other advantage of commodity money is that it is a form of money that does not presuppose capital. Posing his explanation of money in terms of this form, allows Marx to distinguish money from capital. In addition, it conforms to Marx's methodological principle of moving from simple to complex, which is the way thought must proceed in order to reconstruct reality.

It is because of these two features, the objective character of value and the simple character of commodity money, that Marx presents money as commodity money. Neither implies that money must be a commodity. The objectivity of value applies just as much to paper as to commodity money. As Marx's critique of the quantity theory illustrates, the principles derived on the basis of the commodity money assumption carry over to other forms of money. On the other hand, Marx indicates, perhaps in overly subtle ways, that those elements of his account that do apply only to commodity money (such as the stories about gold mining) are temporary expedients. They allow the argument to proceed until the grounds for more complex forms of money can be supplied.

Notes

1. Ong (1983, 33) compares Marx's theory to the "barter based thinking exemplified by Walras's notion of money as a numeraire." He acknowledges that this contradicts other aspects of Marx's theory, but attributes the inconsistency to Marx rather than to a fault in his interpretation. For example, Ong claims that Marx's "demonstration of the necessity of money casts doubt on the validity of the elementary" form as an expression of value (ibid.).
2. Rubin (1927, 127) suggests that the concept of exchange value simply as a quantitative relation could refer to Bailey's position. Showing that he is correct, Marx repeats the same argument throughout his commentary on Bailey (Marx 1861–63b, 127, 128–9, 132, 147, 150).
3. The second and third steps in the derivation of value reflect Marx's account of the way classical political economy came to conceptualize value. He maintains that value is deduced initially from the constancies underlying price fluctuations and, from these, to the recognition that money expresses a common property of commodities (see 1867, 167–68). As will emerge later, the attempt to derive value directly from money results in Bailey's view.
4. I have argued that by "private and independent" labor Marx means that the means of production are private property. See Campbell 1993.
5. As Marx puts it: "the concept of value ends here" (1861–63b, 150). On the absence of continuity, see Marx 1861–63b, 150, 154; and 1867, 155 n., 25; on utility theory, 1862, 164; on time, 1861–63b, 131, 151, 154; and on capital, 1885, 186.

6. In Marx's interpretation, Ricardo regards capitalism as the "eternal natural form of social production" (1867, 174 n., 34). This implies that Ricardo sees no need to explain why products must be exchanged because he regards exchange as the natural way of distributing products. Having assumed exchange is necessary, Ricardo does not know why production presupposes exchange. As a result, he ties exchange to production described in concrete terms, in which meaning, production has no connection to exchange. Marx takes a rather charitable view of this error, saying that Ricardo does not distinguish between concrete and abstract labor (see Marx ibid., 173 n., 33). The importance he attributes to his distinction between them, however, indicates the seriousness of Ricardo's mistake (see ibid., 132).

7. Marx maintains that labor is not quantitatively equal in its natural form (as Ricardo's theory suggests) or in all forms of society. Hence Marx's statement that the historical limitations of Aristotle's society "prevented him from finding out" the basis for the commensurability of commodities does not mean that Aristotle was deluded by these limitations but that the basis for value did not exist in his society. Aristotle would have been wrong to have found "something which is only valid for . . . the production of commodities . . . that the specific social character of private labors carried on independently of each other consists in their equality as human labor" in a society "founded on the labor of slaves" and hence on "the inequality of men and of their labor-powers" (Marx 1867, 167, 152).

8. Marx discusses the idea that money arises from convention in Chapter 2 of *Capital* (1867, 185–6).

9. It seems "that all other commodities universally express their values in a particular commodity because it is money" (Marx 1867, 187). This eliminates Marx's distinction between value and exchange-value. Hence there is no distinction between value and money and "express" means present relative price in money price rather than express value (in the sense of underlying mechanism) in exchange-value (in the sense of phenomenal form). For another statement of the inversion see ibid., 152.

10. As noted earlier, classical political economy, according to Marx, does not deduce the concept of value from money but from the regularities underlying price fluctuations. Ricardo, for example, ignores money.

11. Marx uses the term social labor in the double sense of associated labor and the total labor of society. In his comment on Aristotle, for example, Marx associates the equality of all kinds of labor with a society in which the "commodity-form is the universal form of the product of labor" (1867, 152). Another way in which the universality of the commodity form appears is that Marx makes a distinction between gold functioning as a "single equivalent in isolated exchanges" and its functioning as the general equivalent or money (ibid., 163). In the former case, gold appears to be the *only* equivalent but since exchange occupies a minor place in social production (few products are commodities), it is not the *universal* equivalent.

12. Thus Marx repeats the third step in his derivation of value—that various quantities of different commodities being equal to the same quantity of the same equivalent commodity, must be equal to each other (are "mutually replaceable or of identical magnitude" 1867, 127)—in his discussion of the general value-form (ibid., 159, 10 lb. tea and 40 lb. coffee being both equal to 20 yds. of linen, are equal to each other).

13. For a recent account of method that presents the objectives of science in these terms, see Lawson (1994).

14. Arguments of the same form appear throughout *Capital*. The largest circle, for example, begins with simple circulation, proceeds to capital as underlying mechanism and would end with circulation conceived as the result of capital. Marx suggests its conclusion in Vol. 1 of *Capital* (709), considered presenting it in the "Results" (in Marx 1867, 948–975) and presumably would have presented it in Vol. 3.

15. See Marx 1867, 163. By contrast, Levine thinks that Marx attempts to build the money form out of its aspects. He says: "Marx . . . attempts to consider it [money] as the concretization of the more abstract, or elementary, commodity relations." (Levine 1983, 28). According to Marx, however, it is only "in the process of thinking" that the real entity that is the subject of investigation appears "as a result" (Marx 1953, 101). The subject itself (in this case, money in its fully developed form) is "what is given" to thought or is presupposed by it (ibid., 106, 102).

16. As will be shown when Levine's and Ong's own concepts of money are discussed, they share Bailey's view that exchange value does not express anything. For this reason, if the difference between relative and money price is not taken into account, nothing remains of money. This is an additional reason why they do not see the point of the argument on the simple value form.

17. As noted earlier, Marx attributes Ricardo's trivialization of money to the misconception that capitalist production is "the eternal natural form of social production" with the result that Ricardo does not investigate why exchange is necessary (1867, 174 n., 34). This means that Ricardo also does not consider the need to transform private into social labor. For critiques of Ricardo based on the absence of this transformation see Marx 1961–63b, 131, 136, 137–8; 1861–63a, 164. In addition, Marx's critique of the time chit proposal in the *Grundrisse* is directed against the Ricardian idea that value could be expressed directly in labor time.

18. It seems to Ong, by contrast, that the automatic consequence of commodity money is that money is just a product. He maintains that "Marx does not provide a conception of the social process of bestowal of money's formal quality (since, for him, money is ultimately but a commodity-money" (1983, 36). Marx does say that gold is money "immediately on its emergence from the bowels of the earth" (1867, 187). In this passage, however, he is presupposing that the social action that makes gold money has already occurred and explaining that, because this process "vanishes with its result," the misconception arises that the equivalent has its character independently of its relation to other commodities (i.e., independently of their social action [ibid.]). Levine also interprets Marx to mean that the process of production makes money, money. He states that for "the classical economists, including Marx. . . . money results from a process of commodity production" (1983, 25). His equation of Marx with the classicals shows, however, that by commodity production, he does not really mean commodity production but only production itself (as in Ricardo).

19. Ong (1983, 37) contends that "Marx's claim that 'money is by nature gold and silver' rests on such externally given features" as their durability and scarcity. This misrepresents Marx's position. He argues that rarity is an

important feature of the precious metals as commodity money to the extent that they cannot be available to everyone without production or exchange (Marx 1953, 176).

20. Marx also emphasizes the objective character of value in Volume 2 of *Capital* (see 1885, 576–77). As Ganssmann points out, commodity money was already outdated in Marx's time (1988, 309). This being the case, Marx must have been aware of the unrealisticness of assuming that money is commodity money and must have had positive reasons for doing so. The objective character of value is one such reason.

21. It would be truer to say that for Marx, money like all other commodities has value, but is money because it expresses the value of other commodities.

22. Marx makes a point of citing Jacob's speculation that gold has probably never been paid at its full value (1867, 130). This suggests that, even in the case of gold money, the labor time actually spent in gold production has no empirical relevance. It is evidence that the determination of the value of money by the labor time taken to produce gold is a simplifying assumption or heuristic device.

23. This is why Levine regards the universal equivalent as "the first genuinely positive conception of money" (1983, 28).

24. Levine does consider the private ownership of the means of production in *Needs, Rights and the Market*, where he argues that it is inconsistent with the equality and self-determination of individuals in exchange (1988, 131–2). As in the argument considered here, Levine identifies the purpose of the market system with its implications for need but he is making normative rather than descriptive claim.

25. As noted earlier, the individual determination of need is implicit in Marx's discussion of the exchange process in *Capital* (178–180). Explicit discussions appear in the *Grundrisse* (256, 410, 508).

26. Hence, Marx would answer Levine, as he does Ricardo, that capitalism cannot be regarded as the system of absolute development of needs since "the mass of the producers remain tied to the average level of needs, and must remain tied to it according to the nature of capitalist production" (Marx 1859, 535; see also 520, 527–8).

27. Ong bases his concept of money on the process of money creation through bank lending. He develops central bank credit money from a description of loans issued to an industrial capitalist by a financial capitalist. Thus his view of the constitutive principle of money appears in this first relationship. As he states (1983, 43): For the former [the industrial capitalist] the chief means of starting the productive circuit of capital is the *social judgment* of another who possesses money—the banker—regarding . . . the prowess of this debtor-capitalist. Through such a recognition the debtor-capitalist can advance his debt as a socially acceptable . . . promise of "future money."

28. Ong (1983, 33) argues that, since money does not get its character as universal equivalent from its value, nothing prevents a noncommodity from being money. This is his weak case against Marx; his strong case, to be considered later, is that the supply of gold is exogenous.

29. Ong's proposal, in other words, makes the central bank the same as the time chit bank that makes labor directly social (see Marx 1953, 155–156). Regarding the current banking system, recognizing that the central bank does impose bank losses on the rest of society, Minsky argues that since it

is guaranteeing investment projects, it should impose restrictions on the kinds of projects for which banks issue loans. These restrictions are intended not only to reduce loan losses but to achieve other social goals (increase employment). By implementing them, the bank would become either the ruler of production or the executor of democratically chosen rules (see Minsky 1985, 52–3).

30. Marx suggests that the closest analogy is religion (1867, 165).

31. In answer to Fullarton's claim that money need not have intrinsic value, Marx suggests that money must be a commodity in order to function as the measure of value and standard of price (Marx 1867, 225; see also, 1961–63b, 133). Since the standard of price function is an outgrowth of the measure of value function, it does not involve distinct reasons for money being a commodity.

32. This evidently undermines Levine's (1983, 26) case that "Among the various uses to which Marx puts the labor theory of value, the first, and ultimately most revealing, is that of solving the classical problem of measuring value and specifying a unit of value without reference to money."

33. Marx clearly regards banknotes as money (see Marx 1894, 583, 589). In their simplest form, they are IOUs issued by banks as a means of claiming a share of surplus-value (ibid., 577). The notes that are legal tender, such as those of the Bank of England, are more complex still since they represent govenment credit (ibid., 529).

34. Thus Marx also describes it as the idea that "mutually incommensurable use-values are to be exchanged *en masse* for the total sum of gold or silver in a country" (1867, 220–21 n., 34).

35. More complex versions of the rule involve additional determinants of the quantity of money required for circulation (e.g., adding payments falling due, subtracting payments that cancel each other out) and additional methods of meeting these requirements (e.g., various kinds of debt certificates, see Marx 1867, 237 and 238 n., 54). Marx appeals to the same rule in Volume 3 (1894, 577).

36. In Volume 2 of *Capital*, Marx states that hoards of latent capital are "in the majority of cases . . . nothing more than money withdrawn from domestic circulation which has assumed the form of a hoard in the hands of individual capitalists." Money withdrawn from domestic circulation is coin, and while it may be precious metal coin "it is also possible that [it] consists simply of value tokens." (1885, 396). Thus, when Marx differentiates the functions of money as money from its function as medium circulation by saying that in the former, it is not a symbol he must mean that it does not function as a symbol, not that it has to be the money-commodity.

37. Other instances: Ong maintains that coins "are recognized as the measure of value on the basis of their symbolic status." (1983, 52 n., 3). This is supposed to show that "money is able to measure the value of any particular commodity because [of] the quality of universal equivalence" (ibid., 33) rather than because of its intrinsic value. Marx maintains that money is not a symbol as universal equivalent and in its function as measure of value (see Marx 1867, 185–6). Regarding it as such places it "in the consensual domain occupied by symbols" and denies the objective character of value (Ganssmann 1988:309). Conflating money as universal equivalent and measure of value with its function as means of circulation, Ong main-

tains that "Marx acknowledges" that there is "no role for an intrinsic value in the money object" when he notes, that as medium of circulation "the mere symbolic existence of money suffices" (ibid., 36).

38. See also Marx's rejection of Senior's claim that money functions as means of payment because its value is constant. He maintains instead that "gold and silver . . . function as means of payment because they have become money, that is, the independent embodiment of exchange value" (1859, 144 n.).

39. Even in Volume 1 of *Capital*, Marx states that "credit-money such as bank-notes" can be used to meet payments in times of "monetary famine," meaning that they are real money when they are the form of money (1867, 236–7).

40. Presenting credit only in Volume 3, fulfills the requirement that Marx articulates in the *Contribution*, that the various aspects of money must be presented in their "organic relation . . . with one another [and] with the system of economic categories as a whole" starting from "money in its abstract form . . . within the framework of simple commodity circulation (1859, 186, 187). The failure to proceed in this way from simple to complex causes various aspects of money to be confused with aspects of capital, even among "the best writers on money," Tooke, Fullarton, and Wilson (1867, 225). Marx examines these confusions in Chapter 28 of vol. 3 of *Capital*.

References

Campbell, M. 1993. "Marx's Concept of Economic Relations and the Method of Capital," F. Moseley (ed.), *Marx's Method in Capital*, Atlantic Highlands: Humanities Press.

de Brunhoff, Suzanne, 1973. *Marx on Money*, trans. by Maurice J. Goldbloom, New York: Urizen Books, 1976.

Foley, Duncan. 1983. "On Marx's Theory of Money," *Social Concept* 1:1, pp. 5–19.

Ganssmann, H. 1988. "Money—a Symbolically Generalized Medium of Communication? On the Concept of Money in Recent Sociology," *Economy and Society* 17: 3, pp. 285–316.

Lawson, T. 1994. "A Realist Theory for Economics," in R. Backhouse, (ed.) *New Directions in Economic Methodology*, London: Routledge.

Levine, David. 1983. "Two Options for the Theory of Money," in *Social Concept*, vol. 1, no. 1, pp. 20–29.

———— 1988. *Needs, Rights and the Market*, Boulder: Lynne Reinner Publishers.

Marx, K. 1859. *A Contribution to the Critique of Political Economy*, New York: International Publishers, 1970.

———— 1867. *Capital*, vol. 1, trans. by Ben Fowkes, New York: Vintage Books, 1977.

———— 1885. *Capital*, vol. 2, trans. by David Fernbach, Harmondsworth: Penguin Books, 1992.

———— 1894. *Capital*, vol. 3, trans. by David Fernbach, Harmondsworth: Penguin Books, 1991.

———— 1953. *Grundrisse*, trans. by Martin Nicolaus, New York: Vintage Books, 1977.

———— 1862. *Theories of Surplus Value*, II. Moscow: Progress Publishers, 1968.

———— 1862. *Theories of Surplus Value*, III. Moscow: Progress Publishers, 1968.

Minsky, H. "The Financial Instability Hypothesis: A Restatement," in P. Arestis and T. Skouras (eds.), *Post-Keynesian Economic Theory*, Armonk, NY: M. E. Sharpe.

Ong, Nai-Pew. 1983. "The Logic of Marx's Theory of Money," *Social Concept* 1: 1, pp. 30–54.

Reuten, G. and Williams, M. 1989. *Value-Form and the State*, London and New York: Routledge.

Rubin, I. I., 1927. "Abstract Labor and Value in Marx's System," *Capital and Class* (1978), pp. 107–39.

5

The Development of Marx's Theory of the Distribution of Surplus-Value

Fred Moseley

Marx's theory of the production and distribution of surplus-value is based on a fundamental methodological premise, which has not been sufficiently recognized: that *the total amount of surplus-value is determined prior to and independent of the division of this total amount into individual parts.* The individual parts of surplus-value are then determined at a subsequent stage of the analysis, with the predetermined total amount of surplus-value taken as a given magnitude. This premise was first discussed by Marx in the *Grundrisse* with respect to the equalization of rates of profit across different branches of production. In the second draft of *Capital*, written in 1861–63, parts of which have been only recently published in English, Marx also began with this premise as he worked out his theories of rent, interest, and merchant profit. In the remaining drafts of *Capital*, this fundamental premise is consistently adhered to and emphasized, especially in Volume 3, in which the distribution of surplus-value is the main subject.

Marx expressed this fundamental premise of his theory concerning the prior determination of the total amount of surplus-value in terms of the distinction between the stages of analysis of "capital in general" and "competition" (or "many capitals"). Capital in general refers to the essential properties that all capitals have in common. The most important common property of capitals is their capacity for self-expansion, i.e., their ability to produce surplus-value. Therefore, the main question addressed in the analysis of capital in general is the determination of the total amount of surplus-value produced in the capitalist economy as a whole. Competition refers to the relations among capitals, and, in particular, to the distribution of surplus-value among capitals, first among the different branches of production and then the further

121

division of surplus-value into industrial profit, merchant profit, interest, and rent.

Unfortunately, this fundamental premise of Marx's theory has been almost totally overlooked in the vast literature about Marx's theory, at least in English. In particular, this premise has not been recognized in the long-standing debate over the so-called "transformation problem" in Marx's theory. The main exception to this oversight has been Rosdolsky (1977, pp. 41–50 and 367–75), who emphasized that Marx's explanation of equal rates of profit across industries in the *Grundrisse* was based on this principle (other exceptions have been Mattick 1969, Mattick Jr. 1981, and Foley 1986). However, even Rosdolsky's discussion is limited, because it applies only to the *Grundrisse* and to Marx's theory of equal rates of profit, and not to later drafts of *Capital* nor to the other components of surplus-value.

In an earlier paper (Moseley 1993a), I have attempted to show the importance of this methodological premise for Marx's theory of equal rates of profit and prices of production, i.e., for Marx's solution to the "transformation problem." In particular, I have argued that the widespread interpretation of Marx's theory in terms of linear production theory, which I call the "neo-Ricardian" interpretation, is erroneous because it ignores this fundamental premise of Marx's theory (and for other reasons as well)[1] and is instead based on a very different premise. In Marx's theory, the rate of profit is determined at the level of abstraction of capital in general as the ratio between the total amount of surplus-value and the total capital invested in the capitalist economy as a whole. This rate of profit is then taken as given in the determination of prices of production. In the neo-Ricardian interpretation of Marx's theory, there is no distinction between the levels of abstraction of capital in general and competition. Likewise, there is no recognition of the prior determination of the rate of profit in the analysis of prices of production. Instead, the rate of profit is determined simultaneously along with prices of production. It follows from this fundamental misinterpretation that the main neo-Ricardian criticism of Marx's theory—that Marx's solution to the "transformation problem" is logically incomplete and contradictory—is not correct. If Marx's theory is correctly interpreted, including this premise of the prior determination of the total amount of surplus-value and the general rate of profit, then there is no logical error in his solution to the "transformation problem."

The main purpose of the present paper is to extend this earlier paper by providing substantial further textual evidence of this important methodological premise in Marx's theory of the production and distribution of surplus-value. The various drafts of *Capital* will be examined to show their consistent adherence to this fundamental premise. Not only is Marx's theory of equal rates of profit considered, but also his theory of the other components of surplus-value, in order to demonstrate his consistent adherence to this premise and the logical connection between these different aspects of his theory of the distribution of surplus-value. The burden of interpretation will then be on those—especially the neo-Ricardians—who have so far ignored this fundamental premise of Marx's theory.

1. The *Grundrisse*

The *Grundrisse* (hereafter, G.) is concerned almost entirely with an analysis of capital in general. There is very little discussion of the distribution of surplus-value. The only aspect of the distribution of surplus-value which is discussed is the equalization of profit rates across different branches of production, and this is discussed only very briefly and in passing in a few places. The clearest statement of the premise of the prior determination of the total amount of surplus-value is the following:

> *The total surplus-value . . . can neither grow or decrease by this operation* [the equalization of rates of profit. FM], ever; what is modified thereby is not it, but only its distribution among the different capitals. However, this examination belongs only with that of the many capitals, it does not yet belong here. (G. 760; emphasis added).[2]

A few pages later, Marx comments:

> *The profit of the capitalists as a class, or the profit of capital as such has to exist before it can be distributed,* and it is extremely absurd to try to explain its origin by its distribution. (G. 684; emphasis added)[3]

Thus, although Marx left the elaboration of his theory of equal rates of profit to the subsequent analysis of competition, he was already clear in the *Grundrisse* that this theory would be based on the premise that the total amount of surplus-value is determined prior to its distribution among individual branches of production.

2. The 1861–63 Manuscript[4]

In the summer of 1861, Marx began working on a second draft of *Capital.* He continued to work on this manuscript for the next two years, writing at a very prolific rate and producing what would eventually be published as five volumes. About two-thirds of this manuscript has been previously been published in English as the *Theories of Surplus-Value*. The entire manuscript, including the previously unpublished parts, has recently been published in English as Volumes 30–34 of the *Marx-Engels Collected Works*, which is a translation of the authoritative German collection *Marx-Engels Gesamtausgabe*, published in the 1970s. The publication of this entire manuscript is an important event in Marxian scholarship. This manuscript provides an important link between the *Grundrisse* and *Capital* and should provide many insights into the logical structure and content of *Capital*, similar perhaps to the publication of the English translation of the *Grundrisse* in the 1970s. It should be carefully studied by all those who wish to understand Marx's *Capital*. (Oakley 1983, Chapter 6, written before the publication of the complete English edition, provides a good short introduction to the 1861–63 manuscript.)

Marx began his work on this manuscript with what would later become Part 2 of Volume 1 of Capital ("The Transformation of Money into Capital"), since he had already reworked and published what later became Part 1 as *A Contribution to the Critique of Political Economy*. He wrote drafts of what later became Parts 2–4 of Volume 1, which contain the key chapters of his theory of surplus-value, absolute surplus-value (the working day), and relative surplus-value (technological change). Marx then broke off to work on the *Theories of Surplus-Value*, which was originally intended to be a critical survey of the attempts by the classical economists to explain the origin and determination of surplus-value. Marx's original plan seems to have been to include this critical survey of the theories of surplus-value following his own theory and in the same volume, similar to what he had done for the theories of value and money in the *A Contribution* .... However, Marx soon went far beyond this original intention to discuss not only the production, but also the distribution, of surplus-value. Marx used this extended critique of the classical economists to work out in greater detail his own theory of the distribution of surplus-value. The following discussion will concentrate on those parts of the *Theories of Surplus-Value* and the remaining previously unpublished parts of the 1861–63 manuscript which deal with the distribution of surplus-value.

Marx began his critical survey of the classical economists' theories of surplus-value with the following "general observation":

All economists share the error of examining surplus-value not as such, in its pure form, but in the particular forms of profit and rent. (MECW.30. 348; TSV.I. 40)

Quantitatively, this means that the classical economists shared the error of not distinguishing between the determination of the total amount of surplus-value and the distribution of surplus-value in the specific forms of profit, rent, etc. Thus, Marx had this crucial distinction clearly in mind as he began the *Theories of Surplus-Value*.

Marx then wrote what we know as Volume 1 of *Theories of Surplus-Value*, which is mainly about Smith's theory of value and distribution and the concepts of productive and unproductive labor. Marx's work then took a surprising turn. Instead of next considering Ricardo's theory of surplus-value and perhaps the later Ricardian economists, as Marx originally planned (MECW.31. 583–84, n. 2), Marx next discussed a more recent work, published in 1851, by Rodbertus, who had attempted to develop a new theory of rent along Ricardian lines, but with an attempted solution to Ricardo's problem of absolute rent (Ricardo's theory could not explain how the least fertile land could receive a rent). This subject is out of place in the manuscript both chronologically and logically, since it deals with rent, a form of the distribution of surplus-value, rather than the production of surplus-value. Marx labeled this section of the manuscript a "Digression."

It appears that the immediate reason for this surprising turn was mostly practical and fortuitous. Lassalle had loaned Marx a copy of Rodbertus's book the year before and had recently written to Marx that he wanted his book back (MECW.31. 593, n. 99; TSV. II. 633–34, n. 1). Therefore, Marx studied Rodbertus's book while he still had the opportunity to do so. The book turned out to be more interesting than Marx expected and appears to have stimulated Marx's thinking about rent and about the distribution of surplus-value in general. It started Marx on an extended theoretical excursion for most of the next year, during which he began to work out the details of his own theory of the distribution of surplus-value, based on the premise of the prior determination of the total amount of surplus-value. This important excursion will now be examined in some detail.

2.1 RODBERTUS

Early in the section on Rodbertus, Marx began to emphasize that the theory of rent must be understood in connection with the equalization of profit rates across individual branches of production. Therefore, he began to sketch out the details of his theory of the equalization of profit rates and prices of production (which Marx here called "average prices" or "cost prices") for the first time (MECW.31. 260–64 and 297–305; TSV.II. 25–30 and 64–71). In these sketches, Marx emphasized that the general rate of profit to which all individual rates of profit are equalized is determined by the ratio of the total amount of surplus-value divided by the total amount of capital invested. The total amount of surplus-value, Marx assumed, is determined by a prior analysis of capital in general. This total amount of surplus-value is then distributed among the individual branches of production by means of commodities selling at average prices which differ from their values and which are determined in part by this general rate of profit. In this way, each capital is treated as a "shareholder of the aggregate capital," and receives its share of the total surplus-value, according to its own magnitude. Capitalists are like "hostile brothers [who] divide among themselves the loot of other people's labor" (MECW.31. 264; TSV.II. 29). The total magnitude of this "loot" has already been determined by the prior analysis of capital in general.

Rent is then explained as a further application of this theory of the general rate of profit and prices of production. Rent is a part of the total surplus-value which landlords are able, by their monopoly of the land (and other natural resources), to appropriate for themselves, rather than this surplus-value being distributed among all capitalists. In this theory of rent, the total amount of surplus-value is again taken as a given magnitude, as determined by the prior analysis of capital in general. This total amount of surplus-value is "split" into profit and rent, and rent does not enter into the equalization of profit rates across industries.

> This ownership [of natural resources] is a means of obstructing the process which takes place in the rest of the capitalist spheres of production, and of holding on to this surplus-value created in this particular sphere, so that it is divided between the capitalist and the landowner in that sphere of production itself (MECW.31. 276; TSV.II. 42).

Marx also outlined his general solution to Ricardo's problem of absolute rent, i.e., rent on the least fertile land which is not due to a monopoly price of the agricultural product, (i.e., to a price greater than the value of the product). Marx argued that absolute rent in this sense is possible because the composition of capital in agriculture may be less than the average composition for the total economy (and, in fact, was less in England at the time and tended to be less for all capitalist countries). In this case, the value of agricultural goods is greater than their price of production. Hence the actual price of agricultural goods may rise above their price of production without necessarily being greater than their value. This excess of the actual price over the price of production is the source of absolute rent on the least fertile land. Ricardo and Rodbertus had not been able to explain the possibility of absolute rent because they did not distinguish between the value and the price of production of commodities.

Soon after working on this section on Rodbertus, Marx wrote an important letter to Engels in which he summarized these new theoretical developments. Originally, Marx had planned to consider rent only in Book 2 on landed property, as part of his projected six books on political economy (Marx 1859, 19; SC. 96–97). However, he now realized more clearly that rent is an aspect of the distribution of surplus-value and is intimately connected with the equalization of profit rates. Therefore, he decided to bring the discussion of rent into the first book on Capital, in the later sections on competition and the distribution of surplus-value. The letter to Engels begins:

> I now intend after all to bring the theory of rent already into this volume as a supplementary chapter, i.e., as an illustration of a principle laid down earlier (SC. 120).

Marx then presented a brief sketch of this theory of prices of production (or "cost prices") and his theory of rent. Once again, the total amount of surplus-value and the general rate of profit are taken as given in the determination of "cost-prices" and in the division of surplus-value into profit and rent.

2.2 RICARDO

One of the main conclusions of Marx's discussion of Rodbertus is that both Rodbertus and Ricardo made the mistake, following Smith, of assuming that the cost prices (or prices of production) of individual commodities are equal to their values (i.e., of "identifying cost prices and values") and that this false assumption led to their erroneous theories of rent. Therefore, Marx next discussed "Ricardo's and Smith's Theory of Cost Price." (MECW.31. 387–456; TSV. II., Chapter 10) In this section, Marx argued that Ricardo was not able to provide a satisfactory theory of cost prices because he failed to follow the correct logical method with respect to the production and distribution of surplus-value. Instead of first determining the total amount of surplus-value and the general rate of profit and then determining cost prices on the basis of this predetermined general rate of profit, Ricardo simply assumed a given rate of profit (without explaining its determination) and examined the extent to which the assumption of equal profit rates was consistent with the determination of prices by labor-times. To quote this important methodological criticism at some length:

Ricardo's method is as follows: He begins with the determination of the magnitude of the value of the commodity by labor-time and then examines whether the other economic relations and categories contradict this determination of value or to what extent they modify it. The historical justification of this method of procedure, its scientific necessity in the history of economics, are evident at first sight, but so too is, at the same time, its scientific inadequacy. This inadequacy not only shows itself in the method of presentation (in a formal sense) but leads to erroneous results because it *omits some essential links* and directly seeks to prove the congruity of the economic categories with one another (MECW.390; TSV.II. 164–65; emphasis added).

Instead of postulating this general rate of profit, Ricardo should have examined how far its existence is consistent with the determination of value by labor-time and he would have found that instead of being consistent with it, prima facie, it contradicts it, and that its existence would therefore *have to be explained through a number of intermediary stages*, a procedure very different from merely including it under the law of value. He would then have gained an altogether different insight into the nature of profit and would not have identified it directly with surplus-value (MECW.31. 401; TSV.II. 174; emphasis added).

The most important "essential link" and "intermediary stage" omitted by Ricardo is the prior determination of the total amount of surplus-value and the general rate of profit, which is then taken as given in the subsequent determination of cost prices. Marx summarized his discussion of Ricardo's faulty logical method in the following passage:

> *The equalization of the surplus-values in the different spheres of production does not affect the absolute size of this total surplus-value; but merely alters its distribution among the different spheres of production. The determination of this surplus-value itself, however, only arises out of the determination of value by labor-time.* Without this, the average profit is the average of nothing, pure fancy. And it could then equally well be 1,000 per cent or 10 per cent. . . . One can see that though Ricardo is accused of being too abstract, one would be justified in accusing him of the opposite: *lack of power of abstraction, inability, when dealing with the values of commodities, to forget profits, a factor which confronts him as a result of competition* (MECW.31. 416; TSV.II. 190–91; emphasis added).

Later in the manuscript, after sections on Ricardo's theory of rent, Smith's theory of rent, and Ricardo's theory of surplus-value (which contain nothing new for our purposes), Marx returned to Ricardo's theory of profit. Here again, Marx emphasized that a correct understanding of equal rates of profit requires the "intermediary link" of the prior determination of the total amount of surplus-value. Equal rates of profit are bound to be misunderstood if they:

are not connected by a series of intermediary links with the general laws of value etc: in short, if profit and surplus-value are treated as identical, which is only correct for the aggregate capital. Accordingly, Ricardo has no means for determining the general rate of profit (MECW.32. 61; TSV.II. 427).

Marx also emphasized again the prior determination of the general rate of profit as the ratio of total surplus-value to total capital:

> *The general rate of profit is formed through the total surplus-value produced being calculated on the total capital of society (the class of capitalists).* Each capital, therefore, in each particular branch, represents a portion of a total capital of the same organic composition . . . As such a portion, it draws its dividends from the surplus-value created by the aggregate capital, in accordance with its size . . . The surplus-value thus distributed . . . constitutes the average profit or the general rate of profit, and as such it enters into the costs of production of every sphere of production (MECW.32. 69; TSV.II. 433).

2.3   REVENUE AND ITS SOURCES

The next important section of the 1861–63 manuscript for our purposes is the section entitled "Revenue and Its Sources. Vulgar Political Economy," which is a first draft of what later became Part 7 of Volume 3 of *Capital*. This section includes Marx's first extended discussion of interest, another form of the distribution of surplus-value, besides profit and rent. Marx emphasized that interest, like rent, is a part of the total surplus-value and that the total surplus-value is determined prior to its division into profit, rent, and interest.

> *Interest is therefore nothing but a part of the profit (which, in turn, is itself nothing but surplus-value, unpaid labor)*, which the industrial capitalist pays to the owner of the borrowed capital with which he "works", either exclusively or partially. Interest is a part of profit—of surplus-value—which, established as a special category, is separated from the total profit under its own name, a separation which is by no means based on its origin, but only on the manner in which it is paid out or appropriated (MECW.32. 469; TSV.III. 470–71; emphasis added)

Marx also contrasted his premise of the prior determination of the total amount of value and surplus-value with the diametrically opposed premise of the vulgar economists, according to which the surplus-value is determined as the sum of profit plus interest plus rent.

> But the whole matter is mystified because these different parts of surplus-value [profit, rent, and interest; FM] acquire an independent form, because they accrue to different people, because the titles

to them are based on different elements, and finally because of the autonomy with which certain of these parts of surplus-value confront the production process as its conditions. *From parts into which value can be divided, they become independent elements which constitute value...* (MECW.31. 511; TSV.III. 511; emphasis added).

Finally, Marx also devoted a few pages in this section to a discussion of the relation between interest-bearing capital, mercantile (or commercial) capital, and industrial capital. Marx argued that interest-bearing capital and mercantile capital are derived from or secondary to the basic form of industrial capital. In other words, the analysis of interest-bearing capital and merchant capital follow that of industrial capital, and the incomes received by interest-bearing capital and merchant capital are parts of the total surplus-value produced by industrial capital (or, more precisely, by the labor employed by industrial capital). Marx returned in the next section, to be discussed below, to a more extended discussion of mercantile capital and mercantile profit, yet another form of distribution of the total amount of surplus-value.

2.4 MERCANTILE CAPITAL

We come now to an important part of the 1861–63 manuscript which has only recently been published in English in Volume 33 of the *Marx-Engels Collected Works*. As a direct continuation of the section on "Revenue and its Sources," in which mercantile capital was briefly discussed, two of the next three sections present a more extended discussion of mercantile capital and the mercantile profit derived from it.

Mercantile capital is capital which functions solely in the sphere of circulation, i.e., performs only the pure circulation functions of buying and selling, and activities related to buying and selling (accounting, advertising, credit, etc.). Since according to Marx's theory, these functions by themselves are "unproductive," i.e., produce no value or surplus-value (see Moseley 1992, Chapter 2, for a further discussion of Marx's concept of unproductive labor), the question arises of how this mercantile capital receives a profit, since of course it must, just like any other capital.

Marx's brief answer to this question in this manuscript is that mercantile capital receives its profit as a deduction from the surplus-value produced by industrial capital. As with the other forms of the distribution of surplus-value already discussed, the total amount of surplus-value is determined prior to the deduction of mercantile profit and is taken as given in the analysis of mercantile profit. Marx briefly sketched the general mechanism through which this deduction of mercantile capital from the total surplus-value occurs—through the difference between mercantile capital's buying price and its selling price. This difference enables mercantile capital to recover its cost and to collect the average rate of profit. (Further details of this pricing mechanism are presented in Part 4 of Volume 3 of *Capital*, which will be discussed below).

2.5   CAPITAL AND PROFIT

In between the two sections on mercantile capital just discussed is a section entitled "Third Chapter. Capital and Profit." According to Marx's plan since the *Grundrisse*, the part of his book on "Capital in General" would consist of three chapters: (1) The Production Process of Capital; (2) The Circulation Process of Capital; and (3) Capital and Profit. (MECW.29. 511–16; MECW. 40. 287). At this point in his year-long detour from his draft of Chapter 1 and into the *Theories of Surplus-Value* and the various aspects of the distribution of surplus-value discussed above, Marx decided to write a draft of Chapter 3. (Marx began a separate notebook with the draft of this chapter and wrote "Ultimum" on the front of this notebook, suggesting that this was more of a final draft than the exploratory work of the previous and succeeding notebooks; see MECW.33. 506 n. 4). As we shall see, this draft remained primarily at the level of abstraction of capital in general, although the determination of the average rate of profit was touched upon because it related directly to the subject matter of this chapter. A likely explanation of this decision to write a draft of "Chapter 3" was to explore the relation between this chapter and the various aspects of the distribution of surplus-value that Marx had been working on.

The subject that receives the most attention in this draft of "Chapter 3" on "Capital and Profit" is the tendency of the rate of profit to decline (MECW.33. 104–45), which Marx calls "the most important question in this section" (MECW.33. 91). The chapter also includes an important discussion of the "two transformations of surplus-value into profit," which is more relevant to our subject of the distribution of surplus-value.

In the first transformation, *surplus-value is transformed into profit*, i.e., is related to the total capital invested, and not just to variable capital which, according to Marx's theory, is the source of surplus-value. As a result of this transformation, the source of surplus-value is obliterated and therefore not recognized by the agents of capitalist production. In this first transformation, the magnitude of surplus-value does not change; it is simply related to the total capital, rather than just to variable capital. This first transformation eventually became the subject of Part 1 of Volume 3 ("The Transformation of Surplus-Value into Profit and of the Rate of Surplus-Value into the Rate of Profit").

> Profit—as first transformation of surplus-value—and the rate of profit in this first transformation—expresses surplus-value in proportion to the individual overall capital of which it is the product—treating all parts of this overall capital as uniform, and relating to the whole of it as a homogeneous sum of value, without regard to the organic relation in which the different components of this capital stand towards the creating of its surplus-value (MECW.33. 100).
> Profit, as we are originally faced with it, is thus the same thing as surplus-value, save in a mystified form, though one that necessarily arises from the capitalist mode of production. Because no distinction between constant capital and variable capital can be recognized in the apparent formation of the cost price, the origin of the change in value that occurs in the course of the production process is shifted from the variable capital to the capital as a whole (C.III. 127).

In the second transformation, *profit is transformed into average profit* and the average rate of profit is established. In this second transformation, the total profit is distributed among individual capitals in such a way that the profit appropriated by each individual capital is proportional to the magnitude of the individual capital, rather than equal to the amount of surplus-value actually produced by that capital (or rather by the labor employed by that capital). This redistribution of surplus-value is accomplished by means of the formation of a general or average rate of profit, which is equal to the total profit divided by the total capital, and prices of production based on this average rate of profit. In this second transformation, the amount of profit appropriated by each capital changes, which further obscures the origin of surplus-value. This second transformation eventually became the subject of Part 2 of Volume 3 ("The Transformation of Profit into Average Profit").

> On the basis of the first transformation, therefore, a second takes place, which no longer affects the form alone, but also the substance itself, in that it alters the *absolute magnitude* of profit... This absolute magnitude of profit was untouched by the first transformation (MECW.33. 97).

In this second transformation to average profit, Marx again emphasized clearly that this average rate of profit is determined as the ratio of the total surplus-value to the total capital.

> The empirical, or average, profit can therefore be nothing other than the distribution of that total profit (and the total surplus-value

represented by it or the representation of the total surplus labor) among the individual capitals in each particular sphere of production, in equal proportions ... It therefore represents the result of the particular mode of calculation in which the different capitals divide among themselves aliquot parts of the total profit. *What is available for them to divide among themselves is only determined by the absolute quantity of the total profit or the total surplus-value.* (MECW.33. 99; emphasis added)

Empirical or average profit ... relates the total amount of surplus-value, hence the surplus-value realized by the whole capitalist class, to the total capital, or the capital employed by the whole capitalist class, in exactly this way—it relates the total surplus-value as profit to that total capital of society, without regard to the organic relation in which the individual components of that total capital have participated directly in the production of that total surplus-value ... (MECW.33. 100). The average rate of profit is nothing other than the total surplus-value related to and calculated on this total capital (MECW.33. 104).

Marx also commented that a closer investigation of the determination of the average rate of profit and the consequent distribution of surplus-value "belongs to the chapter on competition" (MECW.33. 94 and 101). Therefore, Marx was still thinking at this time that this third chapter on capital and profit would be concerned only with capital in general. However, the close relation between the "two transformations" of surplus-value into profit required at least some discussion of the average rate of profit in this chapter.

2.6   OUTLINES OF VOLUME 3 OF *CAPITAL*

As mentioned above, after completing the draft of "Capital and Profit," Marx returned to a further discussion of merchant capital, which has already been discussed in section (2.4) above. Marx then returned to the *Theories of Surplus-Value* and wrote three concluding sections on Ramsay, Cherbuliez, and Jones. Marx's main emphasis in these sections was on the glimpses made by these authors of the crucial distinction between constant capital and variable capital and the falling rate of profit that followed from this distinction. For our purposes, the most important parts of these sections are two draft outlines of what later became Volume 3 of *Capital,* which are contained as digressions in the sections on Cherbuliez and Jones.[5] These draft outlines will be discussed in the reverse order in which they appear (about 50 printed pages apart) because the second outline is more general than the first and is clearly presupposed in the latter.

The second outline is for what Marx calls the third "section" (instead of the third "chapter") on "Capital and Profit." This outline is as follows:

1. Conversion of surplus-value into profit. Rate of profit as distinguished from the rate of surplus-value.
2. Conversion of profit into average profit. Formation of the general rate of profit. Transformation of values into prices of production.
3. Adam Smith's and Ricardo's theories of profit and prices of production.
4. Rent. (Illustration of the difference between value and price of production.)
5. History of the so-called Ricardian theory of rent.
6. Law of the fall of the rate of profit. Adam Smith, Ricardo, Carey.
7. Theories of profit . . .
8. Division of profit into industrial profit and interest. Mercantile capital. Money capital.
9. Revenue and its sources. The questions of the relation between production and distribution also to be included here.
10. Reflux movements of money in the process of capitalist production as a whole.
11. Vulgar economy.
12. Conclusion. "Capital and wage labor." (MECW.33. 346–47; TSV.I. 415–16)

The most striking feature of this outline is that the contents of "Capital and Profit" is now radically expanded compared to the draft of just a few months before. It no longer includes just aspects of capital in general (the first transformation of surplus-value into profit and the falling rate of profit), but also includes all the aspects of competition or the distribution of surplus-value which Marx had been working on for the previous year: the general or average rate of profit and prices of production, rent, interest, merchant profit, and revenue and its sources. Evidently, Marx's work on these subjects over the previous year convinced him that they should be included in the third "section" on "Capital and Profit," rather than waiting for a subsequent volume on competition. (Oakley 1983, pp. 82–110, also emphasizes Marx's expansion of the content of "Capital and Profit" to include these aspects of competition and the distribution of surplus-value, besides capital in general.) We can see that this outline is very close to the final version of Volume 3 of *Capital*, which Marx wrote in the following two years (1864–65).[6]

The other outline is a more detailed outline of "the second chapter of Part 3, on 'Capital and Profit,' where the formation of the general rate of profit is dealt with" (MECW.33. 299). (Note that this title presumes the more general outline just discussed of the entire Part 3 on "Capital and Profit.") Excerpts from this outline are:

1. Different organic composition of capitals . . .
2. Differences in the relative value of the parts of different capitals which do not arise from their organic composition . . .
3. The result of those differences is diversity of the rates of profit in different spheres of capitalist production.
4. *For the total capital, however, what has been explained in Chapter 1 holds good. In capitalist production each capital is assumed to be a unit, an aliquot part of the total capital. Formation of the general rate of profit. (Competition).*
5. Transformation of values into prices of production . . .
6. To take up the Ricardian point: the influence of general variations in wages on the general rate of profit and hence on prices of production (MECW.33. 299; TSV.I. 415–16; emphasis added)

Again, this outline is very close to the final version of Part 2 of Volume 3, with (1)–(3) the subjects of Chapter 8, (4)–(5) the subjects of Chapter 9, and (6) the subject of Chapter 11. (Chapters 10 and 12 are not included in this outline). Note especially (4), which is a very important methodological comment and which clearly supports the main point of this paper that the total amount of surplus-value is determined prior to its distribution and is not affected by this distribution. Note also the second sentence of (4), which clarifies the important point that the individual capitals which Marx often used as illustrations in Volume 1 of *Capital* (i.e., in "capitalist production") is not an actual individual capital *per se*, but instead is an ideal representative of the total capital ("is assumed to be a unit, an aliquot part of the total capital"), and thus that the real subject of Volume 1 is this total capital or capital in general. Finally, note also that the "competition" in parentheses clearly indicates that the theory of the equal rates of profit and prices of production belongs at the level of abstraction of competition.

Thus we can see that Marx's year-long study of various aspects of the distribution of surplus-value clarified Marx's thinking on these issues, and led Marx to include them in "Capital and Profit," along with the aspects of capital in general already included. The next major manuscript written by Marx in 1864–65 was the first and only full draft of Volume 3 of *Capital*, as we know it today. Evidently, Marx's work on the 1861–63 manuscript clarified Marx's thinking to such an extent that he was now ready to write this volume. The fact that this first draft, although certainly not polished for publication, is as clear and complete as it is, is further evidence of the clarity Marx achieved while working on the 1861–63 manuscript. To this 1864–65 manuscript of Volume 3 we now turn.

3. Volume 3 of *Capital*

As indicated by Marx's outline just discussed, Volume 3 of *Capital* is primarily concerned with an analysis of the distribution of surplus-value into its component parts—first the equalization of profit rates across branches of production and then the further division of surplus-value into merchant profit, interest, and rent at the level of abstraction of competition. A full discussion of Volume 3 is obviously beyond the scope of this paper. Instead, a brief survey will be presented of each of the specific aspects of the distribution of surplus-value which are discussed in Volume 3 with two main objectives: (1) to provide further support for the main point of this paper—that the total amount of surplus-value is taken as a predetermined magnitude in this analysis of the distribution of surplus-value in Volume 3; and (2) to examine in greater detail Marx's specific theories of the determination of the particular forms of surplus-value. The versions of these specific theories presented in this draft of Volume 3 are Marx's final and most complete versions of these theories.

3.1   EQUAL RATES OF PROFIT AND PRICES OF PRODUCTION[7]

Marx's theory of the equal rates of profit and prices of production presented in Volume 3 may be briefly summarized as follows (see Moseley 1993 for a more thorough discussion): First, the general rate of profit is determined as the ratio of the total amount of surplus-value produced (S) to the total capital invested (C) in the capitalist economy as a whole. Algebraically:

(1) $R = S / C$

As discussed many times above, the total amount of surplus-value (S) is determined at the prior level of analysis of capital in general and is taken as given in the analysis of the distribution of surplus-value. The total amount of capital invested (C) is also taken as given, as the initial sum of money (M) in Marx's "general formula for capital," M-C-M'.

> The prerequisite [of prices of production] is the existence of a general rate of profit... (C.III. 257)
>
>   The general rate of profit is determined in fact (1) by the surplus-value that the total capital produces, (2) by the ratio of this surplus-value to the value of the total capital, (3) and by competition, but only in so far as this is the movement through which the capitals invested in particular spheres of production seek to draw equal dividends from this surplus-value in proportion to their relative size (C.III. 489).

Next, the price of production for each commodity (P_i) is then determined according to the following equation:

(2) $P_i = K_i + R \ C_i$

where K_i is the costs of production of the commodity (the sum of variable capital and constant capital consumed) (a flow variable) and C_i is the total stock of capital invested in the given industry. In this determination of prices of production, the general rate of profit (R) is taken as given, as determined in the prior analysis of capital in general. The magnitudes of individual capitals invested and consumed in each industry (C_i and K_i) are also taken as given, as the sums of money which initiate the circulation of capital in each industry, as is the total capital in the analysis of capital in general. Therefore, prices of production are determined by adding the average profit to the given costs of production for each commodity, with the average profit determined as the product of the general rate of profit and the given capital invested in each industry, and the general rate of profit determined by the prior analysis of capital in general. In this way, the total amount of surplus-value is distributed in such a way that all industries receive the same rate of profit.

> The formula that the price of production of a commodity = k + p, cost price plus profit, can now be stated more exactly; since p = kp') (where p' is the general rate of profit), the price of production = k + kp'. (C.III. 265) [Marx is here ignoring the difference between the stock and flow of capital; FM]
>
> The prices of production arise from an adjustment of commodity values under which, after the reimbursement of the respective capital values consumed in the various spheres of production, the total surplus-value is distributed, not in the proportion in which it is produced in the individual spheres of production, ... but rather in proportion to the size of the capitals advanced ... It is the constant tendency of capitals to bring about, by competition, this adjustment of the total surplus-value which the total capital produces ... (C.III. 895)

The average profit ($= R \ C_i$) included in the price of each commodity will in general not be equal to the amount of surplus-value actually contained in that commodity, and hence the price of production of each commodity will in general not be equal to its value or proportional to the labor-time required to produce it. However, the total amount of surplus-value is not altered by this redistribution of surplus-value among the individual industries according to the total amount of capital invested. Taken all together, the divergences of individual profits from individual surplus-values balance out so that the sum of individual profits is equal to the total amount of surplus-value (S), as determined in the Volume 1 analysis of capital in general. (See Moseley 1993a for an algebraic derivation of this result.)

> We have thus an absolute limit for the value component that forms surplus-value . . . ; this is determined by the excess of the unpaid portion of the working day over its paid portion, i.e., by the value component of the total product in which this surplus labor is realized. If we call this surplus-value whose limits are thus determined profit, when it is calculated on the total capital advanced, as we have already done, then this profit, considered in its absolute amount, is equal to the surplus-value, i.e., it is just as regularly determined in its limits as this is. It is the ratio between the total surplus-value and the total social capital advanced in production. If this capital is 500 . . . and the surplus-value is 100, the absolute limit to the rate of profit is 20 percent. The division of the social profit as measured by this rate among the capitals applied in the various different spheres of production produces prices of production which diverge from commodity values and which are the actual averages governing market prices. *But this divergence from values abolishes neither the determination of prices by values nor the limits imposed on profit by our laws* . . . This surcharge of 20 percent . . . is itself determined by the surplus-value created by the total social capital, and its proportion to the value of this capital; and this is why it is 20 percent and not 10 percent or 100 percent. *The transformation of values into prices of production does not abolish the limits to profit, but simply affects its distribution* among the various particular capitals of which the social capital is composed . . . (C.III. 999–1000; emphasis added)

In my previous paper (Moseley 1993a), I have responded to the widely-accepted neo-Ricardian criticism of Marx's theory of prices of production, that this theory is logically incomplete and contradictory. One of the two main points in my response is that the neo-Ricardian interpretation of Marx's theory does not recognize the distinction between capital in general and competition and the prior determination of the general rate of profit in the analysis of prices of production.[8] If Marx's logical method is followed, including this key premise of the prior determination of the general rate of profit, then there is no logical error in Marx's theory of prices of production.

3.2 COMMERCIAL PROFIT[9]

Commercial capital is what Marx called mercantile capital in the 1861–63 manuscript, i.e., capital engaged in the functions of buying and selling (and related activities). As discussed above, the unique feature of commercial capital is that the circulation functions which it performs do not produce value or surplus-value. Therefore, the question arises of how commercial capital receives a profit if it produces no surplus-value. We have already seen above that Marx's general answer to this question is that commercial capital receives its profit as a deduction from the surplus-value produced by industrial capital and that the mechanism through which this deduction of surplus-value takes place is the difference between the "wholesale" price at which commercial capital purchases commodities from industrial capital and the "retail" price at which commercial capital sells commodities to consumers. The total amount of surplus-value is taken as given and remains the same, but it must now be shared (at equal rates of profit) with commercial capital:

> Since commercial capital does not itself produce any surplus-value, it is clear that *the surplus-value that accrues to it in the form of the average profit forms a portion of the surplus-value produced by the productive capital as a whole.* The question now is this: How does commercial capital attract the part of the surplus-value produced by productive capital that falls to its share? ... It is clear that the merchant can obtain his profit only from the price of the commodities he sells, and also that this profit which he makes on the sale of his commodities must be equal to the difference between his purchase price and his sale price; it must be equal to the excess of the latter over the former (C.III. 395–96; emphasis added).

How then are the purchase price and the selling price of commercial capital determined? Marx first considers the simple case in which there are no additional costs of circulation beyond that necessary to purchase the commodities. The general rate of profit (R') is now determined as the ratio of the predetermined total amount of surplus-value to the sum of industrial capital (C_p) and commercial capital (C_c), not just to the industrial capital as before:

(3) $R' = S / (C_p + C_c) < R = S / C$

Therefore, the general rate of profit is less than what it was in the absence of commercial capital.

Commercial capital's "wholesale" price (WP) (or industrial capital's selling price) is then determined as follows (considering both the total industrial capital and the total commercial capital, rather than individual capitals):

(4) $WP = K_p + R'(C_p)$

where K_p is the cost of production (the sum of variable capital and constant capital consumed). Since $R' < R$, the average profit added to the costs of production by industrial capital is less than in the absence of commercial capital. In this way, industrial capital appropriates a smaller share of the total surplus-value.

The remainder of the total surplus-value is then received by commercial capital by adding the average profit to its buying price to determine its selling or "retail" price (RP):

(5) $RP = WP + R'(C_c)$

This then is Marx's explanation of how commercial capital receives a profit even though it produces no surplus-value. It can easily be shown that the sum of industrial profit and commercial profit determined in this way is equal to the predetermined total amount of surplus-value, and that the "retail" price is equal to the total price of commodities in the earlier case of assuming no commercial capital. Marx presented a numerical example of this method of determination on p. 398 of Volume 3. (Marx gave a similar example in a 1868 letter to Engels, which will be discussed in Section 6 below; see SC. 194–95.)

Marx did not clearly present all the details of the more complicated case with additional costs of circulation (K_c), but the general principles just discussed still apply, with the following modifications: (1) The general rate of profit is even lower because of the greater commercial capital which now includes (K_c). (2) K_c is subtracted from the "wholesale" price and added to the "retail" price, so that the equations for determining these prices become:

(6) $WP = K_p + R'(C_p) - K_c$

(7) $RP = WP + R'(C_c) + K_c$

In this way, commercial capital is able both to recover its additional costs of circulation and to collect the average rate of profit out of the surplus-value produced by industrial capital. Throughout this analysis, Marx assumed that the total amount of surplus-value is predetermined and is not affected by this division into industrial profit and commercial profit. In Marx's examples, the total amount of surplus-value is assumed to be a given $180.[10]

In Volume 2 of *Capital*, Chapter 6 ("The Costs of Circulation"), Marx stated that the "general law" for these costs of circulation is that they are recovered out of the surplus-value produced by productive capital, which is taken as given in this analysis of commercial profit.

> The general law is that all circulation costs that arise simply from a change in the form of the commodity cannot add any value to it. They are simply costs involved in realizing the value or transferring it from one form to another. The capital expended in these costs

(including the labor it commands) belongs to the *faux frais* of capitalist production. The replacement of these costs must come from the surplus product, and *from the standpoint of the capitalist class as a whole it forms a deduction of surplus-value* . . . (C.II. 225–26; emphasis added)

3.3 INTEREST (PART 5)[11]

According to Marx's theory of interest, interest is simply a part of the total surplus-value which the "functioning" capital (either industrial capital or commercial capital) has to pay to the lenders of capital for the use of the lenders' capital. Again, the total amount of surplus-value is predetermined and taken as given and not affected by its division into "profit of enterprise" and interest.

Interest . . . is . . . nothing but a part of the profit, i.e., the surplus-value, which the functioning capitalist, whether industrialist or merchant, must pay to the owner and lender of capital is so far as the capital he uses is not his own but borrowed. (C.III. 493)

Where a given whole such as profit is to be divided into two, the first thing that matters is of course the size of the whole to be divided . . . And the circumstances that determine the magnitude of the profit to be divided, the value product of unpaid labor, are very different from those that determine its distribution among these two types of capitalist . . . (C.III. 482; emphasis added)

Marx argued that there are no general, systematic laws that determine the rate of interest, as there is with the rate of profit. Therefore, there are no general laws that determine the relative shares of "profit of enterprise" and interest in the total surplus-value. The rate of interest is instead determined by the supply of and demand for capital as borrowed funds. For our purposes, the crucial point is that the maximum rate of interest is the rate of profit, which is determined prior to and independently of the division of the total surplus-value into "profit of enterprise" and interest.

With the division into interest and profit of enterprise, the average profit itself sets the limit for the two together. *It supplies the given amount of value they have to share between them, and this is all they have to share.* The specific ratio of this division is accidental here, i.e., it is determined exclusively by competition . . . (C.III. 1001; emphasis added)

3.4 RENT (PART 6)[12]

Marx began his analysis of rent by clearly stating that he was not concerned with a complete analysis of landed property, but only with rent as a form of the distribution of surplus-value.

The analysis of landed property in its various historical forms lies outside the scope of the present work. We are concerned with it *only in so far as a portion of the surplus-value that capital produces falls to the landowner* (C.III. 751; emphasis added).

Marx posed the question of differential rent at the beginning of Chapter 38, in the following way, which also clearly indicates that rent is analyzed as a part of the total surplus-value, which is predetermined and taken as given.

> In our analysis of ground-rent, we intend to proceed first of all from the assumption that products that pay a rent of this kind—which means that *a part of surplus-value . . . is reducible to rent*—are sold like all other commodities at their prices of production . . . The question then arises: How a ground-rent can develop on this assumption, i.e., how a portion of profit can be transformed into ground-rent . . .(C.III. 779; emphasis added)

Marx assumed that agriculture is organized on a capitalist basis, and that capital invested in agriculture receives the same average rate of profit as all other industries. However, agriculture is unique in that productivity differentials of different lands are due in part to unequal natural fertilities, which cannot be eliminated by competition and the transfer of capital. As a result, the price of production of agricultural goods is determined by the labor-time requirements on the least fertile land, rather than the labor-time requirements on the land of average fertility. The greater quantity of goods produced by the same amount of labor on the more fertile lands will sell at the same price as goods produced on the least fertile land. Therefore, the goods produced on the more fertile land will contain a sustainable "surplus profit," i.e., a profit over and above the average rate of profit. This surplus profit is transformed into differential rent that must be paid to landlords because of the landlords' private ownership of the land and thus their monopolization of the benefits of the greater natural fertility.

In Chapter 45, Marx also explained in greater detail the possibility of absolute rent on the least fertile land. Marx argued that absolute rent (which arises even though the price of agricultural goods is not greater than their value) is possible because the composition of capital in agriculture may be less than the average composition for the total economy, in which case the value of agricultural goods will be greater their price of production. Hence the actual price of agricultural goods may rise above their price of production without necessarily being greater than their value, and this excess of the actual price over the price of production is the source of absolute rent on the least fertile land. Because competition among capitalists tends to eliminate a higher than average rate of profit on capital in agriculture, this extra surplus-value accruing to agriculture is appropriated by landlords as absolute rent. Once again, it is clear that rent is a part of a predetermined total amount of surplus-value.[13]

In any case, absolute rent, arising from the excess value over and above the price of production, is simply a part of the agricultural surplus-value, the transformation of this surplus-value into rent, its seizure by the landowner; just as differential rent arises from the transformation of surplus profit into rent, its seizure by landed property, at the governing price of production (C.III. 898).

3.5   REVENUE AND ITS SOURCES (PART 7)[14]

Part 7 is a kind of summary of Marx's theory of the distribution of surplus-value in Volume 3 which has not received the attention it deserves. The main emphasis in this part is on the fundamental premise that the total amount of surplus-value is determined prior to its division into individual parts. A few passages, among many similar passages in Part 7, include:

Profit (profit of enterprise plus interest) and rent are nothing more than characteristic forms assumed by particular portions of the surplus-value in commodities. *The size of the surplus-value sets a quantitative limit for the parts it can be broken down into* (C.III. 971; emphasis added).
The sum of average profit plus ground-rent can never be greater than the quantity of which these are parts, and this is already given before the division. (C.III. 972; emphasis added)

The value freshly added each year by new labor ... can be separated out and resolved into the different revenue forms of wages, profit, and rent; this in no way alters the limits of the value itself, the sum of the value that is divided between these different categories. In the same way, a change in the ratio of these individual portions among themselves cannot affect their sum, this given sum of value. ... What is given first, therefore, is the mass of commodity values to be divided into wages, profit, and rent ... *We have thus an absolute limit for the value component that forms surplus-value and can be broken down into profit and ground-rent; this is determined by the excess of the unpaid portion of the working day over its paid portion,* i.e., by the value component of the total product in which this surplus labor is realized (C.III. 998–99; emphasis added).

Marx also contrasted his premise with essentially the opposite premise of the vulgar economists, according to whom the different forms of revenue—wages, profit, and rent—are themselves independent "sources" of value, rather than being parts of a predetermined total value. Marx called this opposite view the "Trinity Formula" or the "illusions created by competition."

> Thus if the portion of commodity value representing labor freshly added . . . breaks down into different portions, which assume mutually independent shapes in the form of revenues, this does not in any way mean that wages, profit, and ground-rent are now to be considered as the constituent elements, with the governing price of commodities . . . itself arising from their combination or sum . . . *In actual fact commodity value is the quantitative premise, the sum total value of wages, profit, and rent, whatever their relative mutual magnitudes might be.* In the false conception considered here, however, wages, profit and rent are three independent value magnitudes, whose total produces, limits and determines the magnitude of commodity value. (C.III. 1002; emphasis added)

4. Volume 1 of *Capital*

In the final draft of Volume 1 of *Capital*, which was written in 1866–67, there are a number of anticipations of Marx's theory of the distribution of surplus-value in Volume 3, which provide further evidence of Marx's method of first determining the total amount of surplus-value and then analyzing the division of this total amount into individual parts. The main anticipations are: (1) in Chapter 5 (pp. 266–67), a preview of Marx's theories of merchant profit and interest as parts of a predetermined total amount of surplus-value; (2) in Chapter 10, the theory of the determination of the length of the working day by the class struggle between capitalists and workers; (3) in Chapter 11 (pp. 421–22), a preview of Marx's theory of equal rates of profit and prices of production; (4) in Chapter 12, the derivation of technological change as an inherent tendency of capital in general; and (5) in the introduction to Part 7, a preview of Volume 3 as a theory of the distribution of surplus-value into its various fragments. Because of space limitation, it will not be possible to discuss these anticipations in detail (see Moseley 1995 for a further discussion). One example will have to suffice from the introduction to Part 7:

> The capitalist who produces surplus-value, i.e., who extracts unpaid labor directly from the workers and fixes it in commodities, is admittedly the first appropriator of this surplus-value, but he is by no

means its ultimate proprietor. He has to share it afterwards with capitalists who fulfill other functions in social production taken as a whole, with the owner of the land, and with yet other people. *Surplus-value is therefore split up into various parts. Its fragments fall to various categories of person, and take on various mutually independent forms, such as profit, interest, gains made through trade, ground rent, etc. We shall be able to deal with these modified forms of surplus-value only in Volume 3.* (C.I. 709; emphasis added)

The break-up of surplus-value into various fragments does not affect either its nature or the conditions under which it becomes an element of accumulation. (C.I. 710; emphasis added)

5. Letters to Engels, 1867–68

Further evidence of Marx's method of the prior determination of the total amount of surplus-value is provided by three important letters to Engels written in 1867–68, i.e., soon after the publication of the first edition of Volume 1 of *Capital*. In August 1867, Marx wrote that one of the two best points of his book was the determination of the total amount of surplus-value prior to the analysis of the particular forms of surplus-value.

The best points in my book are: . . . 2) the treatment of surplus-value independently of its particular forms. This will be seen especially in the second volume. [Marx's plan at the time was to publish what we know as both Volume 2 and 3 in the "second volume". FM] The treatment of the particular forms by classical economy, which always mixes them up with the general form is a regular hash (SC. 180).[15]

Marx repeated the same point in a letter in January 1868, in which he stated that his treatment of surplus-value was one of the "three fundamentally new elements" of his book:

1) That in contrast to all former political economy, which from the very outset treats the different fragments of surplus-value with their fixed forms of rent, profit, and interest as already given, I first deal with the general form of surplus-value, in which all these fragments are still undifferentiated—in solution, as it were (SC. 186).

Finally, in an important letter in April 1868, Marx outlined for Engels the contents of Volume 3 of *Capital*. Excerpts from this letter clearly indicate that the main subject of Volume 3 is the division of surplus-value into its component parts:

In Book III, we come to the transformation of surplus-value into its different forms and separate component parts.
I. Profit is for us first of all only another name or another category for surplus-value.
II. ... A mean or general rate of profit is formed by competition. *This rate of profit, expressed in absolute terms, can be nothing else than the surplus-value produced (annually) by the capitalist class as a whole in relation to the total capital advanced by society as a whole... (T)he mass of capital belonging to each sphere of production receives an aliquot part of the total surplus-value proportionate to the part of the total social capital which it constitutes...* But this means that the prices of commodities must deviate from their values ... The price thus equalized, which distributes the social surplus equally among the individual capitals in proportion to their size, is the price of production of commodities ...
III. The tendency of the rate of profit to decline ...
IV. Previously we have only dealt with productive capital. Now *modifications occur caused by merchant capital ...*
V. Next comes the *splitting up of this profit into entrepreneur's profit and interest.*
VI. *Transformation of surplus profit into rent.*
VII. At last we have arrived at the *phenomena which serve as the starting point for the vulgar economists:* rent originating from the land, profit (interest) from capital, wages from labor. But from our point of view the thing now looks differently. The apparent movement is explained (SC. 193–95; emphasis added).

6. Conclusion

This paper has presented a considerable amount of textual evidence to support the argument that Marx's theory of the distribution of surplus-value is consistently based throughout the various drafts of *Capital* on the fundamental premise that the total amount of surplus-value is determined prior to and independently of the division of this total amount into individual parts. If anything, Marx became increasingly clear about this premise as he worked out his specific theories of the different forms of revenue into which the total surplus-value is divided.

The burden of interpretation would now seem to be on others—especially the neo-Ricardians—who have heretofore ignored this fundamental premise of Marx's theory, especially in their interpretation of the "transformation problem." I have shown in my earlier paper (Moseley 1993a) that if Marx's theory is correctly interpreted to include this premise, then there is no logical error in his solution to the "transformation problem."

In response, the neo-Ricardians need to show how their interpretation of Marx's theory, and of the "transformation problem" in particular, is consistent with this fundamental premise. Otherwise, it can only be concluded that their criticisms of Marx's theory do not in fact apply to Marx's theory, at least not in terms of Marx's own logical method, but instead apply only to their misguided attempts to interpret Marx's theory in terms of linear production theory.

Notes

1. The other main difference between linear production theory and Marx's theory, and hence the other main error in the neo-Ricardian interpretation of Marx's theory, has to do with the fundamental givens in the two theories. In linear production theory, the fundamental givens are the physical quantities of the technical conditions of production and the real wage. In Marx's theory, the fundamental givens are sums of money which are invested as capital, i.e., the initial M in Marx's "general formula for capital," M-C-M'. This difference is especially relevant to the neo-Ricardian criticism that Marx failed to transform the inputs of constant capital and variable capital from value to prices. I argue that the inputs of constant capital and variable capital are taken as given in money terms and therefore do not need to be "transformed" from values to prices. Others who have made similar arguments are Carchedi 1984 and 1993 and Mattick 1981.
2. The references to Marx in this paper utilize the following shorthand notation:

C.I.	*Capital*, Volume 1.
C.II.	*Capital*, Volume 2.
C.III.	*Capital*, Volume 3.
G.	*Grundrisse.*
MECW.30.	*Marx-Engels, Collected Works*, Volume 30.
MECW.31.	*Marx-Engels, Collected Works*, Volume 31.
MECW.33.	*Marx-Engels, Collected Works*, Volume 33.
SC.	*Selected Correspondence.*
TSV.I.	*Theories of Surplus-Value*, Volume 1.
TSV.II.	*Theories of Surplus-value*, Volume 2.
TSV.III.	*Theories of Surplus-value*, Volume 3.

3. See also G. 435–36.
4. Michael Heinrich (1989) has argued that while working on the 1861–63 manuscript, Marx encountered difficulties in maintaining the distinction between capital in general and competition, and eventually abandoned this distinction. I have argued in Moseley (1995) that Marx encountered no such difficulties while working on this manuscript and that Marx maintained this distinction in the final versions of *Capital*. The present paper provides further textual support for this critique of Heinrich's argument.
5. In the *Theories of Surplus-Value*, these outlines are located at the end of Volume 1, which is different from their actual location in the 1861–63 manuscript and which is misleading in that it makes it appear as if these outlines were written early in the 1861–63 manuscript and before Marx's long theoretical detour during which he worked out the details of his

theory of the distribution of surplus-value and which led to the formulation of these outlines.

6. The "Conversion of profit into average profit," which later became Part 2 of Volume 3 and which is an aspect of the distribution of surplus-value, is discussed before the "law of the fall in the rate of profit," which later became Part 3 of Volume 3 and which is an aspect of capital in general, because of the connection between the "two transformations of surplus-value into profit" discussed in the previous section.

7. Especially Chapter 9.

8. The other main point in my response is that the fundamental givens in Marx's theory are not the physical quantities of the technical conditions and the real wage, as in the neo-Ricardian interpretation, but are instead sums of money invested as capital; see note 1.

9. Especially Chapter 17.

10. The dollar sign is substituted for Marx's pound sign.

11. Especially Chapters 22 and 23.

12. Especially Chapters 38 and 45.

13. It should be noted that Marx's theory does not claim that absolute rent is the *only* source of rent on the least fertile land. The other possible source is monopoly rent, i.e., rent derived from the price of agricultural goods being greater than their value. Therefore, Marx's theory does not *require* that the composition of capital in agriculture be below average, and hence is not invalidated by the composition of capital in agriculture being above average. The reasons why Marx distinguished between absolute rent and monopoly rent were (1) to distinguish whether the source of rent on the least fertile land was surplus-value produced *within* agriculture or surplus-value produced *outside* agriculture, and (2) because Ricardo had argued that monopoly rent was the only source of rent on the least fertile land. As discussed above, Ricardo's mistake was due to his identification of value and price of production.

14. Especially Chapters 49 and 50.

15. This statement is very similar to Marx's "general observation" at the beginning of the *Theories of Surplus-Value*, discussed above.

References

Burkett, Paul (1991). "Some Comments on 'Capital in General' and the Structure of Marx's *Capital*'," *Capital and Class* 44 (Summer), 49–72.

Carchedi, Guglielmo (1984). "The Logic of Prices as Values," *Economy and Society*. 13:4, 431–55.

——— (1993). "Marx's Logic of Inquiry and Price Formation," in Moseley (1993b).

Foley, Duncan (1986). *Understanding Capital: Marx's Economic Theory*. Cambridge, MA: Harvard University Press.

Heinrich, Michael (1989). "Capital in General and the Structure of Marx's *Capital*," *Capital and Class*, No. 38, summer, 63–79.

Marx, Karl (1857–58). *Grundrisse*. Middlesex, England: Penguin Books, 1973.

——— (1859). *A Contribution to the Critique of Political Economy*. New York: International Publishers, 1970.

—— (1861–63). *Theories of Surplus Value,* Volume 1. Moscow: Progress Publishers, 1963.

—— (1861–63). *Theories of Surplus Value,* Volume 2. Moscow: Progress Publishers, 1968.

—— (1861–63). *Theories of Surplus Value,* Volume 3. Moscow: Progress Publishers, 1971

—— (1867). *Capital,* Volume 1. New York: Random House, 1977.

—— (1884). *Capital,* Volume 2. New York: Random House, 1981.

Marx, Karl, and Frederick Engels (n.d.). *Selected Correspondence.* Moscow: Progress Publishers, 1975.

—— (1861–63). *Collected Works,* Volume 30. New York: International Publishers, 1988.

—— (1861–63). *Collected Works,* Volume 31. New York: International Publishers, 1989.

—— (1861–63). *Collected Works,* Volume 33. New York: International Publishers, 1992.

—— (1861–63). *Collected Works,* Volume 40. New York: International Publishers, 1983.

Mattick, Paul (1969). *Marx and Keynes.* Boston: Porter Sargent.

Mattick, Paul Jr (1981). "Some Aspects of the Value-Price Problem," *Économies et Sociétés* 15:6–7, 725–81; repr. *International Journal of Political Economy* 21:4 (1991–92), 9–66.

Moseley, Fred (1993a). "Marx's Logical Method and the Transformation Problem," in Moseley (1993b).

—— (1993b). *Marx's Method in "Capital": A Reexamination.* Atlantic Highlands, NJ: Humanities Press.

—— (1995). "Capital in General and Marx's Logical Method: A Response to Heinrich's Critique," *Capital and Class,* no. 56, summer, 15–48.

Oakley, Allen (1983). *The Making of Marx's Critical Theory: A Bibliographical Analysis.* London: Routledge and Kegan Paul.

Rosdolsky, Roman (1968). *The Making of Marx's 'Capital.'* London: Pluto Press, 1977.

6

The Notion of Tendency in Marx's 1894 Law of Profit

Geert Reuten

1. Introduction

In economics and other social sciences it is difficult to make explanatory general theories that are empirically falsifiable and empirically corroborated (Popper). Current mainstream economists deal with this difficulty by just evading it: (a) They refrain from formulating general empirical theories; (b) Consequently the notion of "law" has by and large disappeared from the economics jargon; (c) Adopting a deductive method they construct mathematical economic models—these are not empirically tested, however, they are "applied."

In some of the recent methodological literature it is being suggested that the classical notion of "tendency" or "tendency law" might be fruitful for developing explanatory devices in economics and other social sciences (Bhaskar 1979, Lawson 1989, Hausman 1992).[1] In this paper I want to look at the actual usage of the concept of tendency in the history of economics, for which I have selected as a case a well-known as well as controversial theory, that is, Marx's 1894 Law of Profit (the three chapters on the tendency of the rate of profit to fall in Volume III of *Capital*).

In mainstream economics, indeed the notion of tendency (if not taken as identical to "trend") merely prevails in its history. Between 1900 and 1940 the concept disappeared from the center of mainstream theorizing. Marshall (1890, 26) still held that: "Nearly all laws of science are statements of tendencies." A number of Marxists, on the other hand, have kept on using notions of tendency—though rarely in constructing new theories.

What is a tendency? The notion of tendency is by no means a clear cut and univocally used concept. Blaug (1992) and Hausman (1992), for example, take it merely to be a *ceteris paribus* statement. I think that such a notion looses a lot of what is interesting about the tendency concept (see Reuten 1996 for a critique of Hausman). The least one can say is that tendencies are about "forces" and (their) "expressions," or about "powers" and (their) "outcomes"—be it natural or social forces/powers (for the purposes of this paper I will use these pairs from now on interchangeably). The main divergent notions are either to see powers as tendentially in operation (thus to link "tendency" to some power entity) *or* to see the outcome as a tendential occurrence. I will briefly expand on these and similar conceptual issues in Section 2. It is my contention, however, that full clarity on such issues cannot be gained by talking *about* them. The case of Marx's law of profit, then, must have the double object of both finding out about Marx's notion of tendency and clarification of possible notions of tendency (Section 3). As we will see there appears to be room for more than one notion of tendency in Marx. While this is a difficulty for interpreting the content of Marx's theory of profit, it makes the case interesting for exploring the notion of tendency—and perhaps learning from it.

A crucial question of course is how we can do empirical research on the basis of tendency laws. Although this is not the subject of this paper, I will make, in Section 4, a few tentative remarks on this issue. Indeed this question motivates my concern for the notion of tendency law. Law? Isn't that a concept that we had happily extinguished from economic research? Yes. With it, indeed, theoretically informed explanation of empirical phenomena: mainstream economics is left with an ever so more elegant but sterile formal framework cut loose from reality (cf. Rosenberg 1992).

2. The Concept of "Tendency": Some General Notions

2.1 UNIVERSAL VERSUS SOCIAL-GENERAL THEORIES AND TENDENCIES VERSUS TRENDS

For a start I want to have two issues out of the way. The first is that tendencies *are* not trends. A trend is a statistical device imposed on or/and observed from empirical figures. On the other hand tendencies might be, but need not be, causative for trends. This needs emphasizing because some current mainstream economists as well as some philosophers of science (e.g., Popper 1957) mix up tendency and trend.

The second is that, in this paper, I am not concerned with so called "trans-historical laws" (sometimes, confusingly, called for short "historical laws"). I make a distinction between (1) trans-historical universal theories ("all human beings are mortal"), (2) historicist theories ("feudalism necessarily develops into capitalism") and (3) social-general theories ("within the domain of capitalism: if prices go up demand slows down"). All natural scientific theories are in fact of a trans-historical kind (evolutionary theories might be classified separately). Some psychological and social theories might be trans-historical. By their *aims* e.g., Freud's, and Maslow's theories are trans-historical. Much of neoclassical economics is by its *aim* trans-historical (as against the modern neoclassical institutionalism).

Much of the "floor" for the mainstream discussion of laws in the social sciences (including economics) has been set by Popper's *The Poverty of Historicism* (1957). For the time being I share his queries about historicist theories in this work. However, in taking "trans-historical" (i.e., universal) theories for the prototype of scientific theories generally, I think he goes much too far. Many (if not most) empirically interesting social scientific theories are of the "social-general" type.

This needs emphasizing, because my "tendency case," discussed in Section 3, is of a social-general type theory. In his *Capital* Marx sets out a theory that is particular to the capitalist mode of production.[2]

2.2 TENDENCIES: LAWS AS "NORMIC LAWS"

In the introduction I referred to problems of the application of a positivist methodology in economics (either in a verificationist or falsificationist variety). Since the 1980s such problems have been well documented in the economics methodology literature. Some years before that, Bhaskar (1975, 1979) provided a rigorous critique of empiricist positivism, centering the discussion on the notions of law and tendency. The kernel of this critique is rather simple.

The foremost problem lies in positivism's inheritance of the Humean concept of law, that is, that laws are constant conjunctions of events (plus some disputed contribution of mind). Though a constant conjunction of events is not always considered as a sufficient condition for a law, it is generally considered as at least a necessary condition. Related to this concept of law is the notion that laws find phenomenal expression as events or states of affairs, and that only the phenomenal is real (Bhaskar 1975, 64; 1979, 158).[3]

Thence the first principle of the positivist account of science is "*the principle of empirical-invariance*, viz. that laws are or depend upon empirical regularities." From this derive theories of causality, explanation, prediction, the symmetry of prediction with explanation, the development of science, etc. The second is *"The principle of instance-confirmation* (or falsification), viz. that laws are confirmed (or falsified) by their instances" (Bhaskar 1979, 159; cf. 1975, 127). From this derive various theories of demarcation and scientific rationality.

The kernel of Bhaskar's critique lies in his application of the distinction between closed and open systems. In the natural sciences (apart from astronomy) experimental situations have the character of closed systems, and it is only in such situations that a *constant* conjunction of events can occur. Outside it, in the open system of the "real world," disturbing or counteracting forces operate. (Thus, for example, the law of gravity will only be related to a constant conjunction in cases where there are no disturbing factors.) Laws then must either be restricted to closed systems (whence they are not universal or general laws), or the empirical status of laws in open systems must be doubted. In the first case the question is why the empirical should be privileged in closed systems:

> The empiricist is now caught in a terrible dilemma: for to the extent that the antecedents of law-like statements are instantiated in open systems, he must sacrifice either the universal character or the empirical status of laws. If, on the other hand, he attempts to avoid this dilemma by restricting the application of laws to closed systems (e.g., by making the satisfaction of a ceteris paribus clause a condition of their applicability), he is faced with the embarrassing question of what governs phenomena in open systems (Bhaskar 1975, 65).

Thus the argument is that from the perspective of empiricism there are no universal or general laws. But even if pure positivism is inapplicable, could not a pragmatic *attempt* be made to apply their criteria— as some methodologists (for example Klant 1972, 1984 and Blaug 1980, 1992) have in fact claimed to do? This would be decisive to the extent that with the positivist methodological criteria the object of study would get reduced to, or identified with, its empirical manifestations (cf. Bhaskar 1979, 167).

For science to be an intelligible activity, Bhaskar argues, the invariance principle must be dispensed with.[4] For Bhaskar the status of laws in both the natural and the social sciences is similar. They are tendencies, or as he also calls them: normic laws.[5] The crucial point is that laws are not open system empirical *regularities* and that open system empirical regularities are not laws: On the one hand, counteraction both by different laws and by accidental/contingent events may prevent the phenomenal expression of normic laws. On the other hand empirical regularities may be the joint outcome of the operation of several laws, or indeed be accidental or contingent; that is there may be empirical regularities for which there is no natural or systemic necessity.

But the similar status of laws in the natural and the social sciences (naturalism) does not imply that social objects can be studied in the same way as natural objects (scientism). The point, mentioned in almost every elementary economics textbook, is that the social sciences do not have the opportunity (ontologically or because of moral objections) to experiment. The domain of social science is not more complex than that of the natural sciences: they are both open systems; *ceteris paribus* and probability are not the unique inventions of economists. Nevertheless, natural scientists, if their conceptual apparatus is similar, may reach agreement on the events produced in an experimental situation (on their relevance and interpretation, different schools may diverge). However, the absence of closed systems in the social sciences seems to imply that there are no decisive test situations for social scientific theories. If that is so, the conclusion to draw from this is not that there are no social laws. There are laws in both the natural and the social sciences but they are tendential. The difference between natural and social science is that the conditions for the identification of laws are different (Bhaskar 1979, 163).

In summary: If one identifies laws with constant conjunctions of events then there are no non-superficial general laws, in natural science or in social science. This does not imply that there can be no laws (this would only be the case if the invariance principle were taken as axiomatic); it only implies that laws (which are always tendential) are *not immediately manifest* in open systems.

2.3   TENDENCIES: POWERS, EFFECTS AND PHENOMENAL RESULTS

This concept of laws as tendential laws, expounded in the previous section, appears to be akin to that of J. S. Mill. Bhaskar (1979, 161) seems to deny this; of course the philosophical foundation of such a concept may be different for them. For those methodologists writing on the issue of tendencies J. S. Mill is a common reference point. In this section, in order to further clarify different notions of tendency, as briefly set out in the introduction, I will reformulate in my own words what I take to be the gist of Mill's view on tendencies in his 1836 essay on method (reprinted in his 1844 collection of essays). My reformulation is restricted to some points relevant to the current discussion. For reasons that will become clear later on, I will make a strict difference between a result and an effect of a tendency. Mill does not always make this strict difference (cf. 1836, 337–38). Nevertheless this is an interpretation of Mill.

In the essay Mill seems to make no distinction in ontological status between the natural and the social to the extent that in both domains certain "powers" or "forces" are operative that produce (phenomenal) *results*. Some results are more complicated than others in that many different powers rather than one or a few different powers are operative so as to produce a result. If we had a full picture of the world[6] we would have for the sum of all powers (P) and results (R):

$$P(1, \ldots n) \rightarrow R(1, \ldots n) \qquad \text{(a)}$$

For each result taken in isolation (e.g., the Result numbered 127) we would know its cause or causes, for example,

$$P(2) \text{ and } P(7) \text{ and } P(8) \rightarrow R(127) \qquad \text{(b)}$$

Now step aside from this case of a full picture. Suppose that in reality we already have grounds to know that $P(i)$ is an operative causal power (borrowed from other sciences or ascertained via induction from within political economy), though we do not know (all of) "its" results. We don't even know if there exists at all a *result* (phenomenal) produced by just this one cause. Then let us take $P(i)$ in isolation (because we don't have a full picture and we wish to study causes one at a time— Mill 1836, 322). Now suppose we have information about the working of $P(i)$. In this case we may have grounds to argue that $P(i)$, in isolation, *tends* to produce or *tendentially* produces an *effect* $F(j)$:

$$P(i) -t\rightarrow F(j) \qquad \text{(c)}$$

(where $-t\rightarrow$ stands for tendency; or perhaps rather "tendential operation")

Note that both effects and results are occurrences even if we may not be able to perceive the *effect* (thus there may not be an *immediate* empirical counterpart for an effect). Note also that there is *no* difference in principle between the latter case of isolation (b) and the former full picture case (a). In fact the full picture case (a) should have been written as:

$$P(1, \ldots n) -t\rightarrow R(1, \ldots n) \qquad \text{(d)}$$

In the case of *result* R(127), in representation (b), we had three different causes P2, P7, P8 *each* producing a *tendency* towards some *effect*, perhaps counteracting each other, the outcome of which is *result* R(127).
    Thus we had, for example:

$$\left. \begin{array}{l} P(2) -t\rightarrow F(12) \\ P(7) -t\rightarrow F(17) \\ P(8) -t\rightarrow F(18) \end{array} \right\} R(127) \qquad \text{(e)}$$

In view of the ontological status of tendencies (see below), it is to be noted that, for Mill, effects may not be less true than results:

That which is true in the abstract, is always true in the concrete with proper *allowances* (Mill 1836, 326).

So far my interpretation of Mill.

In discussing tendencies and the related concepts, one may first of all make a distinction between their status as either epistemological or ontological or onto-epistemological (by the latter I refer to those philosophies (of science) that principally do not want to make a separation between epistemology and ontology—e.g., Hegelian dialectics). If one makes a separation between epistemology and ontology, then the least problematic of the "tendency-related concepts" is that of the phenomenological empirical "result." One might claim existence for the latter, even if we might not be able to perceive it in the absence of thought and theory and their cultural mediation (e.g., snow and sorts of snow, or a rate of profit and sorts of rates of profit). "Results" have at least an onto-epistemological existence. In an onto-epistemological framework "results" and all the other concepts: powers, tendencies, and effects, are in fact all equally problematic. These problems are "solved" in the presentation of their systematic connection—which is a presentation of both theoretical and methodological content. (For the purposes of this paper I will not dwell any more on this onto-epistemological position—see Reuten & Williams 1989, Part 1; Smith 1990, 1993; Arthur 1993.) I will proceed by making an (as if) separation between epistemology and ontology.

Far more problematic then, is the status of the concepts of power, tendency, and effect. Least problematic is the notion of "power." Usually one makes ontological existence claims for "powers" (forces, motives), that is, if one has at least some aim for explanation. What about tendencies and effects? It is clear that one can be an ontological realist for powers and results, while merely allotting an epistemological status for tendencies and effects (they are merely theoretical devices). Ruben (1982, 49–56) claims that this holds for Marx. In his interpretation of Marx, tendencies are merely theoretical simplifications in the face of a lack of

"full" knowledge of all the relevant conditions—tendency claims are in principle replaceable by claims about the conditions sufficient for the occurrence of the kind of event in question.... Under such ideal epistemic conditions, laws entail categorical claims about what actually does occur, and not just what tends to occur... (p. 51).

In terms of the representations above, Ruben's interpretation would mean that Marx might agree with representation (a), though not with representation (d). Nevertheless, Ruben writes, "At any given stage in

our acquisition of knowledge, we may have to accept laws of tendencies as the best we can do for the present..." (p. 55). Anticipating
the next section I can merely say that Ruben's interpretation is interesting, but that other interpretations equally fit the text. Marx
(1894F, 318) uses, for example, the phrase of "an actual tendency of
capitalist production."

Mill indeed seems an ontological realist about tendencies and effects.
(As is Bhaskar—the latter, however, conceives of effects and results as
in different ontological layers.)

These issues of ontology make up half the story of the different notions of tendencies. The other half is about the proper "place" for
"tendency" in a representation similar to (e) above. There are two
main possibilities here. (Note that in my Mill representations I did not
want to take sides as to these possibilities. It is even possible that Mill
takes, in fact, a third, intermediate position, between the two ones
indicated below.)

First: In representation (c) and (d) tendencies may be conceived of
as the operators of the powers. Thus tendencies "belong" to powers.
(It is even stronger to say that, inherently powers are always tendential
in character.) This may, more explicitly, be represented as:

$$P(i)[T] \rightarrow F(j) \qquad\qquad (f)$$

(where **T** implies the tendency is "attached" to the power)

Operating "through" the Effect in a Result (on which more than one
power operates—as in representation (e)—all or some of which we
may not know), we have

$$P(i)[T] \rightarrow F(j) \rightarrow R(j) \qquad\qquad (g)$$

This is what I call the *power notion of tendency*, or sometimes the *tendency as power* notion. It seems almost inevitable that this notion involves an ontological claim of a real existence of a tendency. (Or of a
power being inherently tendential in character.)[7] The Result in this
case may of course diverge from the Effect if we had more powers
operating on the result.

A second notion of tendency, *tendency as expression*, or *tendency as
outcome*, allots tendency to the Result. This may be represented as:

$$P(i) \rightarrow F(j) \rightarrow R(j)[T^*] \qquad\qquad (h)$$

(where **T*** implies tendential outcome)

Although this may involve an ontological claim about the existence of
the Effect (F), this need not be the case. The Effect may indeed be a
theoretical device (as Ruben, we have seen, interprets Marx).

Finally, with respect to Marx there is at least one further difficulty, related to the fact that *Capital* describes a multiple conceptual structure. When Marx uses the term "expression" this is often the expression of a force (power) *at that* conceptual moment in his presentation, perhaps at a still abstract level. Thus we may in fact have a "strain" of forces and expressions. Apparently "expression" would then be rather similar to Effect. However, expressions are often "preceded" by an "immediate" operation of the force/power, which is rather more similar to Effect. The term for a more final empirical "result" is the term "manifestation." There is of course not much point in spelling this out further before we get to the textual analysis, but the easiest way to preempt this is to say that in an equivalent of representation (h) there may follow a string of Effects and Results, of which the final term is a "manifestation" of a power or a string of powers.

3. The Case of Marx's Tendency Law of Profit

In *Capital*, Vol. 3 Marx sets out his famous "Law of the Tendential Fall in the Rate of Profit." The aim of this section is *not* to find out about the details of this theory of Marx, but to find out about the notion of tendency in this theory: is it a "power notion of tendency" or rather a "notion of tendency as outcome" (§2.3).[8]

This tendency law is presented in Part 3 of *Capital* III in three chapters: Chapter 13, the law itself; Chapter 14, counteracting factors; and Chapter 15, development of the law's internal contradictions. (In Marx's manuscript, from which Engels edited the final text after Marx's death, these three chapters are one continuous text—one chapter—not separated by headings or even a blank line.) I have used the following editions:

* Marx 1894G = *Das Kapital* III, German text, edited by Engels
* Marx 1894U = *Capital* III, English translation (of 1894G) by Untermann (1909), Lawrence & Wishart (the main English reference until 1981)
* Marx 1894F = *Capital* III, English translation (of 1894G) by Fernbach (1981), Penguin Books
* Marx 1894M = *Das Kapital* III, printed German manuscript (without Engels' editorial work), edited by Müller, Jungnickel, Lietz, Sander, and Schnickmann, 1992 (this text was not available to Untermann or Fernbach).

In my quotations from these texts all *italics* have been added, while an original emphasis is *underlined*. In general I quote from the English Fernbach translation. All the English quotes below have been checked against the German (1894G), and wherever appropriate additions have been made from the German {in curled brackets}. The 1894G text, again, has been checked against the manuscript text, any additions from the latter appear <in hooked brackets>. Occasional comments of mine within a quote are [in square brackets].

3.1 CHAPTER 13, THE LAW ITSELF

This chapter covers about twenty pages (1894F, pp. 318–338). It opens with a numerical example in which at a constant rate of surplus-value ($e = s/v$) and a rising composition of capital (c/v) the rate of profit ($r = s/(c + v)$ or $R/(c + v)$) is shown to decline. Rewriting the expression in the usual way (Marx does not do this) we have:

$$r = s/(c + v) = (ev)/(c + v) = e/(c/v + 1) \qquad (1)$$

After a comment of about one page the concept of tendency turns up. As we will see, the German text seems ambiguous as to the exact meaning of the term tendency. The Fernbach and the Untermann translations apparently take different positions here. Marx writes (Fernbach's translation of 1981):

> [*] The hypothetical series we constructed at the opening of this chapter therefore expresses the *actual tendency of* capitalist production {die wirkliche Tendenz}.[9] With the progressive decline in the variable capital in relation to the constant capital, *this tendency leads to* a rising organic composition of the total capital, and the *direct result* of this is that the rate of surplus-value, with the level of exploitation of labor remaining the same or even rising, is *expressed* in a steadily falling general rate of profit [**]. (We shall show later on (chap. 14) why this fall does not present itself in such an absolute form, but rather more in the tendency to a progressive fall.) The progressive tendency for the general rate of profit to fall is thus simply {nur} <u>the expression, peculiar to the capitalist mode of production,</u> of the progressive development of the social productivity of labor. This does not mean that the rate of profit may not fall temporarily for other reasons as well, but... [***] (Marx 1894F, 318–19)

Thus we have a tendency (**T**) of the capitalist mode of production (CMP), which has an immediate effect (F) to an expression (E):

$$\text{CMP}[\mathbf{T}] \rightarrow c/v \uparrow \rightarrow (F): eEr \downarrow \qquad (2)$$

The tendency seems to be the power or the operation of the power (see representations (f) and (g) in the previous section). The tendency [**T**] leads to a rising value composition of capital (c/v), the immediate effect (F) of which is that the rate of surplus-value (e) gets expressed (E) in a falling rate of profit (r).

In the translation from the German of the second sentence in the quotation above, there is an important difficulty of interpretation (see the passage from * to **) relating to one kernel of the concept of tendency (power versus expression). The German text reads:

[*] Die <Der> im Eingang hypothetisch aufgestellte Reihe <Fall> drückt also die wirkliche Tendenz der kapitalistischen Produktion aus. *Diese* <*Sie*> *erzeugt* ["produces"—what is it that produces: the tendency, *or* capitalist production?] mit der fortschreitenden relativen Abnahme des variabelen Kapitals gegen das konstante eine steigend <fortwäh­rende> höhere organische Zusammensetzung des Gesamtkapitals, deren *unmittelbare Folge* ist, daß die Rate des Mehrwerts bei gleichbleibendem und selbst bei steigendem Exploitationsgrad der Arbeit sich in einer beständig sinkenden allgemeinen Profitrate *ausdrückt.* [**] Marx 1894G, 222–223; 1894M, 287)

The German text (*diese erzeugt*) leaves room for another interpretation from Fernbach's, that is, the mode of production produces the rise in the organic composition of capital, and this is expressed in the (tendential) fall of the rate of profit. The 1909 translation by Untermann follows this interpretation:

[*] The hypothetical series drawn up at the beginning of this chapter expresses, therefore, the actual tendency of capitalist production. *This mode of production produces* a progressive relative decrease of the variable capital as compared to the constant capital, and consequently a continuously rising organic composition of the total capital. The *immediate result* of this is that the rate of surplus-value ... is represented by {expressed in} a continually falling general rate of profit [**]. (Marx 1894U, 212–213)

In my opinion the Untermann translation is the superior one as it fits the remainder of the quotation from ** onwards (esp. the italicized bit—see the quote from the Fernbach translation which from here on is rather similar to the Untermann translation). Thus we seem to have a "tendency as an expression" notion. The capitalist mode of production (CMP) inherently produces an increasing social productivity of labor (prodtt) and this gets expressed in a tendential fall of the rate of profit (r).

$$[\text{CMP: prodtt} \uparrow] \to c/v \uparrow \to (\text{F}): e(\text{E})r \downarrow [\textbf{T*}] \tag{3}$$

(Cf. representation h in §2.3). It remains to be seen if representation (3) is consistent with the further text of this and the next two chapters.

The larger part of the current chapter (chap. 13, the law as such) is devoted to the concomitance of a (tendential) decline in the rate of profit and a rise in the mass of profit. This concomitance is stressed over and again. We have a "double-edged law of a decline in the profit *rate* (r) coupled with a simultaneous increase in the absolute *mass* of profit (R), arising from the same reasons {causes}" (Marx 1894F, 326; 1894G, 230)

Apart from the quote above, the term *tendency* appears only twice in this chapter. One passage reads:

> Thus *the same* development in the social productivity of labor is *expressed*, with the advance of the capitalist mode of production, on the one hand *in a progressive tendency* for the rate of profit to fall and on the other in a constant [beständigem] growth in the absolute mass of the surplus-value or profit appropriated; so that by and large [im ganzen], the relative decline in the variable capital and profit goes together with an absolute increase in both. (Marx 1894F, 329; Marx 1894G, 233)

Again: the tendency seems the *expression* (now coupled, though, with a second expression). This may be represented as:

$$[\text{CMP: prodtt } \uparrow] \ldots \ldots (e = s/v) \begin{cases} (E)r \downarrow [T^*] \\ (E)R \uparrow \end{cases} \tag{4}$$

This is consistent with representation (3), that is the Tendency as Expression interpretation.[10]

This concludes the kernel of "the law as such" or, as Marx also calls it, "the general law" (e.g., 1894F, 339). For the next chapter (14) it is useful to somewhat further spell it out in terms of representations (3) and (4). In my reading this law is *not* merely about the falling rate of profit itself (its tendential fall). The general law of the CMP is the following (see the first three pages of chap. 13 from which I have quoted above):

α. The CMP brings about a (progressive) increase in the social productivity of labor (the production of absolute and relative surplus-value as expressed in the rate of surplus-value e);

β. A dominant way of realizing this (α) is by increasing the rate of surplus-value *concomitantly* on increasing the organic composition of capital.

γ. Its (α and β) *immediate* effect {Folge} is in a twofold expression, that is in: (a) a fall of the general rate of profit and (b) a rise in the social mass of profit.

This may be represented as:

$$[\text{CMP: prodtt } \uparrow \leftrightarrow e \uparrow] \rightarrow [e \uparrow \leftrightarrow c/v \uparrow] \rightarrow (F): e = s/v \begin{cases} (E)r \downarrow [T] \\ (E)R \uparrow \end{cases} \tag{5}$$

However, the law does not just operate in an immediate manner. (This is about α and β and γ—not merely about the latter or about the latter two.) So the law has the character of only/merely/just {nur} a *tendency* (cf. Marx 1894F, 319; 1894G, 223).

While in the chapter at hand the term tendency has not been used more than the three times referred to, it is nevertheless more often implicitly referred to as in e.g.:

> Viewed abstractly, the rate of profit might remain the same . . . (Marx 1894F, 336; 1894G, 239; 1894M, 319)

or:

> The rate of profit could even rise, if a rise in the rate of surplus-value was coupled with a significant reduction in the value of the elements of constant capital, and fixed capital in particular. *In practice*, however, [!] the rate of profit *will fall in the long run*, as we have already seen. (Marx 1894F, 337; 1894G, 240; compare 1894M, 319)

This last statement "in practice . . . already seen" is remarkable indeed. It is a rather definite statement about the expression of the law—or even its empirical manifestation. (I have found it peculiar considering especially the status of this chapter, i.e., prior to the theory about the counteracting causes that affect on the rate of profit.) It is interesting then to find that this particular sentence is not in Marx's manuscript.[11]

3.2   CHAPTER 14, COUNTERACTING FACTORS

The chapter on the "counteracting factors" {causes}, covers about ten pages (Marx 1894F, 339–348). It opens with an empirical observation, which is followed by a passage that is crucial to the interpretation of what Marx means by a tendency.

> If we consider the enormous development in the productive powers of social labor over the last thirty years {i.e., 1835–65} alone, compared with all earlier periods, and if we consider the enormous mass of fixed capital involved in the overall process of social production quite apart from machinery proper, then instead of the problem that occupied previous economists, the problem of explaining the fall in the profit rate, we have the opposite problem of explaining why this fall is not greater or faster. *Counteracting influences* must be at work, checking and canceling {aufheben} <durchkreuzen> the effect *{Wirkung}* of *the general law* and *giving it*[12] simply {nur} *the character of a tendency*, which is why we have described *the fall* in the general rate of profit *as a tendential fall*. The most general of these factors {Ursachen} are as follows. (Marx 1894F, 339; 1894G, 242; 1894M, 301–02)

This text sustains my interpretation of the general law as a tendency law (representation 5, as particularly comprising all the elements α and β and γ).[13] So we have the general law (chap. 13), which appears to be a tendential one because counteracting influences operate (chap. 14).

The causes are next commented upon under separate headings:

1. More intense exploitation of labor. Concerning an increase in the rate of surplus-value (e), we may distinguish: either such an increase *concomitant* on a rise in the composition of capital (c/v), with c increasing and v decreasing; or, such an increase *independent* of an increase of c (with c/v rising merely as a result). This section is about the latter. With e.g., increasing intensification of labor (or prolongation of the working day) one laborer works up more means of production (c), therefore e rises and, for the same amount of capital, the amount of labor decreases. Hence for a given capital less labor is being exploited more intensively. For a given capital, profit, or the mass of surplus value, s = ev. Each of the two factors on the righthand side, if I am right, are called contrary tendencies *by themselves.* This point, as I will show, is important to the general interpretation of "the law."

> It has already been shown, moreover, and this forms the real secret of the tendential fall in the rate of profit, that the procedures for producing relative surplus-value are based, by and large, either on transforming as much as possible of a given amount of labor into surplus-value or on spending as little as possible labor in general in relation to the capital advanced; so that *the same* reasons {Gründe} that permit the level of exploitation of labor to increase make it impossible to exploit as much labor as before with the same total capital. <The same number of laborers is being exploited more, but a decreased number of laborers is being exploited by the same capital.> These are the counteracting {*widerstreitenden*} tendencies which, while they act to bring about a rise in the rate of surplus-value, simultaneously lead [act] to a fall in the mass of surplus-value produced by a given capital, hence a fall in the rate of profit. (Marx 1894F, 340; 1894G, 243; 1894M, 302)

The last sentence is puzzling. First, "counteracting" seems rather: tendencies that counteract each other (rather than tendencies that act counter to an original tendency). Second, the bit after the comma is perhaps confusing: the fall in r is not the conclusion of the sentence. Rather the "widerstreitenden" tendencies operate on the rate of profit in a nonuniform way.[14]

So it seems now that we have two influences (of the same offspring) that counteract *the law*; and this gives the law a tendential character.

Apart from this we see here introduced a theme that we will meet throughout this chapter, which is that tendency and counteractions (or again counteractions by themselves) are discussed in terms of one and the *same* offspring.

Thus we had in the previous chapter, for the total social capital, a fall in the rate of profit, together with an increase in the mass of profit (due to accumulation of capital and a social rise in variable capital). Now, looking at a *given* capital amount we see e rising and s falling (with v going down). For a conclusion we have:

> It does not annul {aufheben} the general law. But it has the effect {er macht} that this law *operates {wirkt} more as a tendency*, i.e., as a law whose absolute realization is held up, delayed and weakened by counteracting factors {gegenwirkende Umstände}. . . . the same factors tend {streben} both to reduce the rate of profit and to slow down the movement in this direction. (Marx 1894F, 341–42; 1894G, 244–45)

This quotation, in combination with the first one provided from chap. 14 (Marx 1894F, 339), reveals either an inconsistency or a subtle differentiation. In the earlier quotation counteracting influences were said to cancel {aufheben} the law's *operation*, hence its tendency character. Now the "widerstreitenden" influences do not annul {aufheben}, but merely weaken the *general* law, hence the latter's operation as a tendency.

I now turn to the remaining "counteracting factors" on which, in the context of this paper, I can be briefer.

2. Reduction of wages below their value (1894F, 342; this is a section of two sentences only).

> We simply make an *empirical reference* to this point here, as . . . it has nothing to do with the general analysis of capital . . . It is none the less one of the most important factors in stemming [aufhalten] the tendency for the rate of profit to fall. (Marx 1894F, 342)

This is a contingent element, i.e., one exogenous to this law. It is characteristic for Marx to make such an empirical reference.

3. Cheapening of the elements of constant capital (1894F, 342–43). This very important factor is about the price effect of productivity increase on the *value* of constant capital, whence the change in the "technical" composition of capital is not translated in an "aliquot" change in the value composition. (On the general theoretical discussion of this issue, see Moseley 1991, chap. 1.) This issue is related to

> . . . the devaluation of *existing* capital. This too is a factor that steadily operates to stay {aufhalten} the fall in the rate of profit . . . We see here once again how the same factors {Ursachen} that produce

the tendency for the rate of profit to fall also moderate the realization of this tendency. (Marx 1894F, 342–43)

4. The relative surplus population (1894F, 343–44). This section is about the retardation of the rise in c/v, brought about by a rise in unemployment caused by any previous rise in c/v.

> The creation of such a surplus population is inseparable from the development of labor productivity and is accelerated by it, the same development as is expressed in the decline in the rate of profit. . . . here again the same reasons that produce the tendential fall in the rate of profit also produce a counterweight to this tendency, *which paralyses* its effect {Wirkung, operation} to a greater or lesser extent. (Marx 1894F, 343–44)

5. Foreign trade (1894F, 344–47). The cheapening of prices by foreign trade may affect the rise in the organic composition not being translated (to the same extent) in the value composition (c/v).

3.3 CONCLUSIONS TO THE CHAPTER ON THE COUNTERACTING FACTORS

Marx's conclusion is:[15]

> We have shown in general, therefore, how *the same causes* that bring about a fall in the general rate of profit provoke counter-effects {Gegenwirkungen hervorrufen, i.e. *call forth counteractions*} that inhibit this fall, delay it and in part even paralyse it. *These do not annul {aufheben} the law*, but *they weaken its* effect {Wirkung, operation}.[16] . . . The law operates therefore simply as a tendency, whose effect {Wirkung} is decisive only under certain particular circumstances and over long periods. {*So wirkt das Gesetz nur als Tendenz*, dessen Wirkung nur unter bestimmten Umständen und im Verlauf langer Perioden schlagend hervortritt.} <dessen Wirkung nur unter bestimmten Umständen und auf lange perioden ausgedehnt schlagend hervortritt.> (Marx 1894F, 346; 1894G, 249; 1894M, 308)

By now the possibility for another interpretation of Marx's notion of tendency is gradually being revealed. We have seen here and before that in the German text the term "Wirkung" (operation, action) is used consistently to describe the law. (In the English text this is almost consistently translated by "effect.") It would perhaps go too far to reverse back to the "power notion of tendency," nevertheless something like "operators of powers" (see the comment just before and after representation (f) in §2.3) or at least operation of powers (causes) seems at stake.

After all there seem two tendential elements in the operation law.

The first is that for various reasons internal to the law (endogenous reasons) an increase in the rate of surplus value (e) (either that independent of c/v, or that concomitant on c/v) dominates over the effect of c/v on the rate of profit. Hence r ↓ [T*]. The second is that for various reasons—again internal ones—the value composition of capital (c/v) may in fact not rise. It may seem attractive then to represent the tendential character of the general law as follows:

$$[\text{CMP: prodtt} \uparrow \leftrightarrow e \uparrow] \rightarrow [e \uparrow \leftrightarrow c/v \uparrow][\mathbf{T}] \rightarrow (\text{F}): e \begin{cases} (\text{E})r \downarrow [\mathbf{T}^*] \\ \\ (\text{E})R \uparrow \end{cases} \quad (6)$$

However, for the operation of the tendential element [e ↑ ↔ c/v ↑] [T] these have explicitly been called *counteracting tendencies* in the case of s = ev (Section 1 of Chap. 14) *only*; but even here not in a clear cut way. The term "widerstreitenden" tendencies may in fact refer to merely these *themselves* only (i.e., e and v). In the other sections Marx talks rather in terms such as counteractions, not in terms of counteracting tendencies. From this one might infer that representation (6) is wrong. We are stuck, however, with an ambivalence as to the meaning of "Wirkung" (operation, action).

Finally there is the issue of the empirical manifestation: "The law operates therefore simply as a tendency; it is only under certain particular circumstances—stretched over long periods—that its operation comes to the fore in an articulate way." (This is my understanding of Marx 1894M, 308.) Does this mean that this "tendency law" in the long run results in a fall of the rate of profit? This is far from obvious from the quotation. It seems rather that: within a sufficiently long span of time there will always occur a constellation of circumstances for which the rate of profit will actually fall; at other constellations, however, the rate of profit might rise. (Nowhere in the text is there, to be sure, a statement about the average development in the rate of profit). For the time being, therefore, r ↓ [T] in representation (5) seems not operational.

3.4   CHAPTER 15, DEVELOPMENT OF THE LAW'S INTERNAL
        CONTRADICTIONS

This very perceptive chapter comprises about 25 pages (1894F, 349–375). Again, I merely pick out the explicit references to the concept of tendency: there are only few here. Apparently, as we will see, this chapter is not very telling about the notion of tendency. Apparently, then, my current §3.4 cannot add much to the earlier conclusions. However, as I will indicate in my general conclusions, the fact that the term tendency is used so scarcely in this chapter *is* telling. The chapter is in four sections:

1. General considerations (1894F, 349–355). This is a general summary of the process of production in reference to *Capital* I. It provides comments on Ricardo's treatment of the issue.

2. The conflict between the extension of production and valorization (1894F, 355–359). In summary the argument in this section runs as follows. First. "As the capitalist mode of production develops, so the rate of profit falls" (p. 356)—as argued for in Chapter 13. This fall would be counteracted by a decrease in the value (cheapening) of the components of capital (either variable capital ↔ increase in relative surplus-value; or constant capital) (argued for in Chapter 14). This cheapening gives rise to the devaluation of the existing capital. The latter conditions the fall in the rate of profit, and delays it. Second. The mass of labor that capital can command does not depend on its value but rather on the mass of raw and ancillary materials, of machinery and elements of fixed capital, and of means of subsistence, out of which it is composed, whatever their value may be.

These (the first and second points) are two moments of the accumulation process: "sie schliessen einen Widerspruch ein, der sich in widersprechenden Tendenzen und Erscheinungen ausdrückt. Die widerstreitenden Agenten wirken gleichzeitig gegeneinander." This may be translated: they contain a contradiction that is *expressed in contradictory tendencies* and phenomena. The antagonistic agencies act simultaneously in opposition to one another. (Marx 1894G, 259; cf. 1894F, 357.) (Note that this is consistent again with the "tendency as expression" notion.) We have simultaneously: impulses to increase and decrease of the working population; decrease in the rate of profit and devaluation of capital which puts a stop to this fall; development of productivity and a higher composition of capital.

These factors may at one time assert themselves side by side in space, and at another assert themselves in time one after the other; periodically "the conflict of antagonistic agencies finds vent in crises. Crises are never more than momentary violent solutions for the existing contradictions, violent eruptions that re-establish the disturbed balance for the time being."[17]

In the next two sections the term "tendency" does not turn up any more, apart from in a comment on prevailing economic theory (1894F, 366). Section 4 is entitled "Supplementary Remarks" (1894F, 368–75). In the face of the empirical manifestation of the law, Section 3 deserves consideration:

3. Surplus capital alongside surplus population (1894F, 359–368). This section contains the presentation of the process of economic crisis in terms of: concentration, overaccumulation, and devaluation of capital; capital to lie idle or to be destroyed; breakdown of the credit system; stagnation (Stockung) in production; a fall in wages. For our purposes the following quote is important:

> The stagnation in production that has intervened prepares the ground—within the capitalist limits—for a later expansion of production. *And so we go round the whole circle once again.* (Marx 1894F, 363–64; 1894G, 265)

Thus it seems that the fall in the profit rate is a periodical matter rather than a trend-like phenomenon (as quite some commentators on Marx have interpreted him). Of course the "missing sentence" in Marx's manuscript, referred to at the end of my §3.1, backs up my conclusion).

4. Marx's and Marxian Theory: Concluding Remarks

4.1 GENERAL CONCLUSIONS TO THE CASE

Chapter 15 of Marx's *Capital* III has presented the "tendency law" in its cyclical expression, that is in economic crisis/stagnation. Especially the devaluation of capital and the destruction of capital in crises/stagnation is highlighted—the effect of which is a rise in the rate of profit: "And so we go round the whole circle once again."

Why is it that in this last chapter the term tendency has been so scarcely used by Marx? Here the previous two chapters come together. If Marx's were a "power notion of tendency" then we might expect that term to have been used over and again in Chapter 15. For the "expression notion" this may be different. In fact Chapter 15 is about expressions throughout. However, these are the expressions of a complex. Here it is shown how the rate of profit does not fall continuously, but rather cyclically. Thus, we simply do not have the, say, unilateral profit fall of Chapter 13. In Chapters 14 and 15 we see *why* the rate of profit does not fall continuously, and why, therefore, Chapter 13 must formulate a "tendency law."

This backs up my first conclusion: "tendency" refers only to "the general law" of Chapter 13—so it is used merely in reference to that general law. There are no "countertendencies." There are, however, counteracting causes. The latter have been traced, where relevant, to the same offspring of the forces behind the tendential fall in the rate of profit itself—thus the interconnection has been sought.

There are, nevertheless, two exceptions to this. One apparent and one inconsistent to my conclusion. The first has been dealt with in §3.3 (e and v as counteracting themselves). The second is the phrase "*contradictory tendencies*" (1894F, 357) referred to in §3.4 under 2.

A second conclusion relates to the ambivalence as to the meaning of "Wirkung" (operation, action) of "the law"—pointed at in §3.3. It seems after all that the term operation is linked to the expression of the law. This is not so surprising if indeed Marx's is *not* a "power notion of tendency." If we have a force (non-tendential in itself, or ontologically non-tendential) which is not expressed immediately, then indeed we might well conceive of its "working" as tendential. Therefore, my second conclusion is that a "tendency" in the case of Marx discussed here is not a power or force. Tendency refers to the resulting *expression* of force (the working/operation of forces being laid down in a law) to the extent that this expression does not work out univocally, but rather in a contradictory way.

A third and tentative concluding remark concerns the ontology-epistemology question referred to in §2.3. In the text studied I have found no evidence at all that Marx's concept of tendency is an ontological one. It would be rash to conclude from this that his must therefore be an epistemological one (cf. Ruben referred to in §2.3). On the other hand I have also no evidence from this case, that Marx's notion of tendency is not an epistemological one.

4.2   MARXIAN THEORY AND EMPIRICAL RESEARCH: SOME FURTHER AND TENTATIVE CONCLUDING REMARKS

How might one do empirical research on the basis of tendency laws? Having considered the case above, one is bound to be left with this query. This issue deserves a full separate paper, nevertheless I will make a few tentative remarks. In order to make sense of empirical research in the light of tendency laws, I believe one is almost forced to take a position similar to Lawson's (1989, 1992) reworking of Kaldor's notion of "stylized facts." Although Lawson philosophically adopts a realist position to the extent that powers and tendencies have ontologically a real existence, this position is not essential to the problem of empirical research that I am considering.

A tendency for Lawson is "a power that may be exercised and yet unrealised in manifest phenomena." Powers themselves exist "by virtue of certain enduring structures" (1989, 62). Laws then are defined similar as with Bhaskar and Mill (§2.2 above). Although the effects of tendencies, he says, will frequently be modified or hidden by the operation of irregular countervailing mechanisms and so forth, their persistency coupled with the irregular operation of the countervailing influences may allow their effects to "shine through". And to the extent that any manifest phenomenon appears to reveal some degree of uniformity, generality or persistency . . . it would seem to provide a *prima facie* case for supposing that some enduring generative mechanisms are at work. . . . And conceptualisations of such partial regularities, of course, are the obvious candidates for representation as "stylized facts." . . . stylized facts can provide an access to enduring things as indications of possible manifestations of the effects of (possibly a combination of) causal tendencies (Lawson 1989, 65–66).

I believe that a similar procedure is currently the best we have, that is, if we take seriously the notion of tendency law without refraining from serious empirical work on their basis. Indeed, as Lawson indicates, Kaldor (after 1966) was concerned about the increasingly formalistic and sterile non-empirical economics of his day—times have not changed in this respect (see e.g., Rosenberg 1992).

I guess that anyone studying Chapters 13–15 of Marx's *Capital* III (the case of Section 3 above) cannot but be impressed by the conscientious and thorough exhibition of that theory up to minutest detail (given its methodological level of abstraction). It may also appear a very realistic theory, even for those who would not want to share its value theoretical notions. (Schumpeter e.g., it seems, owes much to Marx's approach—see his 1943.)

Nevertheless, that theory is insufficient and must be developed further. Marx's *Capital* is indeed an unfinished project: (a) from the point of view of his own aims (Reuten 1997); (b) in terms of the unclarity of the extent of its theoretical break from classical economics (Reuten 1993); (c) in terms of the unclarity of its methodological break from either "analysis" in Ricardian vein, or dialectics in Hegel's traces (Murray 1988; Smith 1990, 1993; Arthur 1993a, 1993b). One problem, and challenge, is that the latter two aspects hang together.

Such theoretical development cannot be carried out in the absence of thorough empirical research. Indeed (restricting myself to the theory of the case of Section 3) I believe that the kind of empirical research as carried out by Weisskopf (1979), Wolff (1986), Moseley (1991) and Duménil & Lévy (1993, 1997) must be carried out. Especially if these are combined with inter-comparisons and discussion as in Moseley (1991).

Of course, one can have many theoretical objections to such empirical research. Not merely because of their particular operationalization of the theory and the many ad hoc decisions that one is bound to make in the face of poor statistics. One may foremost object to the empirical application of an incomplete theory (as indicated above). I believe that one must have reservations here. However, at the same time I am convinced that such empirical research must be carried out and cannot await theory development.

One argument for this is in the concern for the reclaiming of a "real-world political economy," which comprises the explanation of stylized facts. Of course *what* these latter are is not independent of a (theoretic) discourse. However, their communication and explanation affect the social discourse.

The, related, other argument is in the cross fertilization of methodological, theoretical and empirical research. I firmly believe that methodological, theoretical, and empirical research must be carried out alongside each other, short of the ideal of a really integrated triple approach.

Notes

Acknowledgement: I would like to thank Chris Arthur, Martha Campbell, Paul Mattick Jr., Patrick Murray, Fred Moseley, and Tony Smith for the provocative as well as enjoyable discussions at the "International Symposium on Marxian Theory IV." I am grateful to Fred Moseley for a second round comment. This paper has also much benefitted from the stimulation and the thorough comments of Mary Morgan.

1. Bhaskar 1975 and Cartwright 1989 suggest that the concept of tendency might be useful to grasp explanation in the sciences generally.
2. There are a few exceptions to this: sometimes he discusses the historical emergence of an institution; only rarely does he make a remark about a future society. These exceptions, however, do not concern the systematic of the general theory and have the status of illustrations (Smith 1990). Generally, in his work, Marx conceptually differentiates his categories into trans-historical ones and those applied to a particular epoch or mode of production (see Murray 1988, chap. 10, on determinate abstractions and Arthur 1986, 11–12 and passim, on first-order and second-order mediations). In my case of Section 3 there are no such exceptions: all abstractions are determinate ones.
3. The latter are "empirical results" in the terminology of my next paragraph 2.3.
4. This is what he himself does in expounding his own transcendental realist philosophy of science. However, to agree with Bhaskar's critique of empiricist positivism, one need not subscribe to that philosophy.
5. Note that the basis of *his* argument for this is an ontological distinction of causal laws from patterns of events (Bhaskar 1975, 66; 1979, 11–14). For a critique see Reuten & Williams 1988, 20–22.
6. According to Mill we may hope to reach such an (ideal) full picture via an "upwards" process of induction and a "downwards" process of deduction (Mill 1836, 324–25).

7. In my own political economic cum methodological work (Reuten & Williams 1989 and Reuten 1991) I have used the concept of force/power as inherently tendential. The philosophical basis for it, however, is onto-epistemological rather than ontological.

8. Reading the title above makes one wonder how much weight should be given to that already: "law of the tendency" (the heading in Marx's manuscript reads: "Law of the tendential fall in the general rate of profit with {im} the progression of capitalist production"). In the text this phrase does not turn up any more. Fine & Harris (1979, chap. 4) prefer the term "the law of the tendency of the rate of profit to fall (TRPF)" (see also Fine 1982, chap. 8).

9. The phrase "expresses the *actual* tendency," apparently leaves room for a tendency that does not actualize itself. In Hegelian jargon the terms "wirklich" and "actual" have a quite heavy connotation. However, in the course of this and the following chapters the connotation of this term is not played upon any more. So this seems not very important.

10. The other quotation seems again consistent with the Tendency as Expression interpretation: "We have seen how it is that *the same* reasons that produce a tendential fall in the general rate of profit also bring about an accelerated accumulation of capital and hence a growth in the absolute magnitude or total mass of the surplus labour (surplus-value, profit) appropriated by it. Just as everything is expressed upside down in competition, and hence in the consciousness of its agents, so is this law—I mean this inner and necessary connection between two apparently contradictory phenomena" (1894F, 331; 1894G, 235).

11. At least not in this part of the manuscript. I have checked merely these three chapters. (With respect to the point at hand, it is of secondary interest that pp. 1894F, 332–338 (from the * on p. 332 onwards) or 1894G, 236–241 (at the end of p. 235 separated with a line) have been removed from the second part of the manuscript (1894M, 316–321) to here.) The remarkable sentence at hand has apparently been added so as to link up two subparagraphs of the manuscript.

12. "It" refers to the law and not to the effect (Wirkung): "Es müssen gegenwirkende Einflüsse im Spiel sein, welche die Wirkung des allgemeinen *Gesetzes* durchkreuzen und aufheben und *ihm* nur den Charakter einer Tendenz geben, weshalb wir auch den Fall der allgemeinen Profitrate als einen tendenziellen Fall bezeichnet haben" (1894G, 242).

13. An argument for this point is in the clause "which is why we have described the fall in the general rate of profit as a tendential fall;" this would simply be a tautology if the law were not to comprise the α and β elements.

14. "Dies sind die widerstreitenden <widerstrebenden> Tendenzen, die, während sie auf eine Steigerung in der Rate des Mehrwerts, gleichzeitig auf einen Fall der von einem gegebenen Kapital erzeugten Masse des Mehrwerts und daher der Rate des Profits hinwirken" (1894G, 243; 1894M, 302).

15. The last one and a half page of Section 5 of this chapter seem clearly concluding to this and the previous sections. There follows nevertheless a "supplementary" Section 6 (The increase in share capital—some 8 sentences) in which it is stated that the rate of profit for share capital, which is lower than the average, does not enter the general rate of profit. If it did, then the latter would even be lower than the prevailing general rate. It seems that this Section 6 has rather the character of a footnote.

Apart from the concluding statement to be quoted in the main text, there is the following: "The tendential fall in the rate of profit is linked with a tendential rise in the rate of surplus-value, i.e., in the level of exploitation of labour. . . . The profit rate does not fall because labour becomes less productive but rather because it becomes more productive" (Marx 1894F, 347). The first part of this quote, however, is awkward because so far nothing has been presented that counters a rise in the rate of exploitation. (This is also the first and last time that a 'tendential rise in the rate of surplus value' is being alluded to.)

16. Note again the same inconsistency about the annulment {Aufhebung} of the law.

17. The first sentence of this quote is from the Untermann (p. 249) and the second from the Fernbach translation (p. 357). Immediately after this quote the term tendency turns up once more: "To express this contradiction in the most general terms, it consists in the fact that the capitalist mode of production tends towards an absolute development of the productive forces . . ." I pay no attention to this, as in the manuscript we find, instead of the term "tendency," the phrase "ein streben mit sich führt" (1894M, 323).

References

Arthur 1986. Christopher J. Arthur, *Dialectics of Labor; Marx and His Relation to Hegel* (Oxford/New York: Basil Blackwell 1986).

―――― 1993a. "Hegel's *Logic* and Marx's *Capital*," in F. Moseley (ed.), 1993, pp. 63–88.

―――― 1993b. "Negation of the Negation in Marx's *Capital*," *Rethinking Marxism* 6:4, 49–65.

Bellofiore 1997. Riccardo Bellofiore (ed.) *Marxian Economics: A Centenary Appraisal* (London & New York: Macmillan 1997).

Bhaskar 1975. Roy Bhaskar, *A Realist Theory of Science* (Sussex/New Jersey: Harvester/Humanities 1978).

―――― 1979. *The Possibility of Naturalism; A Philosophical Critique of the Contemporary Human Sciences* (Sussex: Harvester 1979).

Blaug 1980. Mark Blaug, *The Methodology of Economics; or How Economists Explain* (Cambridge: Cambridge University Press 1980).

―――― 1992. idem, second edition.

Cartwright 1989. Nancy Cartwright, *Nature's Capacities and Their Measurement* (Oxford: Clarendon Press 1992).

Duménil & Lévy 1993. Gérard Duménil & Dominique Lévy, *The Economics of the Profit Rate: Competition, Crises and Historical Tendencies in Capitalism,* (Aldershot UK: Edward Elgar 1993).

―――― 1997. "The Three Dynamics of the Third Volume of Marx's Capital," in Bellofiore 1997.

Fine 1992. Ben Fine, *Theories of the Capitalist Economy* (London: Edward Arnold 1992).

Fine & Harris 1979. Ben Fine & Laurence Harris, *Rereading Capital* (London: Macmillan 1979).

Hausman 1992. Daniel M. Hausman, *The Inexact and Separate Science of Economics.* (Cambridge/New York etc.: Cambridge University Press 1992).

Klant 1972. J. J. Klant, *Spelregels voor Economen; de logische structuur van economische theorieën*, 2nd edition 1978 (Leiden: Stenfert Kroese 1978).

——— 1984. *The Rules of the Game; The Logical Structure of Economic Theories.* (Cambridge: Cambridge University Press, 1984).

Lawson 1989. Tony Lawson, "Abstraction, Tendencies and Stylised Facts: A Realist Approach to Economic Analysis," *Cambridge Journal of Economics.* 13: 59–78.

——— 1992. "Abstraction, Tendencies and Stylised Facts," in P. Ekins & M. Max-Neef (eds.), *Real-life Economics; Understanding Wealth Creation.* 21–37 (London/New York: Routledge 1992).

Marshall 1890. Alfred Marshall, *Principles of Economics.* 8th ed. 1820 (London: Macmillan 1972).

Marx 1894G. Karl Marx (ed.) F. Engels, *Das Kapital, Kritik der Politischen Okonomie, Band III, Der Gesamtprozesz der kapitalistischen Produktion.* MEW 25 (Berlin: Dietz Verlag 1972).

——— 1894U. *Capital, A Critique of Political Economy, Volume III, The Process of Capitalist Production as a Whole;* trans. of 1894G by Ernest Untermann (1909) (London: Lawrence & Wishart 1974).

——— 1894F. *Capital, A Critique of Political Economy, Volume III;* trans. of 1894G by David Fernbach (1981) (Harmondsworth: Penguin Books 1981).

——— 1894M. "Gesetz des tendenziellen Falls der allgemeinen Profitrate im Fortschritt der kapitalistischen Produktion," in M. Müller, J. Jungnickel, B. Lietz, C. Sander, und A. Schnickmann (eds.), Karl Marx, Ökonomische Manuskripte 1863–1867, Text Teil 2, *Karl Marx, Friedrich Engels Gesamtausgabe (MEGA)*, Zweite Abteilung, Band 4, Teil 2: 285–340 (Berlin/Amsterdam: Dietz Verlag/Internationales Institut für Sozialgeschichte Amsterdam, 1992).

Mill 1836. John Stuart Mill, "On the Definition of Political Economy; and On the Method of Investigation Proper To It," *London and Westminster Review,* October 1936, repr. in J. S. Mill, *Essays on Some Unsettled Questions of Political Economy* (1844[1], 1877[3]); text of 1844 repr. in, J. M. Robson (ed.), *Collected Works of John Stuart Mill,* vol. IV (1967): 309–339 (Toronto/London: University of Toronto Press/Routledge & Kegan Paul, 1975).

Murray 1988. Patrick Murray, *Marx's Theory of Scientific Knowledge* (New Jersey/London: Humanities Press 1990).

Moseley 1991. Fred Moseley, *The Falling Rate of Profit in the Postwar United States Economy* (London: Macmillan 1991).

——— (ed.) 1993. *Marx's Method in Capital: A Reexamination* (New Jersey: Humanities Press 1993).

——— 1994. "Marx's Economic Theory: True or False? A Marxian Response to Blaug's Appraisal," in Moseley (ed.), *Heterodox Economic Theories: True or False* (Brookfield, VT: Edward Elgar 1994).

Popper 1957. Karl Popper, *The Poverty of Historicism,* 2nd ed. 1960 (London and Henley: Routledge & Kegan Paul 1976).

Reuten 1991. Geert Reuten, "Accumulation of Capital and the Foundation of the Tendency of the Rate of Profit to Fall," *Cambridge Journal of Economics,* 15:1, 79–93.

——— 1993. "The Difficult Labor of a Theory of Social Value; Metaphors and Systematic Dialectics at the Beginning of Marx's *Capital,*" in Moseley (ed.) 1993: 89–113.

——— 1996. Geert Reuten, "A Revision of the Neoclassical Economics Methodology: Appraising Hausman's Mill-Twist, Robbins-Gist, and Popper-Whist," in *The Journal of Economic Methodology*, 3:1, pp. 39–67, 1996.

—— 1997. "Destructive Creativity; institutional arrangements of banking and the logic of capitalist technical change in the perspective of Marx's 1894 law of profit," in Bellofiore 1997.

Reuten & Williams 1988. Geert Reuten & Michael Williams, *The Value-Form Determination of Economic Policy: A Dialectical Theory of Economy, Society and State in the Capitalist Epoch* (Amsterdam: Grüner 1988).

—— 1989. *Value-Form and the State; the Tendencies of Accumulation and the Determination of Economic Policy in Capitalist Society* (London/New York: Routledge 1989).

Rosenberg 1992. Alexander Rosenberg, *Economics—Mathematical Politics or Science of Diminishing Returns?* (Chicago/London: University of Chicago Press 1992).

Ruben 1982. David-Hillel Ruben, "Marx, Necessity and Science," in G. H. R. Parkinson (ed.), *Marx and Marxisms*, 39–56 (Cambridge: Cambridge University Press 1982).

Schumpeter 1943. Joseph A. Schumpeter, *Capitalism, Socialism and Democracy*, 4th ed. 1954 (London: Unwin University Books 1966).

Smith 1990. Tony Smith, *The Logic of Marx's Capital; Replies to Hegelian Criticisms* (Albany: State University of New York Press 1990).

—— 1993. "Marx's *Capital* and Hegelian Dialectical Logic," in Moseley (ed.) 1993, 15–36.

Weisskopf 1979. Thomas E. Weisskopf, "Marxian Crisis Theory and the Rate of Profit in the Postwar U.S. Economy," *Cambridge Journal of Economics*, 3: 341–78.

Wolff 1986. Edward N. Wolff, "The Productivity Slow Down and the Fall in the Rate of Profit in the U.S. Economy 1947–76," *Review of Radical Political Economics*, 18, 87–109.

7

Marx's Theory of Social Forms and Lakatos's Methodology of Scientific Research Programs

Tony Smith

1. Introduction

Imre Lakatos's work has had an influence far beyond the confines of the philosophy of science. As Deborah Redman writes,

> Lakatos is currently the most popular philosopher of science among economists. According to Rosenberg, Milton Friedman's positive methodology is being supplanted by Lakatos's methodology of scientific research programs (MSRP). At any rate, the Kuhnian wave of the seventies is being swallowed up by the Lakatosian program. (Redman 1991, 142)

There have been a number of attempts to comprehend mainstream economics in Lakatosian terms. (Latsis 1976, de Marchi and Blaug, 1991) In contrast, the extent to which the Marxian study of capitalism can be interpreted from this perspective has hardly been explored.[1] In the following sections some provisional steps in this direction will be taken. I shall first introduce a reading of Marx's *Capital* that emphasizes the systematic dialectic of economic categories unifying that work. I shall then ask whether we can arrive at a better understanding of Marx's systematic dialectic through considering how it contributes to a scientific research program in Lakatos's sense of the term. Along the way I shall comment on certain shortcomings in Lakatos's framework, and compare the Marxian research program to neoclassical economics.

Lakatos's work can be understood as a response to the dead-end of naive falsificationism, according to which theories are tested by deducing predictions and then investigating whether the events predicted occur. If they do, this does not verify the theory, for other theories may lead to the prediction as well. But if they do not, the proposed theory is falsified. Scientific progress on this view is a matter of abandoning theories that have been falsified (along with those that are in principle not falsifiable and those that involve only trivial predictions). Naive falsificationism runs into insurmountable difficulties. A prediction regarding concrete occurrences can be derived from theoretical propositions only if a set of conditions specifying the relevant context is added to the argument. Also, a set of auxiliary hypotheses must be accepted as true for any test to be run. This means that disconfirmation of a prediction need not imply that the theory in question is mistaken. The problem could lie with the specifications of the background conditions or with the auxiliary hypotheses. If one is willing to play with these specifications and hypotheses enough, it is possible to save *any* theory from disconfirmation.

For Lakatos, science is not simply a matter of theories, predictions, and confirmations/disconfirmations. The fundamental unit of science is the *research program*, not the individual theory. (Lakatos 1970) A research program includes a hard core, consisting of the basic postulates taken as inviolable by all those participating in the research program; a positive and a negative heuristics, which guide researchers towards the questions that ought to be pursued and the intellectual tools that ought to be employed (and away from questions and tools that ought to be avoided) (Lakatos 1968, 168–73); and a protective belt, consisting of the evolving theories, auxiliary hypotheses, and empirical conventions that make up the "body" of the research program.[2] A research program can be said to make *theoretical progress* if predictions of novel facts are generated within its protective belt. It can be said to make *empirical progress* if those predictions are then corroborated (Lakatos 1970, 118). Finally, there is *heuristic progress* whenever changes in the protective belt are consistent with the hard core of the program and not ad hoc suppositions (Lakatos 1978b, 33–4). All of these notions of progress are to be measured relative to competing research programs.

It is now time to consider Marx's *Capital* in the light of Lakatos's framework.

2. Marx's Systematic Dialectic and the Hard Core of Lakatos's Scientific Research Programs

A LAKATOSIAN READING OF THE SYSTEMATIC DIALECTIC IN *CAPITAL*

A systematic ordering of economic categories can be traced in Marx's *Capital*. It is not possible here to do more than enumerate the main stages of this ordering; more will be said about certain parts of it below. All of the stages in Marx's systematic reconstruction of the capitalist mode of production are determinations of *the value-form*, the most basic structure of generalized commodity exchange. Under this social form labor is undertaken privately. The social necessity of labor can be proven only subsequently, with the selling of the produced commodity. The determinations of the value-form are *the commodity form, the money form,* and the *capital form,* which incorporates the other two. The capital form is in turn developed in three categorial stages. In the first, *capital in production,* Marx considers the dynamic of the capital/wage labor relation, examining labor power as a commodity, exploitation, the labor process, and the drive to accumulate. The second categorial level in the account of the capital form is *capital in circulation.* Topics considered here include the time it takes a unit of capital to proceed through the various stages of accumulation, and the intertwining of investments in the production of means of production with investments in the production of means of consumption. The final determination of the capital form is *capital in distribution,* under which heading Marx discussed how surplus produced by some units of capital is distributed to other units. This takes place within the sphere of industrial capital and between industrial capital and merchant capital, bank capital, and landed capital. On this level of the theory Marx explored how decisions that are rational from the standpoint of an individual unit of capital often have irrational results for the system as a whole, culminating in falling rates of profit and economic crises.

What role does this ordering of the basic social forms of capitalism play in the Marxian theory of capitalism as a whole? Lakatos's methodology of scientific research programs suggests one answer: Marx's dialectic of social forms provides the central part of the "hard core" of the Marxian research program devoted to the study of capitalism.

For Lakatos, the hard core of a research program consists of basic postulates underlying work in the "protective belt" of the research program, postulates taken as relatively inviolable by those contributing to the program. The systematic dialectic of social forms fulfills both criteria. The ordering traces "the intrinsic connection existing between economic categories or the obscure physiology, so to speak, of the bourgeois system" (Marx 1862–63, 165). The value-form, the commodity form, the money form, and the capital form provide the over-arching context within which concrete Marxian research into capitalism, both theoretical and empirical, is performed. The account of these forms thus provides the ultimate premises for arguments regarding concrete institutions and events in capitalism, premises that would be given up by defenders of the program very grudgingly.

In some cases, Marx's argument is that certain social forms are necessary conditions of the possibility of others. Money, for example, is a necessary precondition of capital (Campbell 1993). For a Marxist, this is an empirical claim, not a divine revelation or a transcendental deduction.[3] Nonetheless, within the Marxian program it is difficult to conceive of any ordinary empirical test that could call this assertion into question. Another sort of claim is that social agents operating within certain social forms necessarily tend to act in certain ways. Here too the force of the concept of necessity is so great that no ordinary empirical test calling the claim into question would be accepted by someone working within the research program. If empirical evidence were presented purporting to show that the tension between money as a measure of value and money as a means of circulation had been abolished in capitalism, or that capitalism no longer involved exploitation, no Marxist would accept that evidence at face value. All would assume that the evidence in question was suspect in some fundamental way.

This does not mean that one needs to have studied *Capital* from the standpoint of systematic dialectics prior to undertaking concrete theoretical and empirical work in Marxism. It is certainly possible to contribute to a research program without ever explicitly reflecting on its hard core. Nor am I claiming that anyone who wishes to reflect on the hard core of the Marxian program must turn to systematic dialectics. Most theorizing requires no more than a brief list of assumptions relevant to the task at hand. However, if one wishes to consider in a comprehensive fashion the propositions making up the hard core assumptions of Marxian research regarding capitalism, systematic dialectics has no serious competitors. (Smith 1990, 1993a, b; Reuten and Williams 1989; Arthur 1993; but see Mattick 1993)

THE HARD CORE AND THE COMPARATIVE ASSESSMENT OF SCIENTIFIC
RESEARCH PROGRAMS

For Lakatos, the propositions making up the hard core provide the ultimate assumptions without which concrete theoretical and empirical work cannot be undertaken. In Lakatos's framework, however, these propositions play next to no role in the comparative assessment of different research programs. One program is judged to be superior to another if it generates theories from which predictions of novel facts can be derived, and if those predictions are later corroborated. The theories and predictions should be consistent with the hard core assumptions of the program, but otherwise those assumptions play no role in assessing programs. I believe that this is mistaken. *Ceteris paribus,* one research program is superior to another if (a) the hard core assumptions of one specify real mechanisms in the object realm under

investigation, while those of the other do not, or (b) the specifications
of a set of real mechanisms in the hard core of one program are superior to those proposed in the competing program. I shall illustrate
these points by means of a comparison between the hard cores of
Marxism and neoclassical economics, considering in turn an instrumentalist and a non-instrumentalist reading of the latter.

a) If scientific progress is judged primarily by whether predictions
of novel facts are corroborated, why should we care whether the ultimate assumptions underlying our theories are realistic or not? These
assumptions are in effect instruments used to help derive predictions.
The only relevant question would seem to be whether they effectively
perform the task assigned to them. In this sense Lakatos's account of
the role of the hard core in the methodology of scientific research
programs appears fully compatible with an instrumentalist perspective
(Hands 1991, 71).

Neoclassical economics is plagued by a deep schizophrenia on the
question of instrumentalism (Reuten 1996). As we shall see, there are
those who take its postulates as an accurate representation of human
nature. There are many others who willingly concede that its ultimate
assumptions do not present anything like a realistic picture of economic life. Milton Friedman, for instance, finds a theory with completely unrealistic assumptions quite acceptable, as long as it generates
corroborated predictions.

There are also neoclassicals who cannot quite bring themselves to
accept instrumentalism, even when the logic of their position demands
it. Blaug defends the Lakatosian position "that assumptions do not need
to be tested directly, although it might be useful if they could be, *that
in the final analysis only predictions matter,* and that the validity of an
economic theory is established when the predictions to which it gives
rise are repeatedly corroborated by the evidence." (Blaug 1992, 68;
emphasis added) If "only predictions matter," then *any* assumption, no
matter how wildly implausible, should be accepted as valid if it underlies theories from which corroborated predictions are derived. As far
as I can tell, this is quite inconsistent with the following assertion: "So
long as the tests of the accuracy of predictions remain ambiguous—
that is to say, forever—it will remain important also to test the descriptive accuracy of assumptions and to take the results of these tests seriously"
(Blaug 1992, 233). This implies that assumptions can have explanatory force independent of their role in generating predictions, and
therefore are relevant to comparative assessments of competing research
programs. How this assertion coheres with Blaug's professed
Lakatosianism is unclear.[4]

When we turn to Marx, no evidence of this sort of schizophrenia can be found. Marx accepted a realist agenda.[5] This extends to the propositions making up the hard core of his theory of capitalism, including the systematic ordering of social forms. Each determination of a social form in *Capital* explicates real mechanisms operating in the capitalist mode of production. The presentation of social forms can be assessed in these terms apart from its role in explicating background assumptions for predictions of novel facts.

How is the phrase "real mechanism" to be understood here? Andrew Sayer writes,

> Within social structures there are particular 'positions' associated with certain roles. It is particularly important to distinguish the occupant of a position from the position itself. One of the most pervasive illusions of everyday thinking derives from the attribution of the properties of the position, be they good or bad, to the individual or institution occupying it. Whatever effects result, it is assumed that particular *people* must be responsible; there is little appreciation that the structure of social relations, together with their associated resources, constraints or rules, may determine what happens, even though these structures only exist where people reproduce them. (Sayer 1984, 84–85)

In this context the term "mechanisms" refers to the various ways structures of social relations may "determine what happens." Given a structure of generalized commodity production, for example, the mechanism referred to as "the law of value" kicks in; socially average labor productivity will tend to govern exchange relations. Given the structure of the capital/wage labor relation, the exploitation mechanism kicks in; those who own and control capital will tend to appropriate a surplus-value exceeding the value of the wages received by the work force. Given the structure of the relations among individual units of industrial capital, the mechanism of the redistribution of surplus-value will kick in; units that successfully introduce process and product innovations will win surplus profits. The derivation of a comprehensive ordering of the economic categories in *Capital* is simultaneously the derivation of the most basic real mechanisms in capitalism.

Assume for the moment that there is only a single relevant respect in which two research programs are not similar: the hard core assumptions of one illuminate the workings of the realm under investigation, while those of the other do not. It would be exceedingly odd to say that this made no difference in a comparative assessment of the two programs; the first would seem to have a clear advantage over the second. The hard core of the Marxian program refers to real mechanisms

in capitalism, while the hard core of instrumentalist versions of neoclassical economics does not. Everything else being equal, this provides a reason for considering the former program superior. This reason
is not reducible to the prediction and corroboration of novel facts.

b) I now wish to compare briefly the hard cores of Marxism and
neoclassical economics in the non-instrumentalist reading of the latter.
Here two different sorts of reasons can be given for the superiority of
the Marxian research program, although they too do not have to do
with the predictive power of theories in the protective belt of the
programs. They have to do instead with the different types of claims
made in the two hard cores, and with the explanatory force of those
claims.

For many neoclassical economists, the propositions of the hard core
of their research program refer to features of the economic realm that
hold always and everywhere. For example, in Latsis's view the hard
core of the neoclassical theory of the firm consists of four propositions: profit maximization, perfect knowledge, independence of decisions, and perfect markets (Latsis 1972, 209). The first and third of
these assertions define a transhistorical disposition innate in human
nature, a disposition of "rationality."[6] This disposition may be ham-
pered or even repressed in some institutional contexts; the fourth proposition implies that capitalist market societies provide the only adequate
institutional context for the flourishing of this innate disposition. This
too is a transhistorical claim.[7]

How do things stand with Marxism? Certainly *part* of the hard core
of Marxism includes transhistorical suppositions regarding human beings (Geras 1982). But there is no claim that the assertions formulated in the course of the dialectic of social forms in *Capital* hold always
and everywhere.

Consider the following argument. In capitalism, as in all other modes
of production, the continued reproduction of society depends upon
coordinated labor. Yet in capitalism production is undertaken privately;
producers discover whether they have contributed to social reproduction only later, with the subsequent sale of a commodity for money. In
this manner the universal social power of labor bizarrely comes to appear
in the form of commodities and the abstract symbols of money. When
this money comes to function as capital, the bizarreness is taken a
further step. The capital that purchases social labor in effect proclaims
that this labor is merely part of itself ("variable capital"); it appears
that capital alone accomplishes the reproduction of society. And so
commodities, money, and capital are fetishes in which social labor is
manifested in alien objects. Fetishism is a form of subjectivity neces-

sarily generated by the objective material forms of capitalism. The thesis that economic agents in capitalism are subject to fetishism can be taken as part of the Marxist response to the rationality assumption of neoclassical economics. But while the neoclassical claim (in the non-instrumentalist reading) supposedly refers to a transhistorical disposition, the corresponding Marxist thesis is explicitly limited to a historically specific mode of production. In so far as the aim of the two research programs is to account for events, processes, and structures *in capitalism*, the historically specific nature of the claims made in the hard core of the Marxian program provides a reason to find this program *prima facie* superior to the neoclassical program.[8] This reason is not reducible to the prediction and corroboration of novel facts.

Turning from the different types of claims made in the hard cores of the two programs to the explanatory force of those claims, here too we find much of relevance to a comparative assessment of competing programs, *contra* Lakatos. For Lakatos, the propositions of the hard core do not directly involve falsifiable predictions, and so they themselves do not directly involve explanatory claims. On the realist view of the hard core, however, it is mistaken to limit explanatory claims to the assertions in the protective belt. The hard-core propositions of both Marxian social theory and (non-instrumentalist) neoclassical economics claim to provide explanations of the fundamental mechanisms underlying economic activity under the capital form. If the claims made here by defenders of one program prove to be better warranted and more powerful in scope than those proposed by defenders of the other, this is surely relevant to any comparative assessment. This point is worth developing at some length.

For the non-instrumentalist neoclassical economist, the propositions in the hard core of the neoclassical research program explain how the maximizing behavior of atomized rational individuals determines economic processes. Economic agents are atomized in the sense that the independence of decision making is assumed. They are rational in that economic agents are assumed to chose "in accordance with a preference ordering that is complete and transitive, subject to perfect and costlessly acquired information" (Blaug 1992, 229). And they are maximizers in the sense that competition forces them to optimize in the face of constraints.

The Marxian dialectic of social forms proposes a quite different explanation of the most basic mechanisms at work in capitalism. This can be seen from an examination of the circuit of capital, a device Marx employed to summarize his initial discussion of the commodity, money, and capital forms:

Capital first takes the form of money (M) to be invested. It is then invested in the purchase of two sorts of commodities (C), means of production and labor power. Labor power is set to work in a production process (P), resulting in the output of goods and services in the commodity form (C'). These commodities are then sold in the market. If they can be sold for a money price exceeding the initial money invested (M'), capital may be accumulated and the circuit can begin again. Reference to this circuit explains why seeing the maximizing activity of atomized rational individuals as the basic mechanism at work in capitalism is mistaken.

In the atomistic view, all social relations are external. In the circuit of capital, in contrast, economic agents are internally related to other agents (Ollman 1976). The categories "buyer of labor power" and "seller of labor power," for instance, cannot be defined apart from each other. The atomistic categorization of economic agents is also suspect in that the circuit of capital provides a material basis for various forms of collective identity. All those in the position of buyers of labor power objectively share certain interests, as do all those in the position of selling their labor power. The dialectic of social forms explains how the subjective psychology of individual economic agents (reflected in their "preference sets") is determined within a specific class context, and so cannot claim ontological independence.[9] The immediate preference of the owners and controllers of capital is to accumulate capital; that of the owners of labor power is to obtain access to the means of subsistence. The holders of capital tend to develop a preference to reduce the time it takes for their capital to transverse the circuit of capital; the preference of wage laborers is generally to resist speed-ups in the labor process. These and other preferences are not best seen as private decisions made in isolation from other social agents. They are rooted in the social forms defining capitalism.

Regarding rationality, I have already argued that the Marxist dialectic of social forms purports to explain why the actions of even the most rational economic agents in capitalism are simultaneously permeated by the irrationality of fetishism. Further, nothing in the logic of the capital circuit implies that the preference orderings of economic agents need be complete and transitive. The more we reflect on the psychic manipulations of advertising in capitalism, the less plausible this assumption becomes.

Perhaps the most obvious way the assumptions of the hard core of neoclassical economics distort the real mechanisms at work in capitalism has to do with the supposition that agents possess perfect information. Each step in the capital circuit is characterized by radical uncertainty, due to the strategic concealment of information (Laibman 1993, 238). Also, there are no guarantees that the means of production purchased will provide an adequate return on investment before the technical change has subjected them to "moral obsolescence." Neither are there guarantees that the labor power hired will meet or exceed the social average of labor productivity, that the commodities produced will find buyers, or that money will retain its value over time. If economic agents lack perfect information, if they must make decisions in situations of radical uncertainty, then there is no way for them ever to know in advance what the correct maximizing behavior might be, even if we counterfactually suppose both the capacity and the inclination to solve foot-long Lagrangian equations before acting.

As a result, economic agents in capitalism are often not content to operate "under given constraints." Rather than accepting technology as exogenously given, research and development is incorporated within the capital circuit, thereby changing the constraints under which capital operates. Rather than accepting the constraint of the given wage rate, for instance, labor-saving innovations can be sought. Nor are spatial constraints passively accepted; capital flight to low-wage areas can occur. Likewise, wage laborers need not accept the constraint of the given balance of class forces. They can attempt to organize in order to shift that balance in their favor (Storper and Walker 1989). There is thus an extensive range of phenomena that can be accounted for within the Marxian hard core, phenomena that fall outside the scope of the hard core of neoclassical economics.

It is possible to derive predictions of novel facts from the hard core assumption that the basic mechanism at work in capitalism is the maximization of given preference sets by atomized rational individuals. It is also possible to derive predictions of novel facts from the Marxian dialectic of social forms. Lakatos is not wrong when he notes that the hard core of a research program contributes to scientific explanations in this manner. But he is, I believe, mistaken when he limits the explanatory role of the hard core to this. The hard core of neoclassical economics and the systematic ordering of social forms in *Capital* offer competing explanations of the basic mechanisms at work in capitalism. The relative cogency of these competing explanations, and the relative scope of the phenomena they explain, can in principle be weighed apart from the relative success of the two programs at predicting novel facts. A convincing case can be made that the neoclassical program both rests on an inadequate grasp of the mechanisms at work in capitalism and abstracts from relevant features of this mode of production. It is possible to make this case without introducing predictions of any sort.

It is now time to summarize this over-long section. In *Capital* Marx presented a systematic reconstruction of the social forms that make up the capitalist mode of production. This dialectic of social forms can be seen as an attempt to articulate the hard core of a research program in Lakatos's sense of the term. The ordering of social forms in *Capital* provides a basic framework to orient Marxian studies of capitalism. Also, the assertions making up this systematic progression are not subjected to direct empirical testing in the same manner as other propositions formulated within the Marxian program. Approaching *Capital* with Lakatos's methodology of scientific research programs in mind allows us to appreciate Marx's accomplishment in a new way. Has anyone working in any research program in any discipline ever gone to the lengths Marx did to make the hard-core assumptions of his program explicit?

There are, however, two aspects of Marx's approach that do not fit Lakatos's framework so easily. First, there seems to be a disposition towards instrumentalism latent in Lakatos's position, while Marx's systematic ordering of social forms claims to reconstruct in thought the inner nature of the capitalist mode of production. Second, consideration of the hard core plays next to no role in the comparative assessment of competing research programs for Lakatos. This too can be called into question. The hard core of the neoclassical program (on the non-instrumentalist interpretation) consists of statements taken to hold always and everywhere, while the hard core of Marxism is by and large historically specific. This consideration counts as a major advantage of the Marxian program. And finally there is the question of explanation. For Lakatos, the hard core provides background conditions for theories from which predictions of novel facts are derived, and only the success of these predictions is ultimately relevant to comparative assessments. But the Marxian dialectic of social forms and the hard core of the neoclassical program (on the non-instrumentalist reading) both purport to explain the fundamental mechanisms at work in capitalism. If one of these accounts is more cogent than the other, or if one can explain a greater scope of phenomena than the other, this is surely relevant to any comparative assessment of the competing programs.

In Lakatos's framework there are two other parts of a research program besides the hard core: the heuristics of the program and its protective belt. Can a consideration of these themes add anything further to our understanding of the contribution made by the dialectic of social forms to the Marxian research program?

3. The Theory of Social Forms and the Heuristics of the Marxian Research Program

Marx's account of social forms can be used to formulate a set of precepts making up both a positive and negative heuristic for concrete theoretical and empirical research. This includes both the questions to be asked and the tools to be employed in concrete research. This counts as another significant contribution to the Marxian program.

Concrete theoretical and empirical research begins with some basic question or set of questions. What determines whether a specific question fits within the Marxian research program? It is possible to go through Marx's systematic reconstruction of capitalism step-by-step, and derive a set of general questions for concrete research from the analysis of the various social forms. Part of the positive heuristic of Marxism is that the questions asked in concrete research address the issues raised in the analysis of social forms.

It is obviously not possible to provide a comprehensive list of all the questions for concrete research that can be derived from Marx's systematic ordering of social forms. A quick survey of the main categories in the three volumes of *Capital* leads to the following representative sample. In a given historical period or geographical region, what new areas of social life are being commodified? What is the relationship between social labor and money? What are the various functions of money that come into play in the given context, and how are they in tension with each other? What impact does a given change in the labor process have on the rate of exploitation? What is the balance of class forces at the point of production? What sectors are experiencing the most growth in rates of accumulation? How are organizations restructuring in response to accumulation? Which stages in the circuit of capital provide the biggest barriers to increases in the rate of circulation? To what extent are the rhythms of the different sectors of the economy in sync? How are process and product innovations creating surplus profits for certain firms/sectors in certain regions? What are the trends in the rate of profit, and what are the key factors determining those trends? What are the causes of economic crises? Where do the interests of industrial firms, merchant capital, financial capital, and landlords coincide? Where do they diverge?

As incomplete as this list is, it does suggest how the Marxian ordering of social forms generates a set of questions that define an on-going research program. Of course it is possible to pose a number of these questions within competing programs. Nonetheless, three features make this set of questions unique, taken as a whole. The first and most significant is the centrality of class issues, ranging from direct class conflict at the point of production to the manner in which changes in technology, investment patterns, corporate structure, and so on, affect the balance of class forces.[10] The second has to do with time. The above questions are formulated in a way that implies that capitalism has a history, and that this history matters. Capitalism is based on ceaseless experimentation, a ceaseless process of overcoming certain barriers to accumulation only to come across new ones, whose shape depends on paths chosen in the past (Storper and Walker 1989). Third, these general questions are relevant no matter what specific shape capital may take. They hold whether we are investigating separate firms operating in purely competitive markets, or networks of firms cooperating together in a keiretsu. In these and other possible cases the same fundamental class antagonisms are found, the same tensions between the various functions of money arise, the same stages in the circuit of capital must be transversed, and so on.

This takes us to the negative heuristic of Marxism, the sorts of questions that should be avoided in order to remain consistent with the hard core of the research program. Questions that obscure class dynamics are to be avoided. Questions that imply capitalism does not develop over time are to be rejected. And questions that do not allow for capitalism to take on a variety of shapes are suspect as well. Once again, the contrast with the neoclassical research program is sharp. Its basic questions concern the decisions of isolated individuals, ignore path dependencies, and are particularly unsuited for an understanding of the so-called Japanese model of capitalism. (Gerlach 1992) They are thus to be avoided, given the negative heuristic following from Marx's dialectic of social forms.

Besides generating a set of questions, the heuristics of a research program also define the sorts of intellectual tools that are compatible with the program, as well as the sorts of tools that are to be avoided.[11] It is not possible here to do more than mention briefly a few ways in which the systematic ordering of social forms contributes to this dimension of the Marxian program.

1. The necessary connection between the social forms constituting capitalism and the emergence of fetishism rules out uncritical use of methodological tools that simply reflect surface appearances. The production function calculus is an example of a tool of analysis that is to

be avoided for this reason. This approach assumes that "capital" and "labor" are two independent "factors of production," an assumption that rests on capital fetishism.

2. The hard core claim that capitalism necessarily generates fetishism also implies that the methodological tools of ideology critique ought to be employed. Systematic dialectical method is itself one example of such a tool. The systematic relation between the categories "exploitation" and "market price," for instance, provides a basis for a critique of the ideology of consumer sovereignty.

3. A hard core whose propositions emphasize the historical nature of social forms rules out methodological tools that do not allow for the possibility of historical change. This is why so much of sociobiology is incompatible with the Marxian research program.

4. A hard core emphasizing the possibility of historical change through the social agency of working men and women is incompatible with an uncritical use of survey questionnaires hampering this agency. Consider a survey questionnaire asking respondents whether they would support reducing the tax on capital in order to spur investment and create jobs. This question implies that capital investment naturally flows to where it is needed, unless the "unnatural" interference of state taxation distorts the flow. The question does not challenge the pre-understandings of the addressees, or treat them as subjects capable of rejecting the capital relation. Within the Marxian program methodological instruments should be instruments of social change as well; survey questionnaires that reinforce dominant world views do not meet this criterion.

5. The dynamism of capitalism as analyzed in Marx's progression of social forms is more compatible with certain forms of mathematical analysis than others. The mathematical techniques of static equilibrium theory may be helpful in certain carefully defined investigations. In general, however, there is a great danger that use of these methodological tools will lead to a distortion of an essential dimension of social life. Simultaneous equation systems cannot represent the passage of time, especially the temporal dynamic set off by technological change.[12] In contrast, difference equations can depict significant aspects of the trajectory of an economy over time. For example, it is possible to distinguish how prices at the end of a period of production are distinct from those at its beginning, due to the way prices respond to technological changes (Carchedi 1993). The endogeneity of technical change in capitalism is a fundamental claim of Marx's dialectic of social forms, and so a positive heuristic encouraging the use of mathematical tools incorporating technical change can be directly derived from that dialectic.

6. Another point regarding the methodological limits of mathematics has to do with the issue of realism. The dialectic of social forms uncovers mechanisms that have a material existence in the social world. The use of mathematical techniques is to be avoided whenever those techniques obscure the operation of real mechanisms in capitalism.[13] Mathematical techniques, no matter how convenient their use might be to the social theorist, are never a substitute for the qualitative comprehension of real mechanisms.[14]

4. Marx's Theory of Social Forms and the "Protective Belt" of the Marxian Research Program

For Lakatos, the theories and empirical assertions found in the protective belt are measured by three standards: the degree to which predictions of novel facts can be derived from them, the extent to which these predictions have been corroborated, and the consistency of the theories and empirical assertions with the hard core of the program.

Marxism more than holds its own against competing research programs when measured by the standard of the corroborated prediction of novel facts within the protective belt of the program. Marx's predictions of recurrent crises in capitalism, the persistence of conflicts regarding the length of the working day and the intensity of labor, and the ever-increasing concentration and centralization of capital have been corroborated again and again, to mention just a few examples.[15] Nevertheless, here too the prediction and corroboration of novel facts ought not to be the sole criteria for evaluating whether a research program is progressive or degenerate (given the consistency of the protective belt with the hard core of the program). A consideration of the relationship between Marx's systematic dialectic of categories and concrete work in the protective belt of Marxian theory illustrates this point.

Each category in *Capital* defines a determination of a social form, and each determination specifies a real mechanism at work in the capitalist mode of production. Activity within the protective belt of the Marxian research program attempts to specify how these basic mechanisms operate in specific concrete contexts. However important the role of predictions may be here, that role is a restricted one for three reasons.

First, the mechanisms do not operate in closed systems where conditions remain identical and effects are uniform. And so any attempt to investigate how these mechanisms operate concretely must be formulated in terms of tendencies. In any given case the nonoccurrence of a certain event does not show that there is not a tendency for an event of that sort to occur; it does not even show that there is not a *necessary* tendency in that direction. In any given case, for example, it is always possible for a substantial money reserve to be invested in nonprofit organizations; this does not change the fact that in capitalism it is necessarily the case that substantial money reserves will tend to be invested in order to accumulate capital. And so the corroboration or non-corroboration of a prediction regarding a given concrete event is not an especially interesting matter from this perspective.[16]

A second point emerges from consideration of the architectonic of *Capital*. Marx's systematic dialectic is organized linearly, progressing step-by-step from simple and abstract social forms to more complex and concrete forms. Each subsequent stage in the progression "sublates" those that have gone before, that is, it incorporates earlier ones while going beyond them in some fashion. This might be taken to imply that each time the social theorist reaches a new categorial level he or she should go back to the beginning, and show how all of the mechanisms considered earlier are now modified as a result of the addition of the new determination. This, however, would be an impossible task. Marx never even came close to completing the straightforward linear ordering of the social forms making up capitalism. If he had gone on to attempt to show how the various forms and the mechanisms they generate are modified when operating simultaneously, he would never have finished more than a small portion of Volume 1 of *Capital*. There is simply too much complexity here, generating too high a degree of indeterminacy.

This has direct implications for concrete research in the protective belt of a research program. In the concrete realm a whole range of mechanisms operate simultaneously. Whatever difficulties arise in the course of formulating specific predictions regarding the workings of a given mechanism are dwarfed by those that arise when a variety of mechanisms operate together. In the face of a much higher degree of indeterminacy, the corroboration or lack thereof of specific predictions has even less significance.

Third, in many cases the social forms of capitalism generate tendencies that in specific concrete contexts may come into tension with each other, leading to a higher level of indeterminacy yet again. The capital form necessarily involves a tendency for the owners and controllers of capital to seek to increase the rate of exploitation; everything else being equal, this raises the rate of profit. In Marx's view, the capital form also generates a tendency for the organic composition of capital to rise; everything else being equal, this lowers the rate of profit. There is a tendency built-into the capital form to further capital accumulation through lowering wage costs by deskilling; there is also a tendency built-into the capital form to further capital accumulation through productivity increases demanding higher levels of skill. There is a tendency in the capital form for technical innovation to be spurred by the fear of the "moral obsolescence" of fixed capital; there is also a tendency in the capital form for previous investment in fixed capital to retard technical innovation. In these and similar cases the tendency that dominates in a given concrete context will depend on a variety of contingent historical factors.[17] And so the corroboration/non-corroboration of predictions regarding any given concrete context will have a contingent quality as well.[18]

From the standpoint of a Lakatosian such as Blaug, these three points simply reveal the immunizing strategies that undermine Marxism's claim to be taken seriously as a scientific research program. (Blaug 1992, 60–61) The criticism could not possibly be more misguided. Methodology must adjust to the nature of the objects being studied. If capitalism is an open system rather than a closed system, if a variety of distinct mechanisms operate simultaneously in it, and if it is beset by conflicting tendencies, all of this must be acknowledged in any adequate methodology. Issues of social ontology cannot be removed by methodological fiat. The social ontology of capitalism implies that the corroboration/non-corroboration of predictions will have only restricted significance in any plausible research program, even when we restrict our attention to what Lakatos termed the protective belt of programs.

5. Conclusion

I hope to have established that the systematic dialectic of social forms in *Capital* plays a central role in the Marxian research program. It makes explicit much of the hard core of the Marxian study of capitalism; it generates a set of general questions to orient concrete theoretical and empirical inquiries; and it provides guidance regarding which sorts of intellectual techniques are generally suited to the study of events, processes, and structures in capitalism.

Two other themes were also discussed along the way. Both were treated in a preliminary manner, and both point to the need for further study. The first concerned Lakatos's proclivity to assess competing research programs simply in terms of their relative success at predicting novel facts. I have argued that other factors are relevant as well. Far more significant than prediction is retroduction, defined by Sayer as "(the) mode of inference in which events are explained by postulating (and identifying) mechanisms which are capable of producing them" (Sayer 1984, 97). Perhaps equally important is the question of scope. In principle, a research program that accounts for more phenomena within the object realm in question than its competitors could be judged superior, even if those competitors had a somewhat better record at the prediction of novel facts. In the present work no attempt has been made to fix the precise weight that should be given to prediction, retroduction, and scope in the assessment of competing research programs.

The second topic for further research that has been raised is the comparative assessment of neoclassical economics and the Marxian program for the study of capitalism. I have suggested that the Marxian program is superior on all three relevant grounds, the prediction of novel facts, the account of explanatory mechanisms employed in retroductions, and the scope of the phenomena explained. To establish these claims in detail, however, would require more than a single paper.

Notes

1. To my knowledge the only extensive discussion of Marxian theory from a Lakatosian perspective is found in Glass and Johnson (1989). Their account does not emphasize the main theme of the present essay, Marx's ordering of social forms.

2. The term "protective belt" emphasizes that the theories and empirical assumptions making up this belt are subjected to empirical testing, thereby "protecting" the hard core of the research program from such testing.

3. When Marx discussed the procedures he employed in constructing this dialectic, he took pains to stress that "the point of departure" was the "chaotic conception of the whole" latent in everyday experience in capitalism (Marx 1857–58, 100–01). Systematic dialectics has an empirical basis, and is therefore only relatively inviolable. This is compatible with Lakatos, who insisted that the hard core of a research program hardens slowly, by trial and error (Lakatos 1978a, 48 n. 4, 181).

4. Blaug gives his own reasons for rejecting instrumentalism and its "poor man's version," descriptivism, in the following passage: "[Their] weakness is that of all black-box theorizing that makes predictions without being able to explain why the predictions work: the moment the predictions fail, the theory has to be discarded in toto because it lacks an underlying structure of assumptions, an *explanans* that can be adjusted and improved to make better predictions in the future" (Blaug 1992, 99). But in principle instrumentalists/descriptivists can provide elaborate stories of what is "inside the black box." What distinguishes their view is the claim that there is no way to assess these stories apart from their role in generating corroborated predictions. And this is precisely what Blaug (and Lakatos) elsewhere assert.

5. This does not imply that Marxists need reject instrumentalist laws in contexts where calculating devices are all that is called for (Sayer 1984, 116–17).

6. "The classical rational choice paradigm seems to owe its appeal [to the fact that] it provides a *unified theory* which applies to all human behavior, independent of the particularities of time and place" (Vanberg 1993, 183).
7. The assumption of perfect knowledge is a special case, to which I shall return below.
8. It might be thought that a set of principles explaining economic activity in all human history should be evaluated more favorably than a set of principles with more limited application. Explanatory scope is indeed one criteria in evaluations of competing research agendas. But past a certain point any gain in scope is more than offset by losses in other dimensions. We learn in introductory logic that all persons are mortal, that Socrates was a person, and that Socrates was therefore mortal. But no one requesting an explanation of Socrates's death would be satisfied with the answer that he was mortal. In a similar fashion, no one requesting an explanation of the specific workings of capitalism should be satisfied with general notions that supposedly hold always and everywhere (Murray 1988).
9. This is not to deny that other factors (such as gender and race) are also constitutive of individual identity.
10. I do not mean to suggest that non-class issues such as race or gender fall outside the scope of Marxian research. But the class-specific manner in which racial and gender oppression occurs must always be made explicit.
11. This dimension of a research program was of great importance to Lakatos. In one place, at least, he even suggests that the introduction of new problem-solving techniques is the most important factor in determining whether a research program is progressing, more important than even the prediction of novel facts: "progress is not even so much in the actual novel predictions . . . but in the mathematical and physical novelty of problem-solving techniques which later lead to, and form a part of, a progressive research program" (Lakatos 1978b, 101). It is not clear to me how this statement is consistent with the stress on novel predictions elsewhere in his writings.
12. "Neo-Walrasian closed system models have so far been inadequate—or, at best, grotesquely cumbersome—vehicles for representing the role of ignorance and the passage of time in human affairs . . . Both problems are, it would appear, rooted in the hard-core heuristic routine of modelling the behavior of each individual agent so as to portray his every action as part of a comprehensively planned 'optimal' time-path" (Leijonhufvud 1976, 107).
13. An example of the problems that can arise if this last methodological injunction is ignored is given by Fred Moseley. Define "P" to represent total profits; "S," total surplus-value; and "U," the total expenses of unproductive labor. From the mathematical point of view the equation $P = S - U$ is equivalent to the equation $S = P + U$. However from the perspective of the material forces at work in capitalism, the two could not be more different. There are real mechanisms at work that lead the amount of profit to equal the total amount of surplus-value minus the costs of unproductive labor, as expressed in the first equation. There are no mechanisms that operate along the lines of the second equation; with the level of profits held constant, an increase in unproductive labor does not result in a greater amount of surplus-value (Moseley 1994, 87).

14. "(T)he logical or mathematical manipulation of a hypothetical closed system represented by symbols is a poor guide to causal structure, for the rules governing these kinds of manipulation need not correspond to the laws governing the possible ways-of-acting of real objects; models may be run backwards, effects can be used to calculate ('determine') causes and hence an ability to calculate and 'predict' may rest upon mis-specifications of even the basic asymmetries of causal dependence" (Sayer 1984, 118–19).

15. There has been a quite extensive debate on what exactly the term "novel facts" means. The conclusion of this debate appears to be that the term can be unpacked in a variety of ways, no one of which is reducible to the others (Hands 1991, 96 ff.). Towards the end of his life Lakatos himself stressed that predicting what is already known, but merely "fortuitous" within competing theories, also counts as a prediction of a novel fact. (Lakatos 1978a, 179, 183, 184–5, 186) While economic crises, capital/wage labor conflict, and the concentration and centralization of capital, are phenomena that have been known for quite some time, their persistence is certainly "fortuitous" from the standpoint of the dominant neoclassical paradigm. The fact that Marxian economic theory successfully predicted their persistence is strong evidence for the progressiveness of the Marxian program, as measured by Lakatos's standard.

16. "Falsifications of predictions of contingencies in open systems whose initial state is incompletely known need not be treated as theoretically significant" (Sayer 1984, 190; see also 111–114).

17. In these sorts of cases I believe it is arbitrary to grant one member of the pair priority by terming it "the tendency," reducing the other to the secondary status of a mere "counter-tendency." If both are equally immanent in the capital form, the language of "conflicting tendencies" is less misleading. The term "real contradictions" could even be used, if one did not mind sending the lovers of formal logic into a state of apoplexy.

18. Other matters outside the scope of this paper complicate matters even further. Gender, race, aesthetic experiences, ethical values, and religious commitments, are just some of the features that would have to be introduced to get a full categorization of economic agents. The more dimensions are introduced to the categorization of individual economic agents, the more indeterminate their behavior in any given specific situation.

References

Arthur 1993. Chris Arthur, "Hegel's *Logic* and Marx's *Capital*," in Moseley 1993, 63–88.
Blaug 1991. Mark Blaug, "Afterword," in De Marchi and Blaug 1991, 499–512.
———. 1992. *The Methodology of Economics: Or How Economists Explain.* Second Edition. New York: Cambridge University Press.
Campbell 1993. Martha Campbell, "Marx's Concept of Economic Relations and the Method of *Capital*," in Moseley 1993, 135–156.
Carchedi 1993. Guglielmo Carchedi, "Marx's Logic of Inquiry and Price Formation," in Moseley 1993, 185–216.

de Marchi and Blaug 1991. Neil De Marchi and Mark Blaug, eds., *Appraising Economic Theories* (Aldershot, Hants: Edward Elgar, 1991).

Friedman 1953. Milton Friedman, *Essays in Positive Economics* (Chicago: University of Chicago Press, 1953).

Geras 1982. Norman Geras, *Marx and Human Nature: Refutation of a Legend* (London: New Left Books, 1982).

Gerlach 1992. Michael Gerlach, *Alliance Capitalism: The Social Organization of Japanese Business* (Berkeley: The University of California Press, 1992).

Glass and Johnson 1989. J.C. Glass and W. Johnson, *Economics: Progression, Stagnation, or Degeneration?* (Ames: Iowa State University Press, 1989).

Hands 1991. D. Wade Hands, "The Problem of Excess Content: Economics, Novelty and a Long Popperian Tale," in de Marchi and Blaug 1991, 58–75.

———. 1993. "Popper and Lakatos in Economic Methodology," in Maki, et al. 1993, 61–75.

Laibman 1993. David Laibman, *Value, Technical Change, and Crisis.* (Armonk, N.Y.: M. E. Sharpe, 1993).

Lakatos 1968. Imre Lakatos, "Criticism and the Methodology of Scientific Research Programs." *Proceedings of the Aristotelian Society* 69, 149–86.

———. 1970. "Falsification and the Methodology of Scientific Research Programmes," in Lakatos and Musgrave 1970, 91–196.

———. 1978a. *Philosophical Papers*, vol. 1. (Cambridge: Cambridge University Press, 1978).

———. 1978b. *Philosophical Papers*, vol. 2. (Cambridge: Cambridge University Press, 1978.

Lakatos and Musgrave 1970. I. Lakatos and A. Musgrave, eds., *Criticism and the Growth of Knowledge* (New York: Cambridge University Press, 1970).

Latsis 1972. Spiro Latsis, "Situational Determinism in Economics," *British Journal of the Philosophy of Science* 23, 207–45.

———. ed. 1976. *Method and Appraisal in Economics.* (New York: Cambridge University Press, 1976).

Leijonhufvud 1976. Axel Leijonhufvud, "Schools, 'Revolutions,' and Research Programes In Economic Theory," in Latsis 1976, 65–108.

Maki, Gustafsson, and Knudsen 1993. Uskali Maki, Bo Gustafsson, and Christian Knudsen, eds., *Rationality, Institutions & "Economic Methodology"* (New York: Routledge Press, 1993).

Marx 1857–58. Karl Marx, *Grundrisse*, trans. M. Nicolaus (New York: Vintage, 1973).

———. 1867. *Capital*, vol. 1, trans. Ben Fowkes (Harmondsworth: Penguin, 1967).

———. 1862–63. *Theories of Surplus Value, Volume II*, trans. Emile Burns (Moscow: Progress Publishers, 1963).

Mattick 1993. Paul Mattick Jr., "Marx's Dialectic," in Moseley 1993, 115–134.

Moseley 1993. Fred Moseley, ed., *Marx's Method in Capital: A Reexamination* (New Jersey: Humanities Press, 1993).

———. 1994. "Unproductive Labor and the Rate of Profit: A Reply." *Science and Society* 58:1, 84–92.

Murray 1988. Patrick Murray, *Marx's Theory of Scientific Knowledge.* Atlantic Highlands, N.J.: Humanities Press.

Ollman 1976. Bertell Ollman, *Alienation* (Cambridge: Cambridge University Press, 1976).

Redman 1991. Deborah Redman, *Economics and the Philosophy of Science* (New York: Oxford University Press, 1991).

Reuten 1996. Geert Reuten, "A Revision of the Neoclassical Economics Methodology: Appraising Hausman's Mill-Twist, Robbins-Gist, and Popper-Whist," in *The Journal of Economic Methodology*, 3:1, pp. 39–67, 1996.

Reuten and Williams 1989. Geert Reuten and Michael Williams, *Value-Form and the State* (London: Routledge, 1989).

Sayer 1984. Andrew Sayer, *Method in Social Science: A Realist Approach* (London: Hutchinson, 1984).

Smith 1990. Tony Smith, *The Logic of Marx's Capital* (Albany: State University of New York Press, 1990).

———. 1993a. *Dialectical Social Theory and Its Critics* (Albany: State University of New York Press, 1993).

———. 1993b. "Marx's *Capital* and Hegelian Dialectical Logic," in Moseley 1993, 15–36.

Storper and Walker 1989. Michael Storper and Richard Walker, *The Capitalist Imperative: Territory, Technology, and Industrial Growth* (New York: Blackwell, 1989).

Vanberg 1993. Viktor Vanberg, "Rational Choice, Rule-Following and Institutions: An Evolutionary Perspective," in Maki, et al., 171–200.

Contributors

CHRISTOPHER J. ARTHUR is an Honorary Lecturer of Philosophy at the University of Sussex. He is the author of *The Dialectics of Labor: Marx and His Relation to Hegel* (Basil Blackwell 1986). He is also a member of the Editorial Board of *Radical Philosophy* and *Capital and Class*.

MARTHA CAMPBELL has taught at the University of Denver and Miami University. Her research specialty is Marxian monetary theory.

PAUL MATTICK JR. teaches philosophy at Adelphi University. Editor of the *International Journal of Political Economy*, he is the author of *Social Knowledge: The Nature and Limits of Social Science* (M. E. Sharpe 1986), and has edited *Eighteenth-Century Aesthetics and the Reconstruction of Art* (Cambridge University Press 1993).

FRED MOSELEY teaches economics at Mount Holyoke College. He is the author of *The Falling Rate of Profit in the Postwar United States Economy* (St. Martin's Press 1992) and the editor of *Marx's Method in Capital: A Reexamination* (Humanities Press 1993) and *Heterodox Economic Theories: True or False* (Elgar 1995).

PATRICK MURRAY teaches philosophy at Creighton University. He is the author of *Marx's Theory of Scientific Knowledge* (Humanities Press 1988) and the editor of *Reflections on Commercial Life* (Routledge 1997).

GEERT REUTEN teaches economics at the University of Amsterdam. He is the author of *Value-Form and the State: The Tendencies of Accumulation and the Determination of Economic Policy in Capitalist Society* (with Michael Williams) (Routledge 1989).

TONY SMITH teaches philosophy at Iowa State University. He is the author of *The Logic of Marx's Capital* (SUNY Press 1990), *The Role of Ethics in Social Theory* (SUNY Press 1991), and *Dialectical Theory and Its Critics* (SUNY Press 1992).

Name Index

Albritton, Robert, 7n. 2
Anscombe, Elizabeth, 45
Aristotle, 3, 38–39, 45, 57, 59n. 27, 60n. 34, 95
Arthur, Christopher J., 2, 33n. 1, 36n. 51, 156, 170, 171n. 2, 179

Backhouse, Hans-Georg, 11
Bacon, Francis, 40, 42, 61n. 41
Bailey, Samuel, 61n. 44, 91, 94–97, 100, 104, 107, 108, 112, 114nn. 2, 3, 116n. 16
Banaji, Jairus, 20, 26–27, 35nn. 36, 47, 51, 54
Berkeley, 52, 58n. 14
Bernstein, Richard, 58n. 6
Bhaskar, Roy, 5, 150, 152–54, 157, 169, 171nn. 1, 4, 5
Black, Collison, 56
Blaug, Mark, 49, 151, 153, 176, 180, 183, 192, 193n. 4

Campbell, Martha, 4, 20, 36nn. 51, 61, 40, 48, 49, 61n. 45, 87n. 12, 179
Campus, Antonietta, 55–56
Carchedi, Gugliemo, 147n. 1, 189
Cartwright, Nancy, 171n. 1
Catephores, G., 34n. 11, 35n. 29
Cerutti, Furio, 58n. 2
Cherbuliez, A.-E., 133
Clarke, Simon, 58n. 2
Collins, James, 58nn. 4, 14

Davidson, Donald, 45, 46–47, 57n. 1
DeBrunhoff, Suzanne, 101
Descartes, Rene, 40, 41, 58nn. 11, 14
deMarchi, Neil, 176
Duménil, Gerard, 170
Durkheim, Emile, 67

Echeverria, Rafael, 7n. 2
Eldred, Michael, 34n. 16
Engels, Frederick, 1, 2, 9–21, 24, 33n. 2, 34nn. 24, 25, 35nn. 34, 37, 158

Ferguson, C. E., 55–56
Fernbach, David, 158, 159, 160, 173n. 17
Feuerbach, L., 42, 48
Fine, Ben, 172n. 8
Foley, Duncan, 89, 107, 122
Friedman, Milton, 176, 180
Frisby, David, 60n. 32
Fullarton, John, 118n. 31, 119n. 40

Ganssmann, Heiner, 113, 117n. 20, 118n. 37
Geras, Norman, 182
Gerlach, Michael, 188
Glass, J. C., 193n. 1
Gossen, H., 56
Grossman, Henryk, 16–17, 35n. 36

Hands, Wade, 180, 195n. 15
Harris, Laurence, 172n. 8
Harvey, David, 58n. 2
Hausman, Daniel M., 49, 50, 150, 151
Hegel, G. W. F., 1, 3, 9–10, 12, 20, 33n. 7, 34n. 18, 38, 39, 41, 44, 45, 51, 54, 57, 58nn. 5, 12, 13, 59nn. 19, 23, 61n. 40, 66, 72, 75, 87n. 14, 170
Heinrich, Michael, 147n. 4
Hobbes, Thomas, 42, 61n. 41
Hume, David, 42–43, 47, 52, 59nn. 17, 18, 60n. 30

Jackson, T. A., 33n. 5
James, William, 46–47, 61n. 47

201

Subject Index